FAIR VALUE ACCOUNTING

IN

HISTORICAL PERSPECTIVE

Edited by **IZUMI WATANABE**

Professor Emeritus
Osaka University of Economics

2014
MORIYAMA SHOTEN, Tokyo

FAIR VALUE ACCOUNTING IN HISTORICAL PERSPECTIVE
Copyright © 2014 by Izumi Watanabe

No part of this book may be reproduced in any form
— except for brief quotation (not to exceed 1,000 words)
in a review or professional work — without permission
in writing from the publishers.

Published by Moriyama Shoten, Tokyo, Japan
Hayashi Bldg., 1-10, Kanda-Nishikicho,
Chiyoda-ku, Tokyo, 101-0054, Japan

ISBN978-4-8394-2139-7

List of Contributors

Toshifumi Matsumoto is Professor of Accounting, Waseda University
Noriaki Miyatake is Associate Professor, Osaka University of Economics
Toshitake Miyauchi is Lecturer, Otemon Gakuin University
Norio Takasu is Professor, University of Hyogo.
Takeshi Sugita is Associate Professor, Osaka University of Economics
Izumi Watanabe is Professor Emeritus, Osaka University of Economics
Shigeto Sasaki is Professor, Senshu University
Kei Okajima is Associate Professor, Takushoku University
Hideki Kubota is Professor, Konan University
Takemi Ono is Professor, Tokyo Keizai University

Acknowledgements

This work was supported by JSPS KAKENHI Grant Number 23330151 and supported by Japan Accounting Association. The editor also appreciates that he received a publishing subvention from The Japan Industrial Management and Accounting Institute. We are very grateful.

FOREWORD

The purpose of this book is to reexamine the relationship between the market value and the discounted present value, which form the basis of fair value measurement, and the original role of double-entry bookkeeping. This reexamination looks at modern accounting from the perspective of measurement to uncover what constitutes truly useful information with respect to the presently overused decision making usefulness approach.

The following points were the focus of our efforts. First, we shed light on the basic function of fair value, the measurement method of the Asset and Liability Approach now conquering modern accounting, along with the history behind its appearance, and indicate the current status, themes and problems of fair value accounting. Next, we show just when in history the measurement of current value, which is the specific measurement attribute of fair value, took the stage and point out the discrepancies of current value when used in today's fair value accounting, as well as the various aspects where current value and fair value deviate. Based on this point, we examine the problems facing today's overemphasised usefulness approach for decision making, comparing it to accounting's true nature.

Our aims are to find (1) what role double-entry bookkeeping was invented to fulfill, (2) when current value measurement appeared, (3) what the relationships between current value measurement and acquisition cost valuation and discounted present value are from a historical perspective, and finally (4) sound a warning bell from history with regard to the overuse of the usefulness doctrine (excessive importance placed on the Asset and Liability View), expose the distortions of modern accounting and the dangers lurking in the path of modern accounting from accounting concepts that overemphasise the Asset and Liability View.

What kind of rationale can there be in the accounting view for the recent excessive Asset and Liability View and fair value accounting? I desire to sound a warning bell with the hammer of history to show the perilous journey modern accounting is taking with its core shifts from reliability to usefulness, and from verifiability to relevance.

    Early Spring in 2014,

Editor Izumi Watanabe

Contents

List of Contributors	iii
Acknowledgements	iii
Foreword ·· Izumi Watanabe	v
Introduction ·· Izumi Watanabe	1

Section I: Status and Aspects of Fair Value Accounting

Chapter 1: Fundamental Functions of Accounting and Fair Value Measurement — From the Perspective of Distributable Income Measurement Function — ················· Toshifumi Matsumoto   9
1-1. Introduction   10
1-2. Triangular Relationship in Institutional Accounting Systems   11
1-3. Distribution Capability of Appraisal Gain   18
1-4. Characteristics of Fair Value Accounting   24
1-5. Searching for Distribution Standards in Overall Fair Value Accounting   30
1-6. Conclusion   34

Chapter 2: Advent of Fair Value Accounting and Its Historical Background ·· Noriaki Miyatake   37
2-1. Introduction   38
2-2. S&L Crisis and Expectations toward Current Value Principle   39
2-3. Arrival of Fair Value Accounting   44
2-4. Enron Affairs and Fair Value Accounting   47
2-5. Subprime Loan Problem and Fair Value Accounting   52
2-6. Conclusion   56

Chapter 3: Current Status and Issues of Fair Value Accounting
·· Toshitake Miyauchi   61
3-1. Introduction   62
3-2. Survey Pattern   63
3-3. Accounting Functions and Hardness of Fair Value   64
3-4. The Information Role and Fair Value Accounting   68
3-5. The Contract Role and Fair Value Accounting   78
3-6. Conclusion   80

Chapter 4: Conflict in Fair Value Accounting — The Spell of Realization Principle — ································ Norio Takasu   85
4-1. Introduction   86

viii Fair Value Accounting in Historical Perspective

4-2. Switch of Views of Financial Accounting from the Revenue and Expense View to the Asset and Liability View ... 87
4-3. Problems involved in the Selection of Measurement Attributes in the Asset and Liability View ... 93
4-4. Development of the Revenue and Expense View and the Realization Principle ... 97
4-5. Corporate Risk and Accounting Measurement ... 100
4-6. Conclusion ... 102

Section II: Verification of Fair Value Accounting from the Historical Perspective — From Current Value to Fair Value Measurement — ... 107

Chapter 5: The British East India Company's Market Valuation in the Second Half of the Seventeenth Century (1664-1694) .... Takeshi Sugita 109
5-1. Introduction ... 110
5-2. Overview of EIC and its Method of Selling Imported Commodities ... 111
5-3. Unsold Goods Valuation Method at Closing of Ledger ... 112
5-4. Sale Price-Based Estimation ... 121
5-5. Treatment of Valuation Differences Based on Sale Price, etc. ... 125
5-6. Conclusion ... 127

Chapter 6: Appearance of Current Valuation in Seventeenth and Eighteenth Century Britain — Ledger Entries of Monteage, Malcolm, Hayes and Hamilton — .... Izumi Watanabe 131
6-1. Introduction ... 132
6-2. Advent of Current Valuation ... 134
6-3. Current Valuation of Fixed Assets up to the Eighteenth Century ... 137
6-4. Eighteenth Century fixed Asset Valuation Methods ... 140
6-5. Advent of Current Valuation of Inventory Assets ... 144
6-6. Conclusion ... 150

Chapter 7: Significance of Current Value Information in Nineteenth Century England Corporate Accounting — Statute Companies and General Registered Companies —
.... Shigeto Sasaki 153
7-1. Introduction ... 154
7-2. The Role of Current Value Information in the Accounting Practices of Grand Junction Railway Co. ... 155

7-3. The Role of Market Value Information in the Accounting
Practices of Neuchatel Asphalte Co. ... 169
7-4. The Role of Market Value Information in the Accounting
Practices of Natal Land and Colonization Co. ... 171
7-5. Conclusion ... 174

Chapter 8: The Evolution of Audit Thought on Asset Verification
during the Period 1880-1940: in the UK and the US practices
.... Kei Okajima 177
8-1. Introduction ... 178
8-2. Verification Structure Underlying the British Professional
Audit ... 179
8-3. Conception of "Verification of Assets" ... 183
8-4. American Balance Sheet Audit and Verification of Assets
therein ... 190
8-5. Conclusion ... 199

Chapter 9: Classical Inflation Accounting and Fair Value Measurement .... Hideki Kubota 203
9-1. Introduction ... 204
9-2. Experiments for Systematization of Classical Inflation
Accounting and the New Financial Instruments Project in
the US ... 205
9-3. "Entity Specific Assumptions" versus "Market Participant
Assumptions" ... 210
9-4. History of Acceptance of Valuation at Current Price and Fair
Value Measurement in Japan after World War II ... 212
9-5. Conclusion ... 217

Chapter 10: Various Aspects of Divergence from Fair Value
Accounting in History — Actual Requirements for Application
of Market Value Accounting — .... Takemi Ono 223
10-1. Introduction:Basic Stance Regarding Market Value
Accounting Application ... 224
10-2. An Interpretation of the Financial Crisis and Easing the
Application of Market Value Accounting Application. ... 225
10-3. Function of Liquidity in Market Value Accounting ... 227
10-4. Market Value Deviation Theory and Abandonment of
Market Value When Liquidity is Lost ... 228
10-5. Debating the Appropriateness of Market Value Accounting
Application and its Avoidance ... 234
10-6. Conclusion: Requirement of Market Value Accounting
Application ... 239

Chapter 11: A Warning Bell from History on giving too much Emphasis to the Usefulness Approach ········· Izumi Watanabe 243
11-1. Introduction 244
11-2. True Nature of Accounting: Historical Cost as Guarantor of Evidentiality 245
11-3. Fundamental Role of Double-Entry Bookkeeping as a Pillar of Accounting's Structural Computation 247
11-4. Historical Cost and Current Value: Nothing more than Different Points in Time 250
11-5. Historical Cost and Market Value in Transaction Value Accounting 252
11-6. Discounted Present Value and Feasibility Concept 257
11-7. Retreat of Reliability and Verifiability and Faithful Expressions 259
11-8. Conclusion: Original Role of Accounting 262

Index 267

INTRODUCTION

After the Great East Japan Earthquake & Tsunami of March 11, 2011, the news media repeated the message, over and over again, "Although the heart cannot be seen, heartfelt gestures can... Thoughts cannot be seen, but thoughtfulness can..." *

Even now, these messages still resound in people's minds. This message was part of a television commercial in which a young man sees a pregnant woman get on the train and hesitates, out of shyness perhaps, to give up his seat for her and ends up feeling guilty the rest of the way home. He then sees an elderly woman with heavy bags climbing stairs and walks by slowly, but then decides to go back to help her, taking the load from her, and gently helping her up the stairs. I wonder how many were touched by this scene, which stressed the importance of taking action to help others when most needed, and on practicality, instead of just theorising.

*This impressive message was a quote from Shoji Miyazawa's poem *The Meaning of Gestures*, in which we can find the words as follows: "What is the shape of your *heart*? No one can answer. It can be seen neither by you nor someone else. But can't it? Of course, the *heart* cannot be seen, but *heartfelt behaviour* can be seen. Because they are positive actions that people do for others out of kind-heartedness. The same can be said for *thoughts*. They also cannot be seen, but *thoughtfulness* can because it is linked to acts done for others. When a *warm heart* begets *warm behaviour* and kind thoughts beget kind action, a person's heart and mind come to be beautiful. This is what it means to be human being. (Miyazawa [2010], *The Meaning of Behaviour–For All You Early Adolescents*, Tokyo, pp. 108–109.)

What the author is probably trying to convey here is the existence of a trend in modern society emphasising the importance of concrete measures taken as a means to an end. However, as clearly expressed by the poem, not all events in life generate immediate results. If the heart is not in it, then the behaviour will not be effective and in the absence of thoughts, there can never be any thoughtfulness. Conversely, a heart without its incarnation in the form of behaviour is meaningless, and thoughts without thoughtfulness are akin to words written in sand. Therefore, the heart and behaviour, and thoughts and thoughtfulness, are both two ways of expressing a single concept, and we as human being cannot live meaningfully without having each of them functioning as one.

The basis of the Asset and Liability View is the focus on the "physical" world, or practical actions as a means to an end represented by assets, liabilities and net assets on the balance sheet. However, if such concrete actions are not based on "occurrences," (i. e. when abstract thoughts lead to commercial activities that give rise to the concrete assets and liabilities listed on a balance sheet, or an income statement that shows revenues and expenses), then we must hammer into our minds the fact that assets, liabilities and net assets we believe to exist in the real world will ultimately cease to be.

As a result, under an accounting concept based solely on the Asset and Liability View – or put another way, under today's accounting concept that overemphasises the balance sheet – the real image of transactions cannot be fully grasped and therefore the true nature of accounting can never be represented. The foundation of accounting, and of double-entry bookkeeping that supports its computation structure, must be verifiable by anyone at any time and reliability supported by truth and affirmation that assumes continuous recording, whereby the latter is obtained through the recording of economic events as they occur in real life. Continuous recording based on double-entry accounting, or the Revenue and Expense View, is itself the origin of accounting.

Meanwhile, market valuation which supports the Asset and Liability View was practiced at the same time double-entry bookkeeping came about. As you know, double-entry bookkeeping was developed in the city-states of Northern Italy at the onset of the thirteenth century as a means to annotate claims and debts. Double-entry bookkeeping, invented as an annotation method, blossomed into *Bilancio* (a kind of financial statement of inventory with appropriation of surplus) for physical inventories in the early fourteenth century. Double-entry bookkeeping, which has buttressed the income calculation structure of accounting, came about as the fundamental means of proving transaction facts, and as such the market value assigned at the time a transaction occurs, which then becomes historical cost with the passage of time. The numbers appearing therein must be reliable to all interested parties including investors and creditors.

It is natural that double-entry bookkeeping, which arose as a means of evidencing the correctness of trades instead of the authentic deed, was based on the concept of reliability. Which one is more reliable, the proving side (Revenue and Expense View) or the proved side (Asset and Liability View) ? Needless to say, the answer is clear.

Double-entry bookkeeping is an accurately recorded account based on fact in real transactions. Consequently, it is reliable to all people and has been used for as long as 800 years since its dawn. In other words, it subsists on that reliability underwritten by the facts (accuracy) and verifiability (transparency) of transactions which is the root of accounting. Under today's usefulness approach to the regulation of accounting, we can say that the fundamental significance of reliability has largely been forgotten.

Fair value accounting, the basis of the decision making usefulness approach, finds the roots in ASOBAT in 1966 as follows "We find historical-cost information relevant but not adequate for all purposes. We accordingly recommend that current-cost information as well as historical-cost information should be reported." (AAA [1966], *A Statement of Basic Accounting Theory*, Illinois, p. 19). This accounting concept was spurred into a gallop by the release of SFAC in 1978 leading in due course to the publication of IFRS No.13 "Fair Value Measurement" in 2011. However, we didn't need to wait until the twentieth or twenty-first century for a method that corrects the difference between historical cost and market value, because one was already in existence at the beginning of the thirteenth century at the same time of the appearance of double-entry bookkeeping.

The market valuation of receivables and loan, that is bad debts expense, has already appeared in the oldest account in 1211, and the valuation losses on equipment, furniture and fixtures can be found here and there in the ledgers of fourteenth century Italian merchants. Also, the market valuation of inventory assets is found in the late seventeenth century accounts of the English East India Company, as well as in many ledgers in eighteenth century Great Britain. Double-entry bookkeeping, from its onset, used both historical cost measurement and market value measurement concurrently. In other words, double-entry bookkeeping, the computing structure on which accounting is based, evolved through time encapsulating within it ever since its creation a system that corrects price discrepancies occurring with the passage of time. The prices at which transactions are all recorded are based on market value (present value) at the moment they are executed and the prices assigned merely transfigure into historical cost (past value) at the day of settlement after time has elapsed. In other words, market value measurement accounting can be defined broadly as historical cost accounting (concomitant accounting with both past accounting and present accounting = mixed attribute accounting), or as transaction price accounting.

However, market value, commonly known as current value, differs substantively from fair value, whose root is discounted present value (future value), a central figure in future cash inflow measurements, which first appeared in the 1950s. That is despite its "current" nature. That is because the time axis is fundamentally different depending on whether the posting is a record of an actual transaction based on fact, or some supposed deal based on conjecture. The most basic role of modern accounting is to provide information. But recently, its role as information useful for decision making has been overemphasised causing financial accounting to exceed its original calculation structure framework and thus deviate from the presentation of results based on fact and venture into the enchanted forest of forecasts and expectations. The reason is that in terms of useful information demanded by influential investors and speculators who head investment funds, corporate value information based on future cash flow estimates and forecasts is more useful in decision making than reliable earnings information based on past transaction facts, despite the former potentially containing unconfirmed elements.

Formerly, the FASB examined the useful nature of accounting information in its SFAC No. 1 "Objectives of Financial Reporting," published in November 1978 stating that "financial reporting should provide information that is useful to present and potential investors and creditors and other users in making rational investment, credit, and similar decisions" (par. 34). In addition, to guarantee its usefulness, it placed "relevance" and "reliability" as two equally-important precepts. At that time, everyone was fully aware that useful information had to be reliable. However, the conceptual framework of the 2010 IASB propounds that "to be useful, financial information must not only represent relevant phenomena, but it must also faithfully represent the phenomena that it purports to represent." (IASB [2010] F-4-41).

The SFAC and IFRS, which both initially advocated that it is the reliability of the information that makes it useful, caused rather the shackling of reliability in favour of providing useful information. As a result, verifiability was downgraded from being a fundamental feature of accounting standards formulation to a reinforcement feature, and reliability was removed completely from the reinforcement feature of useful information. This change is akin to madness. Instead, what has been released are faithful representations. What on earth are these representations being faithful to?

Double-entry bookkeeping, which has been supporting computational structure of accounting, has been passed down from generation to generation since the thirteenth century, because it is an income calculation system that is verifiable and reliable by anyone accurately based on the facts of transactions. Under the guise of usefulness and relevance, the Revenue and Expense View which begat accounting has been driven from prominence into a hidden corner. I would go as far as saying, "what and how well grounded are the arguments in such an accounting view?"

Izumi Watanabe

Section I

Status and Aspects of Fair Value Accounting

Chapter 1

Fundamental Functions of Accounting and Fair Value Measurement

― From the Perspective of Distributable Income Measurement Function ―

Toshifumi Matsumoto
Waseda Univercity

Abstract
  Since the end of 20th century Japanese accounting standards have introduced accounting methods from SFAS and IAS/IFRS. The primary objective of these standards is to provide corporate financial information to securities markets, and calculating distributable income is viewed less important. Actually these accounting standards contain a series of methods based on fair value measurements which is linked to recognition of appraisal gains (or unrealized income). The problem is that the recognition of appraisal gains is not limited to the domain of providing the financial information to capital markets but affecting the accounting by Companies Act and corporate tax regulation in Japan.
  Under such circumstances, some argue that the determination of distributable income should be delegate to Companies Act and the Tax Law, or others argue that comprehensive income including appraisal gain can be used as a basis for distributable income. In order to promote this type of debate, the relationship between distributable income and appraisal gains needs to be examined.
  In this chapter, analysis has started from reconfirmation of the importance of accounting as a distributable income calculation system. And then after distribution capability of appraisal gains

recognized by overall fair value accounting is examined, it is pointed out that the overall fair value accounting loses the function as the system of conventional distributable income calculation, and finally its alternative method based on cash flow is implied.

Keywords
functions of accounting, distributable income, overall fair value accounting, comprehensive income, appraisal gains, maintenance of capital, cash flow

1-1. Introduction

In response to the accounting big bang at the end of the last century and the EU's equivalence assessment on Japanese GAAP that followed, the FASB' Statements of financial accounting standards (SFAS), the IAS/IFRS and their accounting methods were introduced in Japanese accounting standards one after the other. Despite the announcement by the Minister of Finance that indicated the postponement of the decision to make IFRS application compulsory at a press briefing[1], as long as international cooperation continues to progress in capital markets around the world, the convergence of these standards to those of Japan and the upward trend in the number of companies applying IFRS in Japan, will likely proceed unabated.

The primary objective of SFAS and IFRS is to provide corporate financial information to the securities markets, adversely both providing information for business administration, and calculating distributable income as the basis for income available for dividend and taxable income are viewed less important. Actually, these accounting standards have introduced a series of treatment methods for fair value accounting (accounting that assumes the measurement of assets and liabilities based on an current exit price, an current entry price, value-in-use and other attributes) which is linked to the recognition of appraisal gains (or unrealized income). These standards, as I will mention later, not only affect Japan's Ordinance of the Ministry of Justice Regarding Corporate Accounts, but are also linked to tax accounting through tax return system based on approved final accounts.

Under such circumstances, some argue that the determination

---
[1] Financial Services Agency [2011], Business Accounting Council [2009].

of income available for dividend and taxable income are not the functions of financial accounting anymore and should be delegated to Companies Act and the Tax Law as their own function. Others argue that comprehensive income including appraisal gain can be used as the calculation basis for income available for dividend and taxable income. However, in order to promote this type of debate, the relationship between distributable income and appraisal gain needs to be examined. In this Chapter, I will clarify the limits of fair value accounting from the perspective of distributable income calculation and search for ways to recover those functions in fair value accounting system.

1-2. Triangular Relationship in Institutional Accounting Systems

(1) Three basic accounting functions

Looking back through the history of accounting, the root of the ledger is the recording of accounts receivable and accounts payable[2]. It is natural to consider that, as this entails, the fundamental function of accounting is to provide information necessary for management of assets and liabilitiies and for operation of a company.

When companies take on the form of joint investment whereby dividends are normally paid out to contributors of capital, it becomes necessary to calculate distributable income from the viewpoint of business maintenance. When doing so, if there are borrowings from banks, the calculation of distributable income bears the function of adjusting the interest of the proprietor and the creditors, and when corporation tax becomes a general system, the calculation of distributable income marks the starting point for the calculation of taxable income. Moreover, as capital procurement through stocks and bonds becomes commonplace with the expansion of economic scale, providing business information to securities markets is added to the functions of accounting.

When considering the above, we can assume that the following functions are expected to accounting at the very least.

(1) provision of information for business administration (record

---

[2] For example, Katano [1952], pp. 46–48.

of transactions, record of costs, evaluation of performance, etc.) (2) calculation of distributable income (income available for dividend, taxable income) (3) provision of corporate financial information to securities markets.

Among these functions, the provision of information to securities markets is thought to be the most important nowadays, and the remaining functions increasingly are left out of discussions all together. However, as far as the calculation of income available for dividend and taxable income is based on accounting system, and it goes by Companies Act and Tax Law, both functions of accounting is indispensable.

Table 1-1 is a verification of the importance of distributable income calculation function of accounting judding from the amount of relating resource allocations. Practically, this table shows the amount of total new capital procurement[3] by new share issues, the amount of dividend, and the amount of income taxes for Nikkei 225 Stock Average adoption brand, for the six-year period from FY2006[4] to FY2011. As presented here, from the perspective of resource allocation amounts, the distributable income calculation function is not inferior to the information provision function to securities markets.

---

[3] With respect to the information provision to securities markets function, the capital procurement amount from the sale of bonds should be added and, if the information provision function is to cover all capital markets in general, then the capital procurement amount from bank loans should also be added. However, because the procurement and settlement amounts are offset for these items on the balance sheet, the new procurement amount cannot be calculated from the account balance. Therefore, Table 1−1 does not show these items.

[4] From this fiscal year, the statement of changes in net assets showing the increase in capital from new issuances has been published.

Table 1-1: Accounting functions from the perspective of resource allocation amount

225 Nikkei Average adoption brand: FY2006 to FY2011 (nonconsolidated)	
Capital increase	10,103,678 million yen
(increase in capital a/c by new share issuance)	(5,069,906 million yen)
(increase in capital reserve a/c by new share issuance)	(5,033,772 million yen)
Dividend from surplus	24,507,892 million yen
Corporate income taxes	18,028,339 million yen

(Compiled from the Nikkei NEEDS-Financial QUEST)

(2) Change of the triangle relationship in three institutional accounting systems

— From net income to comprehensive income —

After World War II, in Japan, accounting regulated by former Commercial Law (tax laws) fulfilled the function of distributable (taxable) income calculation while accounting regulated by former Securities and Exchange Act fulfilled the function of providing information to securities markets.

Specifically, dividends and taxable income were calculated based on financial statements prepared in accordance with accounting regulations by the former Commercial Law, and the financial statements slightly revised were published on securities markets as a part of securities reports. This is the so-called triangle relationship between three institutional accounting systems (after this, "triangle relationship") whereby the accounting rules in the Commercial Law played the role of keystone.

However, in recent years, there have been significant changes to this framework. With the 2006 enforcement of the Companies Act came the abolition of provisions regarding corporate accounts and, in its place ordinance of the Ministry of justice regarding corporate accounts was enacted[5].

---

[5] The following explains the reason for the delegation of accounting regulations by the ordinance. "The globalization of corporate activity in recent years necessitated an international system of corporate comparison. International accounting standards came to be formulated thus requiring Japan to respond rapidly. As a result, the Revised Commercial Law of 2002 halted the stipulation by law from the items that stock companies should ascribe and record in their balance sheets to the asset

The ordinance substantially mandated the almost complete adoption of the ASBJ (Accounting Standards board of Japan) accounting standards[6], meaning that the responsibility for practically formulating this Ministry of justice was transferred from the Ministry of Justice to the ASBJ.

On the other hand, the relationship between the Financial Instruments and Exchange Act (former Securities and Exchange Act) and the Tax Law has changed and revisions to accounting standards by the ASBJ began to affect the Tax Law. Its precedent example is the 2000 revision of the Tax Law. In this revision the appraisal gain or loss of securities available for sale was to be added to income depending on certain conditions. This resulted from the adoption of "accounting standards for financial instruments" published in 1999 by Business Accounting Council of Financial Services Agency[7], the accounting standards setting body before the ASBJ. Moreover, in 2008, the ASBJ removed last-in first-out methods from the valuation methods of inventory[8] leading to the abolition thereof from the Tax Law[9].

---

valuation rules (the continental law method), and delegated it to the Ministry of Justice. (Izumida, Sato, Mitsuhashi [2008], p. 8).

[6] Upon the 2009 partial revision of the Ordinance on Company Accounting, the Ministry of Justice stated the following on its website HP under the title "Purpose of Revision": "This Revision consists of necessary corrections to the Ordinance on Company Accounting (2006 Ministry of Justice Ordinance No. 12) based on the delegation of the Companies Act (2005, Act No. 86) following the release of accounting standards on business combinations by the Accounting Standards Board of Japan and the recent revisions of related laws and regulations as a result of the requirement to converge with international accounting standards, as well as the partial revision of the Ordinance for Enforcement of the Companies Act (2006, Ministry of Justice Ordinance No. 12) based on the delegation of the said Act as a result of calls for various revisions from related parties".

(http://wwwmoj.gojp/MINJI/minji179.html)

[7] In 1998 The Securities Bureau of Ministry of Finance separated and became independent from Ministry of Finance as Financial Services Agency.

[8] ASBJ [2008a]

[9] Ministry of finance stated in 2009 that "in light of the revision of inventory asset valuation rules effected from the perspective of the international convergence of company accounting standards (September 26, 2008; ASBJ "Accounting Standard for Valuation of Inventories"), for the valuation of inventories in terms of taxation, upon the implementation of necessary transitional measures, last-in first-out method and simple average method shall be excluded from selectable valuation methods (Ordinance 28-1) ".

Like this, the previous situation where the accounting rules provided by the Commercial Law was working as the key stone has changed into the present situation where with the initiative of Financial Instruments and Exchange Act the accounting standards of the ASBJ are affecting the entire institutional accounting system.

The notable point here is a change in quality of Japan's accounting standards. The traditional accounting standards (typically the former Commercial Law's accounting rules and the corporate accounting principles issued by the Business Accounting Council of the Ministry of Finance), which supported the previous triangle relationship, were constructed based on cost-realization principles (after this, abbreviated to "cost-realization principles model"), in other words, revenue and expense view. On the other hand the aimed ultimate calculation structure of IFRS, to which Japan's accounting standards have been subject over the years for convergence, is presumed to be an accounting system which is based on the equity valuation model constructed on the relationship "fair value of assets + goodwill − fair value of liabilities = net assets = corporate value for stockholders[10]". Actually, SFAS and IFRS have adopted various accounting methods that make up this model one after another. Then, Japan's accounting standards are also changing from the conventional cost-realization principles model to so-called "mixed attribute model" or "hybrid type of accounting[11]" which partially integrates fair value accounting through the convergence with these accounting standards[12].

Table 1-2 shows a process of capital circulation of a monufacturing company. As indicated therein, the object of measurement based on fair value (an current exit price, an current entry price, value-in-use or discounted present value of expected cash flows) is not limited to the constituent items of "other comprehensive income" (difference in revaluation of other marketable securities, deferred gains or losses on hedges, foreign currency translation adjustment, difference in revaluation of land, etc.). Even in the calculation of current net income (operating income), fair value measurements are adopted and, as a result, current net income differs greatly from that of the former cost-realization principles model. This is so-called hybrid type of

---

[10] Tokuga [2011], pp. 93−102. Tsujiyama [2003], pp. 73−74.
[11] Ishikawa [2008], pp. 61−79.
[12] See Ishikawa [2008], pp. 175−216 for a detailed analysis of changes in the triangle relationship.

16 Fair Value Accounting in Historical Perspective

Table 1-2: Adoption of fair value accounting methods into cost-realization principles modl

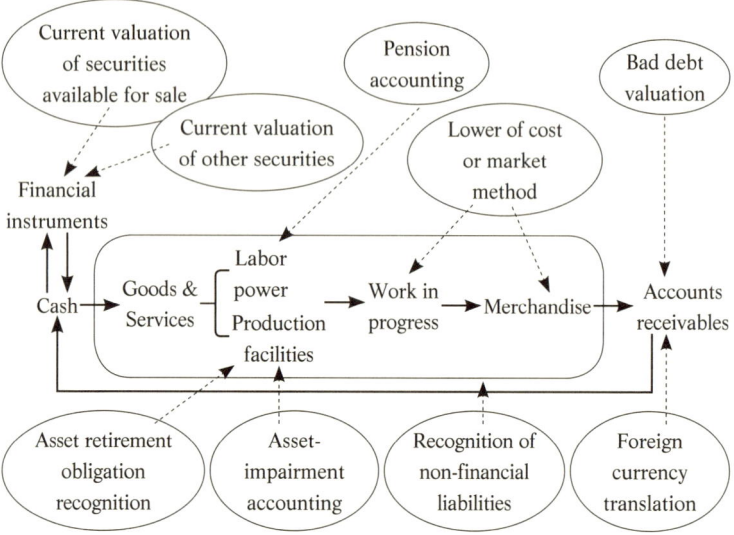

accounting meaning the transformation of the operating income or current net income into "partially comprehensive income[13]".

A typical example of this change is the accounting treatment of appraisal gain[14] on securities available for sale. Under the former Commercial Law, appraisal gain on securities available for sale was excluded from income available for dividend. But now, it is included in it by the Companies Act[15] enacted in 2006.

---

[13] In Japan's accounting system, valuation differences of assets and liabilities based on fair value measurements are divided into the following three types.

(1) Items difficult to recognize even if a valuation gain occurs (ex.: constituent factors of retirement benefit cost);

(2) Items easy to recognize that are calculated into net income (ex.: securities available for sale valuation difference); and

(3) Other items accounted for as other comprehensive income (ex.: difference in revaluation of other marketable securities); among them, (1) and (2) items cause the transformation of the so-called operating income or current net income into "comprehensive income".

[14] ASBJ [2008].

[15] The former Commercial Law admitted the current price valuation of the following asset items.

Chapter 1: Fundamental Functions of Accounting and Fair Value Measurement 17

However, no problems have arisen so far as a result of the above treatment. Table 1-3 is a tabulation of the appraisal gain, appraisal loss, and impairment loss for Nikkei 225 Stock Average adoption brand since the enactment of the Companies Act. As the figures indicate, the amount of appraisal loss accounted is much larger than the amount of appraisal gain. This is why no problem has arisen practically even if the appraisal gain for certain items is recognized.

Table 1-3: Appraisal gain, appraisal loss and impairment loss[16] added to current net income

225 Nikkei Average adoption brands: FY2006 to FY2011 (nonconsolidated)	
appraisal gain of securities available for sale	29, 311 million yen
appraisal gain of derivatives	17, 133 million yen
appraisal loss of securities available for sale	9, 969, 046 million yen
appraisal loss of investment securities	918, 210 million yen
appraisal loss of derivatives	25, 793 million yen
impairment loss	1, 939, 641 million yen

An essential feature of fair value accounting is to assume the

---

Monetary claims with market price (Article 30, par. 3 of the Ordinance for Enforcement of the Commercial Law); -Corporate bonds, national government bonds, regional government bonds and other securities with market price (Article 31, par. 2 and 3 of the Code); and -Shares with market price other than shares of subsidiaries (Article 32, par. 2 of the Code).

However, the Law stipulated that "if the total amount of the market price set thereto exceeds the total amount of acquisition price of the asset, the amount of net assets accounted for in the balance sheet that increased due to the market value set" is deducted in the calculation of distributable earnings. This was the same for the calculation of the maximum amount of interim dividend. But this treatment was abolished by Companies Act and the excess amount is now included in the distributable earnings. Regarding the dividend system of the current Companies Act, see, for example, Izumi, Sato, Mitsuhashi [2008], pp. 170–177, and Ochiai, Kanda, Kondo [2010], pp. 212–213.

[16] To find the general trend relating to the recognition of valuation differences, I tabulated in this table figures for the past 6 years since the enactment of the Companies Act, from FY2006 to FY2011, reported by the 225 Nikkei Average adoption brand.

recognition of appraisal gain. Although fair value measurements are currently resulted in substantially an application of the lower of cost or market basis, once the economic environment will change, there is the possibility that the amount of appraisal gain exceeds the amount of appraisal loss even in the Japanese mixed attribute model. This likelihood will increase as the introduction of fair value accounting methods into the current mixed attribute model advances.

Based on this understanding, when considering fair value accounting from the perspective of the distributable income calculation, the debate focuses on the following two points. The first is the distribution capability of the net appraisal gain (meaning the amount of appraisal gain in excess of the appraisal loss), and the other is the distributable income calculation method in the situation that the fair value measurements would be strengthened in the current accounting system.

1-3. Distribution Capability of Appraisal Gain

(1) Recognition of appraisal gain and funds available for distribution

The debate on appraisal gain recognition has been made from two points of view. One is the measurement of business performance and the other is the calculation of distributable income.

Firstly, under the traditional realization and earnings process approach (cost-realization principles model), not only the appraisal gain of goods and services occurring prior to sale, but also the appraisal gain from assets or liabilities under management have never been recognized as the achievement of business activities of an enterprise. The basic requirement for revenue recognition of this approach is the completion of an earnings process, where the sale of goods and services or the disposal of assets has been considered to be the fundamental sign of the completion. Meanwhile, recognition of earnings brings the outflow of cash (taxes, dividends). Therefore the existence of cash (fund) for distribution is necessary when earnings are recognized. The point of time to meet these requirements is generally when monetary assets is acquired through the sale of goods and services or the disposal of invested assets. Because of this, appraisal gain generated prior to sale is not recognized as revenue without the financial proof, or as unrealized income.

Against this traditional concept came the promulgation that strongly emphasizes the recognition of appraisal gain of marketable financial instruments[17]. First, the basis for the recognition of appraisal gain for the purpose of performance measurement is summarized as follows. "Financial assets held for resale are assets managed with the objective of increasing their intrinsic value within the range of permissible risk, therefore, there can only be market value as the basis for measuring the conditions for attaining the management objective. The crucial fact upon the valuation of the performance of that type of financial asset is not the extent to which sales proceeds operational at the discretion of the administrator or the asset manager were acquired during the fiscal term, but rather to what extent the total market value of the assets under management during the fiscal term has grown and therefore to what extent has grown the appraisal gain realizable at any time" (Daigo [1994], pp. 61-63). This concept is already being reflected in the accounting standards of countries worldwide including Japan.

Next, the basis for recognition of appraisal gain as the purpose for calculating distributable income is described as follows. "In both appraisal gain indicates current fiscal term asset performance and the amount can be easily transformed into fund of its equivalent, it sufficiently provides suitability as income available for distribution" (Daigo [1994], pp. 66-67). "If flexible supply of funds is required, rather than realized income as an aggregate of transaction profits which has been earned and used up conveniently for many purposes in the period, appraisal gains of securities retaining the liquidity in that it is cashable at any time at the end of the year are more appropriate income for distributions" (Daigo [1993], p. 31)[18].

Meanwhile, in response to this opinion, there is the view that negates the distribution capability of appraisal gain from the perspective of creditor protection as follows. "Securities whose value went up also bear the risk of a fall in value. The value of an

---

[17] Daigo [1993], Daigo [1994], Yanaga [2001], pp. 188-198.

[18] When disposing of securities to obtain the necessary cash for the distribution of valuation gains, those gains are partially realized. For example, assume that a company has securities of its acquisition cost 1000, current value 1200. If disposing of 200 worth of securities to distribute 200 in valuation gains from the securities, its acquisition cost would be 167 (= total acquisition cost 1000 × disposal price 200 ÷ current value 1200), resulting in a gain of 33. Put another way, the amount of 33 obtained from selling price 200 is recognized as realized and distributed.

enterprise is dependent on the valuation of risk. The more conservative is valuation, the lower the corporate value becomes. For this reason, even if the value of the securities goes up, there is no guarantee that the value of the company itself will go up the same amount. In such a case, if dividends are paid out only on the basis of the amount, then post-dividend corporate value will fall to the level lower than that before the rise in the price of securities. After the paying of a cash dividend to shareholders, the resulting decrease in corporate value is borne by the creditors" (Saito [1991], p. 10).

An explanation of the above is provided as follows. The assumption behind this debate is the dividend payout of capital gains without the disposal of securities. Here, if there is no surplus fund, then dividend funds has to be procured from some external sources. However, "if paying dividends quickly after procuring capital from the issuance of new shares to existing shareholders, then the enterprise is merely paying back to the shareholders the cash it received from them in the first place with therefore absolutely no economic significance. Even when having paid dividends to shareholders using funds contributed from a third party, this is merely a transfer of some of the equity of existing shareholders to that third party" (Saito [1991], p. 11). "In the end, a meaningful capital procurement method would result in borrowings, but if such borrowings were paid as dividends, while the company would have the same assets as before the loan was taken out, it would just have more debt than before. As long as the new obligations are not subordinate, they will increase the redemption risk of existing obligations and with a decrease in the value thereof comes a fall in the price of already issued corporate bonds" (Saito [1991], p. 11). In answer to this, "if only distributing realized gains, then the interests of creditors are not damaged" (Saito [1991], p. 12)[19].

(2) Distribution of appraisal gain and maintenance of capital

Under the shareholders' limited liability system, the sole collateral for creditors is corporate assets. Because of this, the Commercial Law, from the perspective of creditors protection, has come to show the principles of capital to secure certain assets when measuring distributable income. There are two aspects to this principle, one is the doctrine of capital maintenance which, as

---

[19] Saito [2009], pp. 137-151, provides a detailed examination of this problem.

presented in Table 1-4, requires that a company keeps its net assets (amount of assets exceeding liabilities), over and above its base amount (capital)[20], and the other is doctrine of the capital immutability that requires the maintenance of the initial capital amount itself[21].

Table 1-4: Meaning of the capital maintenance doctrine

Balance sheet

	Assets	Liabilities	
Net assets		(Capital) Net assets to be maintained	Shareholders' equity
		Distributable income	

Table 1-5 is a comparison of the effect on capital by differences in historical cost basis, lower of cost or market basis, fair value (market price) basis concerning securities valuation. As shown in the following example, on a historical cost basis the maintenance of capital requirement cannot be fulfilled if the current value drops[22].

In other words, lower of cost or market basis and fair value basis comply with the doctrine of the capital maintenance, however, the recognition and distribution of appraisal gain by fair value basis may infringe upon the doctrine of the capital immutability. It is explained in detail below.

---

[20] The portion not included in capital is excluded from dividend assets as legal capital surplus. That is to say capital contributed by shareholders is essentially the basic amount of net assets to be maintained.

[21] Tanaka calls the principle requiring the maintenance of the same amount of assets as capital the "capital maintenance doctrine," and the principle requiring that a certain proportion of capital be in the form of real property and that certain strict statutory procedures must be followed if desiring to decrease the amount of real property the "capital immutability doctrine." (Tanaka [1982], pp. 114-115). For details on the capital framework of the former Commercial Law, see Ishii [1967], pp. 37-40, Kishida [1991], pp. 360-362, and Maeda [2009], pp. 19-24.

[22] This point is probably one of the shortcomings of historical cost accounting (Yanaga [2001], pp. 193-194).

Fair Value Accounting in Historical Perspective

Table 1-5: Asset valuation criteria and maintenance of capital

Ex.: Incorporation with 100 in capital paid in cash converted into 100 worth of securities purchased at end of Term 0.

	Term 0	Term 1	Term 2	Term 3
Fair value (market value) of securities	100	80	110	90
Real net assets	100	80	110	90
① Valuation of securities based on acquisition cost	100	100	100	100
Capital	100	100	100	100
Net assets exceeding capital	0	(20)	10	(10)
② Valuation of securities based on lower of cost or market basis (clear-off and re-enter)	100	80	100	90
Capital	100	80	100	90
Net assets exceeding capital	0	0	10	0
③ Valuation of securities based on their fair value	100	80	110	90
Capital	100	80	110	90
Net assets exceeding capital	0	0	0	0

【Example】
(1) At end of Term 0, 100 in cash invested as capital for a new incorporation and then diverted for the purchase of 100 worth of securities.
(2) At end of Term 1, 50 in cash borrowed and 50 in appraisal gain from valuation of securities was distributed as dividends.
(3) At end of Term 2, the market value of securities drops to 120.
(4) Securities were disposed for 110 during Term 3.

In this example the disposal of securities acquired 110 at 100, and therefore this is a successful investment. However, regardless of this, as shown in Table 1-6, the amount of capital at the completion of the investment is 60 and therefore the 100 at the start of the investment is not maintained.

This is because 40 of the 50 in appraisal gain paid out as divi-

Chapter 1: Fundamental Functions of Accounting and Fair Value Measurement 23

Table 1-6: Fair value measurements and doctrine of the capital immutability

	Term 0	Term 1	Term 2	Term 3
	Purchase	Holding	Holding	Disposal during term
Current value of securities	100	150	120	110
Balance sheet:				
Cash	0	0	0	110
Securities (current value)	100	150	120	0
Borrowings	0	50	50	50
Capital	100	100	100	100
Surplus	0	50	(30)	(40)
Income statement:				
Appraisal gain on securities		50	(30)	0
Gain from disposal of securities		0	0	(10)
Income		50	(30)	(10)
Cash flow:				
Cash receipts from disposal of securities		0	0	110
Cash receipts from borrowings		50	0	0
Cash paid for Dividends		(50)	0	0
Net cash flow		0	0	110
Capital	100	100	70	60
Net assets	100	100	70	60

(Note) In fair value accounting, appraisal gain and revenue from sales are not differentiated. They are shown in different accounts here to clarify the difference of transaction.

dends during the investment period became "pie in the sky" due to a drop in its value. In other words, after having distributed the appraisal gain, if a condition "appraisal gain＞realized gain" would happen, the amount of capital at the end of the investment is lower than at the start, even if the investment itself is a success. In order to avoid such an infringement of the doctrine of the capital immutability, distribution must occur after the actual realization of the appraisal gain[23].

1-4. Characteristics of Fair Value Accounting

(1) Measurement based on value-in-use and accounting for appraisal gain

The current accounting system has the mixed attribute model structure with fair value accounting incorporated in the cost-realization principles model. However, with regard to appraisal gain generated from assets and liabilities other than securities available for sale and derivatives, its recognition is not permitted as a general rule[24].

Further, when comparing calculation structure on a theoretical level, the most substantial difference between overall fair value accounting and the mixed attribute model is that the former fundamentally assumes the recognition of appraisal gain not only for investment assets, but also for tangible fixed assets, other operating assets and intangibles, liabilities.

In this calculation structure, if deeming comprehensive income as distributable income including appraisal gain, then the amount of income and funds will deviate considerably thus necessitating the borrowing of a large amount of money (operating assets committed to business purposes cannot be easily disposed of like securities available for sale).

In fair value accounting, valuation is effected based on an current exit price, an current entry price, value-in-use and other aspects. Among them if value-in-use is selected as a measurement attribute for tangible fixed assets and intangible fixed assets, then there is no upper limit to the appraisal gain recognized as a result thereof. This is because, unlike the cost allocation method under which the unamortized balance of the acquisition cost is the upper

---

[23] From the viewpoint affirming the distribution of valuation gains, the decrease in value of securities after valuation gain distribution is deemed as a new failed investment post-distribution. In such a case, the decrease in capital is caused by the occurrence of a loss and therefore can be interpreted as not infringing on the doctrine of capital immutability.

[24] However, in pension accounting, valuation gain may be added to distributable income through the written off of actuarial gain or loss (=market value of plan assets-book value of pension assets with the expected return on plan assets added thereto) bringing down post-employment benefit costs.

Table 1-7: Properties of value-in-use and appraisal gain

At estimate	End of Term	0	1	2	3	4	Total
End of Term	Value-in-use						
0	709	−600	*200*	*200*	*200*	*200*	200
1	454	−600	**200**	*200*	*100*	*200*	100
2	1,859	−600	**200**	**200**	*1,000*	*1,000*	1800
3	190	−600	**200**	**200**	**200**	*200*	200
4	0	−600	**200**	**200**	**200**	**200**	200
	(1) Value-in-use	709	454	1,859	190	0	Total
	(2) Appraisal gain or loss	709	−255	1,405	−1,669	−190	0
	(3) Real CF	−600	200	200	200	200	200
	(4) Income	109	−55	1,605	−1,469	10	200
	(5) Cash deficit	−709	255	−1,405	1,669	190	0

(Note) (1) Value-in-use is the discounted present value of the future cash flow forecasts at the end of each fiscal term (portion in italics), with a discount rate of 5%. In gothic script is (3) the actual cash flow and the income for each fiscal term is the total of the actual cash flow and (2) the appraisal gain or loss (=term-end value-in-use minus the beginning of term value-in-use). (5) Cash deficit is the difference between income and CF (= (3) − (4)).

limit of the valuation amount, there is no upper limit to the expected amount of future cash flow, which is the essential element for value-in-use calculation.

Table 1-7 shows the properties of value-in-use. For example, if valuating operating assets based on value-in-use and distributing the appraisal gain recognized as a result thereof as is, then, as shown in the example in the table, a large gap occurs between income and actual cash flow (funds needed for distribution), and additional borrowings become necessary.

However, new borrowings not only weaken the financial position (damage the interests of creditors) of an enterprise by increasing the debt ratio as stated above, but by distributing appraisal gain before a project is completed and the gain is realized, the risk of bearing considerable loss of initial capital (net assets) appears.

(2) Overall fair value accounting calculation structure

Here, I assume again overall fair value accounting (all assets and liabilities accounted for applying fair value measurements) in its ideal form to verify its calculation structure through a comparison with other models. According to the comprehensive income calculation formula of "comprehensive income = current net income + other comprehensive income", appraisal gain or loss not added to current net income is itemized independently as "other comprehensive income". What enables this separate itemization is just the existence of the current net income calculation system based on continuous record of daily transactions. In contrast, overall fair value accounting adopts the process "fair value measurements of assets and liabilities ⇒ measurement of revenues and expenses ⇒ measurement of comprehensive income", then, continuous record of daily transactions is not necessary in principle. As a result, not only the calculation of current net income becomes impossible, the means to classify the realized and unrealized portions of the difference in revaluation of assets and liabilities are taken away. The following is the verification based on a simple example.

【Example】

Balance sheet at the beginning of the term

Cash	20	Borrowings	50
Machinery	40	Capital	100
Securities	30		
Land	60		
	150		150

Chapter 1: Fundamental Functions of Accounting and Fair Value Measurement 27

Midterm transaction and accounts closure data

		Transaction amount	Term-end book value	Term-end current value
(1)	Sales	200		
(2)	Purchases	120		
(3)	Business expenses (sales, general and administrative)	30		
(4)	Depreciation	5		
(5)	Receivables		30	25
(6)	Inventories		20	25
(7)	Machinery		35	45
(8)	Securities (investment)		30	45
(9)	Land		60	70
(10)	Intellectual property			40
(11)	Payables		24	24
(12)	Borrowings		50	47

(a) Cost-realization principles model

If assets are valued based on acquisition cost (cost allocation) and revenue (income) is recognized at the time of realization, then the following statement is drafted.

Term-end balance sheet

Cash	64	Payables	24
Receivables	25	Borrowings	50
Inventories	20	Capital	100
Machinery	35	Retained earnings	60
Securities	30		
Land	60		
	234		234

Income statement

Cost of goods sold	100	Sales	200
Business expenses	30		
Depreciation	5		
Bad debt	5		
Net income	60		
	200		200

(Note) bad debt 5 = (5) term-end receivables 30 − the current value thereof (recoverable amount) 25

Cash flow Statement

Sales	170
Purchases	96
Expenses	30
Cash flow from operating activities	44
Beg. of term balance	20
Term-end balance	64

(b) Mixed attribute model

The mixed attribute model can be interpreted in two ways as follows. First as an accounting system that measures current net income and comprehensive income doubly, where specific asset and liability items' difference in revaluation is added as "other comprehensive income" to current net income calculated by cost-realization principles model in principle.

If making this the formal mixed attribute model, the other way of interpreting it would be as an accounting system that partially incorporates fair value accounting methods in the process of measuring current net income by conventional cost allocation. In such a case, current net income (or operating income) essentially becomes comprehensive income.

The current comprehensive income measurement does not belong specifically to any of these interpretations but rather bears the qualities of both. That's because as current net income and comprehensive income are calculated simultaneously (formal mixed attribute model), on the other hand, the incorporation one after the other of fair value accounting methods into the current net income measurement process resulted in the current model in which comprehensive income elements are factored into current net income (substantial mixed attribute model).

Based on the previous Example, financial statements by formal mixed attribute model are obtained as follows (cash flows statement is omitted).

Term-end balance sheet

Cash	64	Payables	24
Receivables	25	Borrowings	50
Inventories	20	Capital	100
Machinery	35	Retained earnings	60
Securities	45	Accumulated other comprehensive income	25
Land	70		
	259		259

Profit and loss and comprehensive income statement

Cost of goods soled	100	Sales	200
Business expenses	30		
Depreciation	5		
Bad debt	5		
Net income	60		
	200		200
		Other securities Valuation difference	15
Other comprehensive income	25	Land valuation difference	10
	25		25
		Net income	60
Comprehensive income	85	Other comprehensive income	25
	85		85

(c) Overall fair value accounting

The term overall fair value accounting here means an accounting model whose purpose is to draft a balance sheet whereby "assets−liabilities=net assets=corporate value for stockholders". This is merely an ideal type and not occurring in real life. Assumed therein is the net assets which is the difference between discounted present value of expected cash inflows as total assets and discounted present value of expected cash outflows as total liabilities presents corporate value for stockholders. In practice, after having measured each individual asset and liability item based on fair value, surplus revenue factors (goodwill) are added in as brands and intellectual property. If applying this concept to the previous Example, the following statements result (cash flow statement is omitted).

Term-end balance sheet

Cash	64	Payables	24
Receivables	25	Borrowings	47
Inventories	25	Capital	100
Machinery	45	Comprehensive income	143
Securities	45		
Land	70		
Intellectual property	40		
	314		314

Comprehensive income statement

Increase in payable	24	Increase in cash	44
Comprehensive income	143	Increase in receivable	25
		Increase in inventories	25
		Increase in machinery	5
		Increase in securities	15
		Increase in land	10
		Increase in intellectual property	40
		Decrease in loans	3
	167		167

1-5. Searching for Distribution Standards in Overall Fair Value Accounting

For marketable securities that can be liquidated at any time, the distribution of resulting appraisal gain is debated. In overall fair value accounting, the calculation structure has all assets and liabilities subject to appraisal gain recognition. Furthermore unlike the current exit value (current realizable value, liability transfer price) or entry value (replacement cost), with which there are market price restrictions to the amount of appraisal gain recognized, for value-in-use, there are theoretically no limits to recognize appraisal gain. Today financial accounting system is moving more and more towards fair value accounting. In this situation, if adopting the position of denying the distribution of appraisal gain, it becomes necessary to identify appraisal gain from comprehensive income and remove it from distributable income.

Needless to say, as long as the current mixed attribute model is maintained, no extraordinary issues will arise. That's because if the transformation of current net income into comprehensive income doesn't go any further, we will be able to extract appraisal gain from the ledger and deduct net appraisal gain from distributable income. Problems occur when the financial accounting system switches from the current mixed attribute model to overall fair value accounting[25]. As stated above, if the ultimate goal of overall fair value accounting is to present corporate value for stockholders by the amount of net assets on balance sheet, then that accounting system will lose its function of separating the realized and unrealized portions of difference in revaluation (comprehensive income). (See the Example in the previous section). In such a case, if adopting the position of denying the distribution of unrealized gain (appraisal gain), then overall fair value accounting cannot calculate distributable income.

Despite the above, if the measurement of distributable income is still required in overall fair value accounting, this will have to be done under some methods. In such a case, the following methods

---

[25] The Nikkei's morning edition on November 6, 2006 had an article headlined "Europe and US agree to abolish net income, Japan will be unable to manage gains from disposal of shares". The reasons are as follows: "The expert bodies that formulate the corporate accounting standards of European countries and the United States agreed to the future abolishment of "net income" account items from the income statement and their integration into the "comprehensive income" account item, which reflects the fluctuation of the current value of held assets such as shares. The two most significant accounting standards in the world have moved toward a focus on comprehensive income, therefore Japan's standards will inevitably be affected. There will most likely be a call for countermeasures originating from Japanese corporations owning stock cross-holdings. In comprehensive income concept, current value fluctuations of shares and other assets subject to current valuation are reflected in the figure. This agreement will prohibit the recognition of gains from actual disposals of assets (recycling) because their gains are once recognized at term-end based on current value".

This plan can be undersood as follows that the abolition of net income and recycling is a pretentious attempt to switch the mixed attribute model comprehensive income calculation for the overall fair value accounting comprehensive income measurement. That's because net income and recycling point to the symbolic existence of mixed accounting whereby net income measurement based on the realization principle are preserved within comprehensive income measurement. Put another way, by abolishing term net income, the related realized and earned income measurement system may be hollowed out in one swift move. This plan ended in failure, but it doesn't mean that such a trial cannot find its way back to the surface in the future.

are considered.

(a) Carrying out the accounting based on cost-realization principles in parallel with overall fair value accounting to calculate distributable income

(b) Keeping continuous records of acquisition cost and appraised value for asset and liability accounts and calculate distributable income deducting net appraisal gain from accumulated comprehensive income

(c) Calculating substitute amount of distributable income from cash flow statement

As verified above, as long as realized earnings are distributed at the completion of the earnings process, the interests of creditors will not be violated. What meets this requirement is the cost-realization principles model, which supports triangle relationship before the accounting big bang. (a) is a method whereby this accounting system is applied in concert with overall fair value accounting and the current net income calculated based thereon can be not only the foundation for income available for dividend and taxable income, but also a type of managerial accounting information that indicates operating results not influenced by market price fluctuations[26].

Moreover, even if the current financial accounting system would transfer to overall fair value accounting, continuous record of daily transactions would remain essential to corporate management and therefore the recording system that has always backed the conventional cost-realization principles model would be maintained. (b) is a method that presupposes the above system whereby appraisal gain is extracted from the figures of term-end valuations and acquisition costs of assets and liabilities, and it essentially substitutes (a). The above method assumes continuous record of daily transactions and the performance measurements based thereon, however overall fair value accounting in itself does not necessitate continuous record of daily transactions. And the statement of comprehensive income drafted as a result of revaluation only presents the causes of changes in net assets and does not differentiate between realized and unrealized portions. In the quest for distribution standards with such restrictions, a clue is provided by cash flows from operating activities (hereinafter, CFO). An arrangement of the relationship between CFO and current net

---

[26] Matsumoto [2008], pp. 56-59.

Chapter 1: Fundamental Functions of Accounting and Fair Value Measurement   33

income results in the following formula (1).
　(1) CFO = current net income + depreciation + impairment loss
　　− increase of receivables − increase of inventories + increase of payables
　　− appraisal gain on assets + appraisal loss on assets − appraisal gain on liabilities + appraisal loss on liabilities (increase of provisions)
　　= current net income + depreciation + impairment loss
　　+ increase of working capital
　　− appraisal gain on assets + appraisal loss on assets − appraisal gain on liabilities + appraisal loss on liabilities

Within the above, because the increase of working capital is offset in a relatively short time, if removed it from the above formula (1), the following formula (2) results.
　(2) CFO = <u>current net income + depreciation + impairment loss − appraisal gain on assets + appraisal loss on assets − appraisal gain on liabilities + appraisal loss on liabilities</u>

Here, when calling the amount resulting from subtracting appraisal gain or loss from current net income (the underlined portion) the "income before adjustments", the formula (2) is abridged further as follows (3).
　(3) CFO = income before adjustments + depreciation + impairment loss

This income before adjustments is current net income without appraisal gain or loss on assets or liabilities, and represents the amount resulting from realized revenue minus allocated cost. The portion without asset and liability appraisal loss may exceed the amount of current net income, however, distributable income requirements seem to be satisfied somehow or other[27]. Therefore, the above formula can be expressed as follows (4).
　(4) Distributable amount = CFO − payback amount (depreciation + impairment loss)

This relationship will not change even under overall fair value accounting. Therefore, when the income statement is switched to the statement of comprehensive income under overall fair value

---

[27] As shown in Table 1−5, when peering through the cost principle (when not recognizing valuation loss), the capital amount may not be retained. However, cost principle accounting has been known as the calculation structure for distributable income. For this reason, "somehow or other" is stated here.

accounting, and the distributable income calculation function is lost, the distributable amount is measured by formula (4). However, to do this, the amount of depreciation, unnecessary under overall fair value accounting, has to be calculated. This also makes possible the measurement of impairment loss[28].

Note that, here, to show the relationship between CFO and current net income, the indirect method (difference analysis between income and cash flow) is used, however, overall fair value accounting's statement of comprehensive income has no current net income, depreciation, appraisal gain or loss on assets or liabilities items. Therefore, in overall fair value accounting, CFO is calculated by the direct method (cause analysis of cash flow).

1-6. Conclusion

Despite having lost its former vigor, Japan's accounting standards have been strongly influenced by fair value accounting since the accounting big bang. In this Chapter, in light of this trend, I examined the problems of fair value accounting from the perspective of one of accounting's basic functions, the calculation of distributable income. Originally, the priority (sole purpose) of fair value accounting is to provide information to capital markets and it can be understood as an accounting model whose intention is to present measurements of corporate value for stockholders. If so, then the recognition of appraisal gain unsuited for dividend distribution and tax imposition becomes essential and, although the possibility is small, if overall fair value accounting is effected in earnest, its calculation structure will not allow the separation of appraisal gain from comprehensive income. However, even if the calculation structure of accounting would have greatly transformed, and as a result thereof the use of financial statements

---

[28] This is the payback amount deducted from CFO. The point at issue here is whether to restrict the deduction to the conventional depreciation cost (in this case, impairment loss is included in asset valuation loss and deleted from formula (2)), or recognize impairment loss also as payback in the same way as depreciation cost. In overall fair value accounting, it is necessary to effect depreciation measurements individually because these factors are buried in the valuation differences of tangible assets (= term-end valuation amount − beginning of term valuation amount = new investment amount − retirement/disposal amount + increment amount − depreciation amount − impairment amount).

becomes obsolete for the purpose of calculating income available for dividend and taxable income, this doesn't mean that society will not be needing measurements of distributable income.

What is necessary in this situation is a distributable income measurement method based on (overall) fair value accounting. Specifically, conceivable way is either keeping the continuous transaction recording system which supported the conventional cost-realization principles or overturning the concept of distributable income and calculating it from operating cash flow as a substitute conventional distributable income.

However, even in such a case, measurements are impossible without the depreciation data based on conventional cost allocation system. Here may be the essential function of accounting.

The current financial accounting system stops at the mixed attribute model stage and has yet to attain the level of overall fair value accounting that presents genuine corporate value for stockholders by the amount of net assets. The current mixed attribute model can be interpreted as the result of having gradually introduced fair value measurements with the goal of rendering the above unrealizable information. However, this is akin to starting extremely difficult surgery on a patient who, despite completing relatively simple tasks, ends up being abandoned on the operating table because the method to treat the core problem was not found.

The current mixed attribute model looks like a patchwork pattern that partially incorporates fair value accounting methods in the cost-realization principles model and, it neither is a calculation system for distributable income (earnings) excluding market influence, nor presents net assets as the true corporate value for stockholders.

At present, current net income calculated under the mixed attribute model substitutes for distributable income. However, going forward, if accounting standards and/or the economic environment change drastically, this method may become ineffective. When this happens, the way of separating and purifying distributable income calculation from the information provision function of accounting will likely come to the surface up as a hard problem that should be solved in financial accounting area.

[References in English]
ASBJ [2008a], *Accounting Standard for Valuation of Inventories*.

ASBJ [2008b], *Accounting Standards for Financial Instruments*.
ASBJ [2010],*Accounting Standards for the Presentation of Comprehensive Income*.
Business Accounting Council [2009], *Draft Interim Report: Application of Inter-national Financial Reporting Standards (IFRS) in Japan*.
Financial Services Agency [2011], *About the Examination about the IFRS Application, 21st June*.
Ministry of finance [2009], *Reference Materials Revision-related in 2009 (including Economic Crisis Measures-related Taxation System Measures) (Corporation Tax Relations)*

[References in Japanese]

Daigo, Satoshi [1993]," On the Accounting Treatment of Increases in Market Value of Securities", *Kaikei (Accounting)* Vol. 143, No. 5.
────── [1994]," Relevancy of Market Value Accounting to Performance Evaluation and Distributable Income Determination", *Kaikei (Accounting)*, Vol. 146, No. 5.
Ishii, Teruhisa [1967], *Companies Act volume 1*, Keiso Syobo Publishing Co., Ltd.
Ishikawa, Junji [2008], *Changing Contemporary Accounting*, Nippon Hyouron sha Co., Ltd.
Izumida, Ei-ichi, Toshiaki Sato, Mitsuhashi Seiya [2008], *Company Act on Accounting*, Shinzan Books Co., Ltd.
Katano, Ichiro [1952], *A.C.littleton, Accounting Evolution to 1900*, Dobunkan Shuppan.
Kishida, Masao [1991], *Seminar : Introductory Companies act*, Nikkei Publishing Inc.
Maeda, Tsuneo [2009], *Introductory Companies Act 12th ed.*,Yuhikaku Publishing Co., Ltd.
Matsumoto, Toshifumi [2008]," The Intersection of Financial Accounting and Manage-ment Accounting ─ An Analysis of Features of Jsox, Asset Impairment Accounting and Comprehensive Income Concept ─ ", *Kaikei (Accounting)*, Vol. 173, No. 5.
Ochiai, Seiichi, Hideki Kanda, Mitsuo Kondo [2010],*Commercial Law volume 2 -Company- 8th ed*", Yuhikaku Publishing Co., Ltd..
Saito, Shizuki [1991]," Realization Principle and the Cost Basis Re-examined", *Kaikei (Accounting)*, Vol. 140 No. 2.
────── [2009], *Study on Accounting Standards,* Chuokeizai-sha, Inc.
Tanaka, Seiji [1982], *Full Revision Company Law Detailed Explanation Volume1*, Keiso Shobo Publishing Co., Ltd.
Tsujiyama, Eiko [2003]," The International Movement on Performance Reporting and the Challenges of Accounting Research",*Kaikei (Accounting)*, Vol. 163 No. 2.
Tokuga, Yoshihiro [2011], "Accounts Profit Model and Net Equity Valuation Model", *Kigyokaikei (Accountig)*, Vol. 63, Vo. 1.
Yanaga, Masao [2001], *Corporate accounting and law*, Saiensu-sha Co., Publishers.

Chapter 2

Advent of Fair Value Accounting and Its Historical Background

Noriaki Miyatake
Osaka University of Economics

Abstract

The Savings & Loan crisis of the 1980s resulted in an increase in criticism towards accounting standards based on the historical cost principle and an emphasis on the need for current value accounting. From around 1980, the revenue of S&Ls started deteriorating rapidly, and the accounting standard they should have complied to, was RAP, instead of GAAP. The RAP was a relaxed accounting standard to aid the S&Ls that merely delayed their eventual demise.

The GAO claimed that, if accounting standards were based on current value, the regulators should be able to implement appropriate measures before the crisis deepens, and thus the introduction of current value was advocated. Around 1990, current value accounting saw a sharp increase in supporters amongst congressmen and regulatory agencies. The FASB launched its Project on Accounting for Financial Instruments in 1986 inaugurating the examination of accounting standards for financial instruments as hopes grew for an increase in the role of current value accounting.

Enron witnessed rapid growth in the 1990s becoming America's 7th largest enterprise just 15 years after its founding. However, after peaking in 2000, its stock value plummeted in early 2001 with the burst of the "dot com" bubble and subsequently its shady accounting practices utilizing SPEs and giant losses became evident leading to its bankruptcy. The Enron debacle greatly impacted the U.S. accounting framework and corporate governance, which hitherto had been lauded both domestically and internationally as the best in the world.

On September 15, 2008, investment banking powerhouse Lehman Brothers collapsed and the subprime loan problem metastasized into a global financial crisis. The piling of losses by major financial institutions in the wake of chaotic markets led to demands to the SEC, FASB and IASB from market players and governments for a change in how fair value is measured with respect to financial instruments shedding light on the limitations of the fair value accounting.

Keywords

fair value, S&L crisis, regulatory accounting practices (RAP), project on accounting for financial instruments, Enron debacle, sub-prime loan problem

2-1. Introduction

The American Accounting Association (AAA) defined accounting in their *A Statement of Basic Accounting Theory* (*ASOBAT*) published in 1966 as "the process of identifying, measuring, and communicating economic information to permit informed judgment and decisions by users of the information[1]." This definition is very famous and is the catalyst that led to the emergence of the decision making usefulness approach.

The focus on decision-making usefulness intensified after 1978 when the FASB published its Statement of Financial Accounting Concepts (SFAC). SFAC No.1 *Objectives of Financial Reporting by Business Enterprises* states that "financial reporting should provide information that is useful to present and potential investors and creditors and other users in making rational investment, credit, and similar decisions[2]." Then, SFAC No.2 *Qualitative Characteris-*

---

[1] AAA [1966], p. 1.
[2] FASB [1978], para. 34.

tics of Accounting Information provides that "since a preference that possible errors in measurement be in the direction of understatement rather than overstatement of net income and net assets introduces a bias into financial reporting, conservatism tends to conflict with significant qualitative characteristics, such as representational faithfulness, neutrality, and comparability (including consistency)[3]."

This led to the 2011 publication of IFRS 13 *Fair Value Measurement*, which defines fair value as the price that would be received to sell an asset or paid to transfer a liability in an orderly transaction between market participants at the measurement date (i.e.: an exit price)[4]. IFRS 13 came to be as a result of an agreement between the IASB and FASB in 2009 to coordinate efforts with regard to fair value measurement[5]. Consequently, the above definition likely became the most authoritative in recent years. But not all questions and contradictions regarding fair value accounting have been addressed to date and there remain several issues such as applicable scope and evaluation method.

In this Chapter, I will mainly focus on the advent of fair value accounting in the U.S. and its historical background, and offer an analysis. I will consider the birth of fair value accounting and its significance mainly in terms of the S&L crisis of the '80s, which was partly the result of an insistence on fair value measurement, the Enron crisis of 2001 that caused accounting distrust due to diverse derivative trading and window dressing, and the subprime loan problem which surfaced in 2007 and led to the fall of Lehman Brothers in September 2008 bringing with it a global financial catastrophe.

2-2. S&L Crisis and Expectations toward Current Value Principle

(1) Overview of S&Ls

Savings and Loan Associations (a.k.a. S&Ls), a type of financial institution that specializes in savings deposits and home loans

---

[3] FASB [1980], para. 92.
[4] IASB [2011], para. 9.
[5] IASB [2011], para. BC9-BC18.

have their roots in the "friendly" savings associations that sprouted up in England and Scotland in the early 1800s[6]. In the same century in America, these same friendly savings societies gave birth to mutual savings banks, which grew significantly along with building societies that encouraged home ownership. The owners of these societies, their members, demanded cooperation in raising capital for the societies, meaning that those who already owned a home were asked to contribute capital as required so that it could be lent out for home building purposes. To the common laborer, these societies were very appealing. The first building society was established in 1840, and by 1890, they had grown in number to about 5000 with as much as $300 million in assets.

Building societies grew to the point that they started receiving deposits from individuals with no plans to build a home. The expansion of the American middle class made them take on the role of savings banks and later developing into S&Ls, whose historical roots are a mix of elements including friendly savings, mutual savings and building societies. Like other financial institutions, these societies suffered great losses in the Stock Market Crash of 1929 and the Great Depression that followed, however, S&Ls continued to grow thereafter until faced with a crisis in the 1980s.

(2) S&L crisis and historical background

Impacted by the Vietnam War and the Oil Shocks, America in the 1970s and 80s went through a serious inflationary period. Paul Volker, Federal Reserve Board Chairman from 1979, intensified monetary restraints and raised the prime rate to a maximum of 20%, a great leap upwards from the 12% charged up to that point, which had the effect of taming inflation but such a drastic increase in interest rates pushed the country into a recession. Housing starts, which peaked at 2,020,000 in 1978, went down to 1,290,000 in 1980 and 1,060,000 in 1982, half the annual total just four years earlier. S&Ls also shrank in number from 4,613 in 1980 to 3,825 in 1982[7]. Subsequently, the economy recovered with the help of the tax decreases and deregulations known as "Reaganomics," named after then-President Reagan, however, these measures led to an expansion of the "twin deficits" (budget

---

[6] Hoshino [1998], pp. 13-16.
[7] Eichler, N., [1989], pp. 71-72.

and trade).

The deposit interest liberalization of 1982 brought a sharp increase in bank insolvencies and, from 1988, they became pandemic[8]. The management of S&Ls deteriorated exponentially and every part of the country witnessed depositor runs on banks. The insurer of S&L deposits, the Federal Savings and Loan Insurance Corporation (FSLIC) had to outlay large amounts to bail out the S&Ls and settle claims and fell into the red by 1986.

In 1989, the first Bush administration enacted the Financial Institutions Reform, Recovery and Enforcement Act to rehabilitate the S&Ls. The FSLIC suspended operations, which were then transferred to the hitherto commercial bank insurer, the Federal Deposit Insurance Corporation (FDIC). In addition, the Resolution Trust Corporation (RTC) was established. Between 1980 and 1994, 1,617 banks closed their doors, among them were 1,295 S&Ls. That fourteen-year period witnessed about 70% of the 2,221 total bankruptcies filed between 1934 and 2002[9].

The following are considered as the causes of the operational difficulties faced by S&Ls in the 1980s[10]. (1) Mismatched terms: S&Ls basically procured capital from short-term deposits (debt) that was put to use as long-term home mortgages (assets), however, the inflation of the 70s and the interest rate laxing of the 80s brought more and more term mismatches that depressed interest revenues and caused back spreads; (2) Intensified competition with other types of financial institutions: With securities firm-issued MMFs greatly affecting the market, large amounts of deposits flowed from S&Ls to those securities firms; and (3) Expansion into non-housing sectors: Deregulation led to vast increases in capital management such as purchases of marketable securities and loans to private enterprise, however, these constituted unfamiliar territory to many and high-risk/high-return investments.

(3) S&L accounting problems

For the aforementioned reasons, the S&Ls' earnings situation deteriorated drastically starting from around 1980 and many saw

---

[8] Hamamoto [1996], p. 24.
[9] Kataoka [2004], pp. 3-4.
[10] Hoshino [1998], p. 40. Note that Hoshino [1998], provides other multiple causes (7 total).

their net assets begin to drop. Their regulator, the Federal Home Loan Bank Board (FHLBB) monitored operating conditions based on their capital adequacy ratio. When troubles began, the Board responded simply by lowering the minimum required ratio and enacting a defacto easing of equity regulations by adding accounting items that include equity and eliminating asset account items[11].

The accounting standard to which the reports filed by the S&Ls to the FHLBB had to comply was not GAAP but rather the Regulatory Accounting Practices (RAP). The authority responsible for formulating RAP was the FHLBB and, before the S&L crisis became evident, there were almost no discrepancies between RAP and GAAP. However, at the onset of the debacle, the FHLBB proceeded to revise RAP causing its deviation from GAAP that alleviated the superficial decrease in net assets without addressing the sharp deterioration of the banks' operating environment[12]. Significant accounting rules that were revised at that time include (1) deferral of loss on the sale of loans and (2) mark-up of fixed assets[13].

(1) allowed for the deferral of losses from the sale of collateral loans as intangible assets and amortize over the average remaining period thereof. The objective of this rule was to encourage the disposal of low-yield fixed-interest loans by the S&Ls and generate fees that exceed amortization expenses for such losses by loaning out again sales revenues.

(2) allowed the increasing of book values of fixed assets held up to the appraisal value whereby the resulting valuation gains pushed up nominal net assets and decreased the risk of capital adequacy ratio rule violations by many S&Ls[14].

Sadly, these measures did nothing more than temporarily extend their operation and the mid-80s saw a sharp rise in S&L closures. As the financial burden of deposit insurance payments ballooned to an enormous sum, Congress and the media started blaming RAP for causing the crisis and GAAP was once again in center stage[15].

---

[11] Sawabe [1998], pp. 97-98.
[12] Watanabe [1998], p. 98.
[13] Margavio [1993], pp. 17-19.
[14] Davis & Hill [1993], p. 70.
[15] Federal government expenditures needed to bail out or liquidate the S&L industry totaled $481 billion, including bond yields for capital procurement. The total

(4) GAAP criticism and current value accounting expectations

Although criticism towards RAP led to a return to GAAP, this did not bring an end to the crisis. It was the amount of net assets of the bankrupted S&Ls that highlighted the need for a deposit insurance mechanism, but since GAAP is applied to going concerns, it did not meet the expectations of those looking for a solution.

The General Accounting Office (GAO) complained of the complexity of estimating the amount of bailout capital necessary for the S&Ls (via the FSLIC) based on their financial statements using GAAP under the historical cost principle[16]. Because historical cost accounting ignores fluctuations in market value generated by financial instruments, financial statements cannot provide indications of interest rate risk. Moreover, holding gains are realized through the disposal of financial assets at a market value higher than the book value, meaning that bank managers are incentivized to engage in "gain trading" in the books.

From around 1990, current value accounting rapidly gained support among congressmen and regulators, notably SEC Chairman Breeden and Office of Thrift Supervision (OTS) Director Ryan who stressed the usefulness of current value accounting[17]. This turn of events sparked a search for a current value based accounting system as part of a greater effort to reform the financial system. The participation of the SEC, which pushed for the introduction of the current value principle, meant that this problem did not end with the S&Ls' accounting but encompassed the entire accounting framework. Criticism toward RAP for triggering the S&L crisis may have been one of the reasons for demanding that GAAP provide for the measurement and disclosure of financial investments.

---

included $87.9 billion in RTC costs for handling the settlements of as many as 747 S&Ls up to their dissolution in 1995, as well as $64.7 billion in FSLIC handling costs (The Nikkei, July 13, 1996, Evening Edition, p. 2).

[16] General Accounting Office [1991], pp. 20–24.

[17] Oishi [2012], pp. 176–177. Note that OTS is not controlled by the Office of the Comptroller of the Currency: OCC).

2-3. Arrival of Fair Value Accounting

(1) FASB's project on financial instruments

The FASB launched its project on accounting for financial instruments in 1986 as a vehicle to examine financial instrument accounting standards at a time when expectations toward current value accounting abounded. This move was not only to counteract the S&L crisis but also to shed light on the realities of derivative trading, which was continuing to expand in volume.

Events that shook the stock markets in the late 80s and early 90s include "Black Monday" (October 19, 1987) on which the Dow Jones Industrial Average fell an unprecedented $508, or 22.6%, P&G's gigantic losses on interest rate swaps in 1994, huge losses on the structured loans of California's Orange County, and the 1995 bankruptcy of the U.K.'s Barings Bank, dubbed the "Queen's Bank", from losses incurred from the derivative trades of a single employee.

The project concluded that, although there was a need for a comprehensive and top-to-bottom integrated accounting standard that handled recognition, measurement and disclosure, such a standard could not be realized over a short period. Therefore, it advised that the examination of "disclosure" in the notes be conducted in phase 1, and the examination of "recognition and measurement" in the financial statements be conducted in phase 2[18].

(2) Phase 1 of the project on financial instruments[19]

SFAS No.105 *Disclosure of Information about Financial Instruments with Off-Balance-Sheet Risk and Financial Instruments with Concentrations of Credit* Risk published in 1990 provided the first results of the project on financial instruments and stipulated rules for the disclosure of information on financial instruments. disclosure requirements were divided into three main categories: (1) Disclosure of Extent, Nature, and Terms of Financial Instruments with Off-Balance-Sheet Risk, (2) Disclosure of Credit Risk of Financial Instruments with Off-Balance-Sheet Credit Risk, (3) Disclosure of Concentrations of Credit Risk of

---

[18] Suzuki [2002], p. 7. Note that phase 3 was to constitute "classification of liabilities and capital," however, the regulator concentrated in phases 1 and 2.

[19] Yamada [1995], pp. 72-75.

All Financial Instruments.

SFAS No.107 *Disclosures about Fair Value of Financial Instruments* published the following year calls for the disclosure of the fair value of all financial instruments by all businesses regardless of whether they are recognized on the balance sheet. For financial instruments, that includes both assets and debt. This standard has two major aspects: (1) if fair value can be estimated, the method and important assumptions used in the estimation of the relevant financial instruments must be disclosed, and (2) if fair value cannot be estimated, information regarding the estimation of the financial instruments in question (ex.: book value, effective interest, maturity date) and the reasons why fair value cannot be estimated must be disclosed.

Phase 1 concluded with the release of SFAS No. 105 and No. 107, however, as derivative trading volume increased thereafter, many pointed to the former's inadequate disclosure of the risks inherent in derivatives, which were limited to disclosure as off-balance sheet risks. For options, SFAS No. 105 only requires the disclosure of put options and not call options, which have no off-balance sheet risk, leaving investors potentially unable to fully comprehend the intention of and facts behind an enterprise's acquisition of financial instruments disclosed under No. 105. For this reason, a new examination of ways to improve derivative disclosure was begun leading to the publication of SFAS No.119 *Disclosure about Derivative Financial Instruments and Fair Value of Financial Instruments* in 1994.

SFAS No. 119 may be divided into two parts, new areas of derivative-related disclosures and a revision of No. 105 and 107. There were three new areas of disclosure: (1) disclosure of the same scope, nature and conditions prescribed by No. 105 of derivatives not subject thereto by holding purpose (trading and other purposes); (2) disclosure of the average fair value during the term and the end of term fair value, and quantitative information on net gain and loss on transactions and other items; and (3) disclosure of holding purpose and financial statement indications of derivatives held for purposes other than trading, as well as mainly qualitative information on account items relating thereto if such were held for hedging futures. SFAS No. 105 and No. 107 were revised to add a few disclosure items based on the results of the application thereof, require disclosure by holding purpose and call for new disclosure items relating to derivatives.

(3) Phase 2 of the project on financial instruments[20]

SFAS No. 114 *Accounting by Creditors for Impairment of a Loan* published in 1993 handles standards regarding the recognition, measurement and disclosure of impairment loss on loans[21]. The recognition of impairment loss is required when the possibility heightens of the inability to collect the entire loan amount (total principal and interest) as provided for in a contract. The measurement method of impairment loss using the discounted present value calculated after discounting the future cash flow forecast by the effective interest rate is provided for as the principle method (some cases allow for measurement based on market price and collateral property fair value). The handling and disclosure items relating to the recognition of revenue after impairment loss was recognized are also stipulated.

SFAS No. 115 *Accounting for Certain Investments in Debt and Equity Securities* of 1993 targeted not all financial instruments but only equity securities and debt securities whose fair value could be easily calculated setting forth the handling of their accounting treatment and reporting. It also categorizes subject marketable securities based on holding purpose into three types and presents a respective accounting treatment method and disclosure standards applicable to each. (1) Held-to-Maturity Securities: Valuated by the amortized cost method on the balance sheet (whereby current term amortizations of premiums or discounts are accounted for in current term profits). (2) Trading Securities: Measured based on fair value on the balance sheet with any resulting unrealized valuation gain or loss accounted in current term profits. (3) Available-for-Sale Securities: All other securities not applicable to (1) or (2) among equity and debt instruments whose fair value is easily determinable. Although such are measured using fair value on the balance sheet, unrealized valuation gain or loss is not accounted to current term profits but rather reported separately in the equity section.

Hoshino (1998) states that SFAS No. 115 was published as a result of the S&L crisis indicating "to increase the variability of periodical gain or loss and equity, financial institutions subject to equity regulations that hold vast amounts of financial assets want to avoid accounting impact and to do so implement various mana-

---

[20] Yamada [1995], pp. 73–74.
[21] SFAS No. 114 was revised to become SFAS No. 118 [1994], "Accounting by Creditors for Impairment of a Loan-Income Recognition and Disclosures".

gerial measures and face various economic effects" (p. 151). In addition, No. 115 classified marketable securities into three types by holding purpose each with a different applicable valuation method, however, "because this approach invites arbitrariness when classifying marketable securities and the possibility of using accounting information to soften the accounting impact resulting from such classification, among other effects, the risk problem may be further complicated" (p. 155).

2-4. Enron Affairs and Fair Value Accounting

(1) Enron

The precursor of Enron was the result of the 1985 merger between a Nebraska gas company called "InterNorth Inc." and a Texas company called "Houston Natural Gas" (HNG), which took the name "Enron" the following year. With HNG's Kenneth Lay at the helm as CEO, the new medium-size company's activities at that time were uneventful, consisting of supplying natural gas through pipelines running across America's wilderness, a typical old economy enterprise. During the 1980s, Enron stated in 1987 that its goal was to become the No. 1 natural gas company in North America and, by 1990, it had actually attained it with a 15% share of the market[22]. While Enron expanded its natural gas business globally, it planned power plant constructions at various locations and branched out into the electric power supply business.

This management style changed drastically with the deregulation of the 1990s, which saw the market entry of a series of new players and the creation of a new energy market to ensure smooth trading. This deregulation was the result of Kenneth Lay's personal relations with President George H.W. Bush and Enron's lobbying efforts with respect to both the Republican and Democratic Parties.

Enron grew exponentially with the help of variegated derivatives trading in this newly formed market. They handled not only futures, options and other relatively easy to understand instruments, but also new derivatives that dealt with weather and broadband lines. Enron continued to grow well into the 90s after Bill Clinton came to power in 1993 and, in 2000, was ranked 7th in sales among U.S. corporations by Fortune magazine[23].

---

[22] Oshima and Yajima [2002], p. 34.

However, after peaking in the spring of 2000, the IT bubble started crumbling and Enron's stock price stopped climbing[24]. Enron announced in October 2001 that it had been accounting huge losses through Special Purpose Entities (SPE) outside the scope of consolidation and was reversing about $1.2 billion in equity as a result. The following November, the company reported a revision of several years of financial statements and sought to merge with Dynergy in a desperate plea for survival, however, the deal fell through and Enron subsequently filled under Chapter 11 of the Bankruptcy Code on December 2, 2001.

Enron also planned a move into the Japanese market establishing "Enron Japan" in 2000 to realize plans for the construction of a thermal power plant. But Enron collapsed prior to any making any real progress and its Japan subsidiary falled for bankruptcy immediately thereafter.

(2) **Historical background**

The 1990s, the period of Enron's sharp rise, was the decade that followed an era of global turmoil marked by the dissolution of the Soviet Union after the end of the Cold War, the democratization of Eastern European countries, the unification of East and West Germany, the burst of Japan's real estate bubble and the invasion of Kuwait by Iraq sparking the Gulf War. However, optimism abounded thanks to the overall favorable U.S. economy under the Clinton administration, which began in 1993, the so-called "New Economy" driven by the IT revolution and continuous, globalization-fueled, inflation-free economic growth. This optimism was also based on the idea of the success of democracy with America as the "sole victor" and only superpower.

Despite the positive economic conditions on the whole, huge losses were being reported on countless occasions in the area of derivative trading. The more IT advanced, the more complicated and large scale derivatives became. Hedge funds were also greatly popular during this period. The sale of pound using the Bank of England in 1992 by George Soros' Quantum Fund is a famous

---

[23] No. 1 that year was Exxon Mobil, and No.'s 6 and 8 sandwiching Enron were Citigroup and IBM.

[24] Enron's stock price could barely reach $10 for years after its establishment in 1985, but it skyrocketed to over $80 in 2000 after climbing sharply starting in the mid-90s.

example of hedge fund activity at that time. The latter half of the 90s was marked by the Asian currency crisis of 1997 and the Russian financial crisis the following year. The ensuing violent market fluctuations impacted financial institutions and hedge funds placing highly leveraged bets to the tune of several times their own capital outlay. Even the "Dream Team" fund Long-Term Capital Management (LTCM), whose ranks included two Nobel laureates, essentially collapsed under the strain of humongous losses.

Regardless of the series of crises, derivatives and hedge funds continued to expand enjoying a rise in average share value. However, the year 2000 began with the fall of the dot-coms caused partly by the sharp rise of NASDAQ, the market's counteraction of the IT boom and a hike in interest rates starting from the latter half of 1999. After exceeding $1,000 for the first time in 1995, NASDAQ, heavy with high-tech and IT stocks, saw a rapid increase to over $5,000 in March 2000, its highest level ever. The bubble burst not only erased its dramatic increase but pushed the market down to $1,100 by the end of 2002, returning to its level in the latter half of 1996.

(3) Enron and fair value accounting

Enron's accounting practices were characterized by (1) the inflation of profits using SPEs and placement of assets and debt off the balance sheet, (2) huge stock options-based compensation of managers and executives, and (3) exaggerated revenue figures resulting from an aggressive utilization of fair value accounting. Regarding (1), as already indicated by much advanced research, Enron made use of the rule that allowed for the exclusion of SPEs capitalized externally at 3% or more of total equity from the scope of consolidation to justify transferring its losses to SPEs that spotlighted a facade of soaring profits. In its efforts to recruit external sources of capital for some of its non-consolidated SPEs, Enron would offer help in fund procurement and some cases involved its employees. These SPEs were initially established to be excluded from consolidation[25].

---

[25] Because Enron did not post SPE debts that should have been included in the scope of consolidation, its total liabilities as of end of 1999 were shown as being $700 million less than the real amount. From the latter half of 2000 to 2001, a period of 15 months, revenues from the sale of assets to SPEs and other machinations increased

The distribution of stock options in itself, as mentioned in (2), is allowed and CEO Kenneth Lay and his successor Jeffrey Skilling, along with multiple executives, received massive remunerations to the tune of several tens of millions of dollars. However, if the high stock price from which these payments were made was the product of accounting improprieties, then these practices constitute nothing else but criminal activity.

(3) is considered the result of the 1998 publication of SFAS No. 133 *Accounting for Derivative Instruments and Hedging Activities*, which required all derivatives to be measured based on fair value and posted on the balance sheet with any net differences in fair value accounted as a current term gain or loss or other comprehensive income[26]. As derivative trading volume expanded, the market saw repeated cases of gigantic losses and fair value-based measurement was expected to heighten the level of transparency of derivatives. However, Enron used it merely to boost its own stock price.

At a time when the electric power market was still young, Enron was a major player. Many participated in short-term futures transactions, which were lively, but few dealt in the long-term and there was much wiggle room for price manipulation. Takatera (2004) states that "the early recognition of profits by enterprises in the 1990s (particularly Enron) was promoted by fair value accounting, which expanded from market value accounting to current value accounting" (P.206).

(4) Post-Enron movements

The Enron debacle had a tremendous impact on the United States' accounting framework and corporate governance, which had hitherto been lauded as the best in the world both domestically and internationally. Questions arose as to whether the huge executive payouts based on stock options resulting from accounting irregularities using SPEs constituted insider trading. Execs dumped their shares just before the price tanked leaving general investors and employees to suffer huge losses. Enron employees were not only encouraged to invest directly in Enron stocks but

---

earnings by $1 billion. Mr. Powers, who was in charge of internal investigations, said that over 70% of net earnings recorded during this period did not exist. (The Nikkei, February 6, 2002, Evening Edition p. 1)

[26] Chuo Aoyama Audit Corporation [2005], p. 57.

also purchased shares as part of their 401k pension plans. In addition, Enron utilized California power outages for making profits and its actions resulted in several criminal and civil lawsuits.

The Enron affair was also a failure of corporate governance. According to U.S. Senate subcommittee members, the outside directors of Enron's audit committee, Arthur Andersen LLP, had received reports of the company's risky accounting practices over 2 years prior to its bankruptcy. Enron's board of directors even approved some of the off-the-books transactions using SPEs entwined with Enron derivatives, despite understanding the extreme risks being taken[27].

The neutrality of audit firms and analysts also posed a major problem. Andersen, one of the so-called "Big 5" accounting firms, was Enron's auditor. The issue of an audit firm acquiring a remuneration for audits from the target company was compounded by Andersen's acquisition of revenue for consulting work leading many to surmise that it purposefully overlooked Enron's window-dressing. Andersen subsequently destroyed all documents relating to Enron and in 2002, a year after the latter's collapse, it was forced to dissolve after allegations of overlooking Worldcom window-dressing which led to the mass exodus of its clients.

To cope with the distrust towards the accounting framework and corporate governance, the SEC demanded in 2002 that the CEO and CFO of every public company in America draft a written oath affirming the accuracy of its accounting statements. The same year, the Public Company Accounting Reform and Investor Protection Act, a.k.a. the "Sarbanes-Oxley," or "SOX," Act, was enacted. The SOX Act's main objectives include (1) to strengthen the quality control and independence of audits, (2) to reform corporate governance and tighten and clarify corporate responsibility, and (3) to fortify disclosure requirements[28]. The accounting system was changed by (1) increasing the external source capitalization minimum requirement for SPEs to be accounted for outside the scope of consolidation from 3% to 10%, (2) requiring a detailed explanation of publicly announced figures that exclude extraordinary losses, etc. at the discretion of the company such as "real pro-

---

[27] The Nikkei, July 8, 2002, Morning Edition, p. 9.
[28] See KPMG AZSA LLC's website (http://www.azsa.or.jp/b_info/keyword/sox.html).

fit" and "proforma profit[29]", and (3) the expensing of stock options by the publication of the Revised SFAS No. 123 *Share-Based Payment* in 2004.

2-5. Subprime Loan Problem and Fair Value Accounting

(1) Subprime loan problem and its historical background (pre-Lehman)

Subprime loans are home mortgages designed for people with relatively low credit and income whose issuance increased with the rise of home values. The bonds created to securitize sub-primes, called "Mortgage-Backed Securities" (MBS), proliferated worldwide, but a decline in home values that increased defaults on those sub-primes sparked a financial crisis that led to the collapse of Lehman Brothers, or the "Lehman Shock." A downward trend in home values became apparent towards the end of 2006, falling to about 30% of their peak in 2006 by the end of 2008. The mortgage delinquency rate had grown from around 13% at end of '06 to a monstrous 40% by '08 and, during the same period, sub-prime loan MBS dropped some 60% in value, even those rated "triple A," with BBB-rated MBS losing over 90% of their value[30].

The start of 2007 was marked by the bankruptcies of sub-prime loan issuers, their number increasing sharply by the following year. Large banks were announcing big valuation losses one after the other, doubtful accounts were disposed and financial instruments were being sold off to secure cash, triggering declines in financial instrument prices including MBS. The downgrading of "monoline" financial insurers made matters worse as it caused the downgrading of financial instruments that were highly-rated due their backing by trusted, "triple A" rated monoline insurance. Then in March 2008, Bear Stearns essentially went belly-up and

---

[29] There is also the EBITDA (earnings before interest, taxes, depreciation, and amortization) published by Worldcom. Managers were strongly pressured by the market to calculate the gains expected by Wall Street as proforma gains and the gains actually posted were the result of a calculation close resembling the same (Izumi Watanabe, "Excessive Management of Gains," The Nikkei, August 20, 2002, Morning Edition, p. 26).

[30] Bank of Japan [2009], p. 25. Note that the MBS handling commercial properties also fell approx. 30% (AAA-rated) and approx. 80% (BBB-rated).

was bought out by JPMorgan Chase[31].

Next, in July, Government Sponsored Enterprises (GSE) Fannie Mae and Freddie Mac fell into hard times and were placed under the stewardship of the government. Their main business was home mortgages and they owned a substantial quantity of MBS. Debt instruments issued by these GSEs that were held overseas amounted to $1.3 billion thus generating a systemic risk if not bailed out by the government[32].

(2) Subprime loan problem and historical background (post-Lehman)

On September 15, 2008, investment bank giant Lehman Brothers closed its doors and the subprime loan problem had already metastasized into a global financial crisis. Its collapse led some MMFs, known to be safe investments, to dip below par.

On the same day of Lehman's demise, another megabank, Merrill Lynch, was acquired by Bank of America. That month, 2 out of the remaining 5 large investment banks, namely Morgan Stanley and Goldman Sachs, accepted financial assistance from the U.S. government and FRB and became bank holding companies[33]. Another top five investment bank, Bear Stearns, was completely eradicated just 6 months after its bankruptcy. Also that month, America's largest S&L, Washington Mutual, dissolved and mega-insurer AIG underwent troubles that called for a government lifeline that placed it in public hands. More financial institutions would face crises and reorganizations. Citigroup received government aid while Wachovia acquired Wells Fargo. This financial crisis' tentacles also reached the automotive industry. April 2009 witnessed the bankruptcy of Chrysler, and June that year saw GM's demise.

Not long after the world started getting back on its feet from this financial Medusa, a European sovereign debt crisis originating in Greece came to the surface. This debt crisis not only affected

---

[31] For details on the financial institution operating crisis and the government's response thereto, see Okina [2010], pp. 12–13.

[32] Kobayashi [2008], p. 18.

[33] Both investment banks became bank holding companies enabling the handling of deposits as commercial banks. Although subject to monitoring by the FRB, which is more stringent than the SEC, it became possible to accept liquidity assistance through FRB capital infusions (Kobayashi [2008], p. 19).

Portugal and Ireland but also threatened large-scale economies like Italy and Spain. Meanwhile, the American economy was settling in comparison to the tumultuous "Lehman Shock" aftermath period. New York's Dow Jones Industrial Average fell to $6,600 in March 2009, less than half its peak of $14,000 in October 2007. However, by the end of 2009, it had jumped back to over $10,400 and then recovered to a level exceeding $13,000 at the end of September 2012 amidst fears of the European financial crisis.

(3) Subprime loan problem and fair value accounting

Takatera and Kusano (2009) state that one of the subprime loans related accounting issues, accounting for sales of securitization transactions, actually preceded subprime accounting. "As if the formula used by banks for lending symbolically switched from the book value/hold to maturity model (holding a loan to term) to the composition/sale model (securitize and sell loans), banks began recognizing early (or post in advance) gains (or losses including negative gains) based on short-term principle accounting linked to sale accounting (disposal of securitized transactions by selling) and fair value accounting prior to sub-prime loan accounting" (p. 179).

An example of this is the accounting for sale of securitized transactions by New Century Financial (NCF)[34]. An overview is provided as follows. NCF executed a sales agreement with a loan buyer (investor) and sold the loan for a price above face value. The agreement stated that, upon satisfaction of certain requirements, NCF would buyback the loan from the investor. Although NCF needed to set aside a large reserve in preparation for buybacks, it did not do so. NCF collapsed relatively early after the world learned of the sub-prime loan problem, and the aforementioned accounting treatment is considered one of the causes.

Supposedly, even if that company had put aside sufficient reserves, experts conjecture that handling the aforementioned 90% decrease in the value of MBS would have been a daunting task. The Lehman Shock drove down the value of a wide spectrum of financial instruments, not just MBS, and large financial institutions saw an increase in losses that one after the other either led them down the path of bankruptcy, or government assistance. In addition to direct transactions, banks were using off-the-books

---

[34] Takatera and Kusano [2009], p. 181, authors summarize p. 181.

"Structured Investment Vehicles" (SIV), whose regulations were relatively lax, to invest in financial instruments. There were many cases where these SIVs had neither employees nor offices and were managing assets in name alone with the banks that established them acting as asset managers. In January 2007, there were 55 such SIVs but most went bankrupt causing their parent banks to suffer more losses[35].

The expansion in losses incurred by large financial institutions as a result of market turmoil led to pressure from the markets themselves and the government on the SEC, FASB and IASB to force a change of the fair value measurement of financial instruments. Those three regulators responded and the limitations of fair value accounting were brought to light. In the U.S., the SEC's authority to suspend SFAS No. 157 *Fair Value Measurements* was reaffirmed by the Emergency Economic Stabilization Act enacted after the Lehman Shock. The FASB published the FASB Staff Position (FSP) FSP FAS157-3 *Determining the Fair Value of a Financial Asset When the Market for That Asset Is Not Active* and FSP FAS157-4 *Determining Fair Value When the Volume and Level of Activity for the Asset or Liability Have Significantly Decreased and Identifying Transactions That Are Not Orderly* which allowed companies to not employ fair value when such is determined as being a market value with low liquidity or a clearance sale price.

The IASB revised IAS No. 39 *Financial Instruments: Recognition and Measurement* after considering the recognition of changes of financial instrument classification only in rare cases of SFAS No. 115 applicability[36]. This revision allowed, in rare cases, for the switching of classifications of debt instruments held for "trading" purposes to "Held-to-Maturity" or "Available-for-Sale", and the reclassification of loans made for "trading" purposes with the intention of securitization to "loans and receivables". IASB was criticized for their lack of due process in this revision despite imposed time limitations[37].

---

[35] Ueda [2010], pp. 27-28.
[36] Yamada, Kaneko and Hiramatsu [2009], p. 89.
[37] The background is provided in detail by Yamada, Kaneko and Hiramatsu [2009], pp. 87-93.

2-6. Conclusion

In this chapter, in discussing the historical background of the advent of fair value accounting, I indicated the problems with GAAP based on the historical cost principle arising as a result of the S&L crisis and pointed to the heightened expectations toward current value accounting as one of the culprits. However, in light of the Enron affair and subprime loan problem, there are evident defects in the accounting for unrealized gains and the measurement method of financial instruments, among others, based on current value accounting and later fair value accounting. Based on the historical cost principle, unrealized valuation gains are not accounted for in the ledger, therefore, it is generally not accounted for in the same way as valuation losses. Losses are posted off-balance sheet, so they are not revealed even if a company's financial conditions deteriorate. This is particularly true regarding fixed assets whose high values greatly affect enterprises as a whole. When contradictions become too substantial to hide, huge losses suddenly jump to the surface. This is what happened to the S&Ls.

On the other hand, when measuring the fair value of financial instruments without a clear market price, there is the risk of failing to remove arbitrariness resulting in the posting of excessive unrealized valuation gains. If this results in an increase in stock value or dividends or large executive remunerations, then that company's survival may be in question. This is what happened to Enron.

One way to avoid this situation is to apply the low cost method, however, in financial crises such as when economic bubble burst, posting or cutting out valuation losses may result in a decrease in financial asset value. This was the pattern of the sub-prime problem and the confusion resulting from fair value application.

Accounting systems and standards have been improved each time there occurred a financial crisis or cases of accounting improprieties following the Enron affair. However, preventing these problems from occurring in the future armed only with the power of accounting is extremely difficult. Controlling economic booms and busts and formulating appropriate penalties and rules to safeguard against illegal activities and "gray-zone" practices exceeds the role of accounting.

Nevertheless, an accounting system that includes disclosure requirements bears certain responsibilities toward the financial system and can potentially fulfill an important role in resolving the aforementioned problems. Examples would include the further revision of the scope of consolidation and the clear classification of unrealized and realized gains. Although the consolidation scope was supposed to have been strengthened after the Enron scandal, the same mistakes were repeated during the subprime debacle (increase of off-balance-sheet transactions using SIVs). The classification of gains restricts excessive dividends and executive remunerations thus allowing a company to prevent large capital outflows from its coffers, maintain its ability to counteract valuation losses in time of economic downturns, and anticipate effects that enhance survivability.

In an age when the financial economy greatly exceeds the real economy in scale, the importance of fair value accounting seems to have risen. However, on the other side of the coin, as actualized by the Lehman Shock, the sharp increase in valuation losses and changes in standards brought upon by political pressure, exposed the imperfections of fair value accounting. Fair value accounting may have been one of the causes of the global financial crisis.

[References in English]
AAA [1966], *A Statement of Accounting Basic Theory*. Davis, H. and J.W. Hill [1993], "The Association Between S & Ls' Deviation from GAAP and Their Survival", *Journal of Accounting and Public Policy*, Vol. 12, No. 1.
Eichler, N. [1989], *The Thrift Debacle*, Berkeley.
FASB [1976], *An Analysis of Issues Related to Conceptual Framework for Financial Accounting and Reporting: Elements of Financial Statements and Their Measurement, FASB Discussion Memorandum*.
―――― [1978], *Objectives of Financial Reporting by Business Enterprises, Statement of Financial Accounting Concepts No. 1*.
―――― [1980], *Qualitative Characteristics of Accounting Information, Statement of Financial Accounting Concepts No. 2*.
General Accounting Office [1989], Troubled Financial Institutions: Solutions to the Thrift Industry Problem, GAO/GGD-89-47.
―――― [1991], *Failed Banks : Accounting and Auditing Reform Urgently Needed*, GAO/AMFD 91-43.
Hill, J.W. and R.W. Ingram [1989], "Selection of GAAP or RAP in the Savings and Loan industry," *The Accounting Review*, No. 4.
IASB [2011], *Fair Value Measurement No.13*, IFRS.
Lev, Baruch [2003], "Corporate Earnings: Facts and Fiction", *Journal of Economic Perspectives*, 17 (2).
Levitt, Arthur [1998], "The Numbers Game", *NYU Center For Law and Business*, New York.
Margavio,G.W. [1993], "The Savings and Loan Debacle: The Culmination of

Three Decades of Conflicting Regulation, Deregulation, and Re-Regulation, *The Accounting Historians Journal*, Vol. 20, No. 1.

Hodge,Frank D. [2003], "Investors' perceptions of earnings quality, auditor independence, and the usefulness of audited financial information", *Accounting Horizons*, Vol. 17.

Neef,Dale [2003], *Managing Corporate Reputation and Risk*, Elsevier.

Nissim,Penman [2008], *Principles for the Application of Fair value accounting*, Columbia Business School.

Thomas.C.William [2002], "The Rise and Fall of Enron" ,*Journal of Accountancy*, Vol. 13, No. 4.

Razaee,Z. and J.T.Lee [1995], "Market Value Accounting Standards in the United States and their Significance for the Global Banking Industry", *The International Journal of Accounting*, Vol. 30, No. 3.

Report of the Staff to the Senate Committee on Governmental Affairs [2002], *Financial Oversight of Enron: The SEC and Private Sector Watchdogs*.

Walton,Peter [2007], *The Routledge Companion to Fair Value and Financial Reporting*, New York.

【References in Japanese】

Ando, Hideyoshi [2007], *A Study on Accounting*, Chuokeizaisha, Inc.

Chuo Aoyama Kansa Hojin [2005], *American Accounting Principles: 2006 edition*, Toyokeizai-Shinposha.

Hamamoto, Michimasa [1996], "The S&L Crisis and Accounting Policies in the U.S.", *Kaikei Kensa Kenkyu (Accounting Auditing Reserch)*, No. 14.

Hoshino Ichiro [1998], *Accountings research on the financial crisis*, Dobunkan Shuppan.

Kataoka, Hisayoshi [2004], "Deposit Insurance Premium System in the U.S. and Canada", *Yokin Hoken Kenkyu (Study on Deposit Insurance)*, Vol. 1.

Kitamura, Keiko [2011], *Fair Value measurement: Significance and limitations*, Japan Accounting Association Special Committee.

Kobayashi, Shinya [2008], "The Collapse of American Type Financial Capitalism", *Kinyu Zaisei jijo (Financial Affairs)*, No. 2008-13, October.

Koga, Chitoshi [2009], *Innovation of financial Accounting*, Chuokeizai-sha, Inc.

―――― [1999], *Derivative Accounting*, Moriyama Shoten.

Kusano,Toyomi [2007], "Integration between hedge funds", *Economist*, No. 2007-31,July.

Kusano, Masaki [2005], *Income Accounting Theory*, Moriyama Shoten.

Nihon Ginko (the Bank of Japan) [2009], *Kinyu Shijyo Report (Report on the financial market)*, No. 2009, July.

Obinata,Takashi. [2012], *Financial crisis and accounting regulation: fallacy of the fair value accounting mesurement*, Chuoukeizai-sha, Inc.

Oishi, keiichi [2012], "Framework of Financial Regulations", Obinata, Takashi [2012], *Finacial Crisis & Accounting Regulation*, Chuokeizai-sha Inc.

Okina, Yuri [2010], *Financial Crisis and Prudence Policy*, Nikkei Publishing Inc.

Okumura, Koichi ([2000], "A big wave of power liberalization: Enron hits japan", *Economist*, No. 2009-12, September.
───── [2001],"This is Enron", *Economist*, No. 2001-13, March.
Okumura, Hiroshi [2002], *The Enron Shock: A Crisis for Corporations*, NTT-Publishing Co., Ltd.
Oshima, Haruyuki, and Atsushi, Yashima [2002], *There is Something Wrong With the U.S.*, NHK-Publishing, Inc.
Saito, Shizuki [2007], *Discussion Material : Conceptual Framework of Financial Accounting*, Chuokeizai-sha, Inc.
Sawabe, Norio [1998], *Global Financial Regulations and Accounting Systems*, Koyo Shobou.
Suzuki, Naoyuki [2002], "Historical View of American Accounting Standards Until the Proposal for Jeneral Fair Value Accounting of Financial Instruments", *Nihon Ginko Kinyu Kenkyujo Discussion Paper (Bank of Japan Institute for Monetary and Economic Studies Discussion Paper)*, No. 2002-J-6
Takasu, Norio [2012],"Establishment of Decision Making Usefulness Approach and Formation of Conceptual Framework ── From a Viewpoint of Accounting Regulation in America ── ", Chiba, Junichi and Tsuneo, Nakano eds., *History of Accounts and Accounting*, Chuokeizai-sha Inc., pp. 373-409.
Takatera, Sadao [2004], "Early income Recognition in Aggressive Accounting", *Osaka Keidai Ronsyu*, Vol. 55, No. 1.
Takatera, Sadao, Masaki,Kusano [2009], "A Critical Study in Subprime Accounting", *Osaka Keidai Ronsyu*, Vol. 59, No. 6.
Takayanagi, Kazuo [2005], *The Enron Affair and American Corporate Law*, Chuo University Press.
Tsunogaya, Noriyuki [2009], *Discounted Present Value Accounting*, Moriyama Shoten.
Ueda, Kazuo [2010], *World Finance Over Sight of World Finance and Economic Crisis*, Keio University Press Inc.
Urasaki, Naohiro [2002], *Fair Value Accounting*, Moriyama Shoten.
Watanabe, Izumi [2012], A Warning Bell from History on The Excessive Usefulness Approach of Decision Making, Working Paper of Osaka University of Economics, No. 2012-1, April.
Yamada, Tatsumi [1995], "Research and Survey on Trends in American Financial Accounting Standard in Connection With Financial Instruments", *Shoji Homu (Judicial Affairs of Commercial Matter)*, No. 1402, No. 1995 -5, October.
Yamada, Tatsumi, and Akira, Kaneko and Kazuo, Hiramatsu [2009], "Present Situation and Problems of IFRS", *Zeikei Tsushin*, No. 64-1.

Chapter 3

Current Status and Issues of Fair Value Accounting

Toshitake Miyauchi
Otemon Gakuin University

Abstract
 Because of the convergence of International Financial Reporting Standards and national accounting standards, or more precisely the adoption of International Financial Reporting Standards in many countries worldwide, the amount of accounting information that is based on fair value measurements is on the rise within national accounting standards. This includes cases of mandatory application of International Financial Reporting Standards that point to fair value accounting, as witnessed in Europe. The number of account items that measure fair value went up, meaning that the number of companies practicing financial reporting based on International Financial Reporting Standards rose resulting in the fast-paced accumulation of empirical research analysis results on the economic consequences that fair value accounting engenders.
 The purpose of this paper is to determine whether fair value accounting improves the information role, or whether it has any effect on the contract role, based on a survey of such empirical results. The conclusion of this paper is that fair value accounting does not necessarily improve the information role and may negatively affect the contract role, in the case of financial contracts,

because of the unreliability and high volatility of fair value measurements.

Keywords
Fair value, hardness, investment decision role, contract role, reliability, value relevance, debt covenants

3-1. Introduction

The new formulation, revision or abolition of national accounting standards based on the outlook of convergence with, or adoption of, International Financial Reporting Standards (hereinafter referred to as "IFRS,") is increasing the amount of accounting information based on fair value measurements within national accounting standards worldwide. Actually, there are several fair value concepts embedded into Japan's accounting standards. Since fiscal 2005, E.U. states have required companies to apply IFRS when drafting their consolidated financial statements and, since fiscal 2009, Japan has allowed the application of IFRS in the disclosure of financial statements resulting in an increase in the number of companies adopting an IFRS-based financial reporting system. Such a rise in the quantity of account items that measure fair value, or rise in the quantity of companies reporting on the basis of IFRS, whose core espouses fair value measurement, is leading to the rapid piling up of results of analyses of empirical research focused on the economic consequences of fair value accounting.

The purpose of this research is to survey these empirical results in order to shed light on the current status and issues involving the functions of accounting which fair value accounting affects. Specifically, this survey is to learn whether fair value accounting has improved the information role and whether it has any impact whatsoever on the contract role.

The composition of this paper is provided as follows. Section 2 will classify the descriptive style taken by the surveys and clarify the style of this paper. Section 3 points out the accounting functions in which fair value accounting is emphasized and examines the extent of the hardness of fair value accounting. Sections 4 and 5 show the effect fair value accounting has on the information role as well as on the contract role. Lastly, a conclusion to the argument will be provided.

3-2. Survey Pattern

In this research, a survey on the economic consequences brought upon to the information role and contract role as a result of the expansion and progression of fair value accounting is planned, however, there exists Obinata [2011], Shuto [2011] and Tokuga [2011]. In writing survey paper, we have a choice of descriptive style.

The first style is the "status and issues clarification type survey" whereby prior research is conducted extensively on a certain topic and, by reporting the facts known inductively, current conditions such as what is clarified (or not clarified), what contradicting research results are presented (what should be tested in future research), etc. are brought to light with regard to that topic generating issues encompassing it. Obinata [2011] and Shuto [2011] adopted the above style in their paper. The former indicates that, based on an overview of a great multitude of empirical literatures on fair value, the expansion of fair value accounting brings with it two grave defects, namely more opportunities for discretionary reporting on the part of managers and the deterioration of the usefulness of reports. The latter surveys whether the information role of accounting is improved by the introduction or increase of accounting standards that require fair value measurements presenting the possibility that fair value accounting does not necessarily improve the information role.

The second style is the "hypothesis testing type survey." In research that is commonly called "empirical," sample companies are extracted to test the suitability of a hypothesis to be proven based on the data provided thereby. This style was applied to the surveys. Specifically, after establishing a hypothesis to be proven, a comprehensive survey of research results is conducted based on samples of empirical results taken from already published journals to support or reject the hypothesis. For example, although he employed the wording "accounting standards" (not "empirical results"), this is the style Obinata [2002][1] is thought to employ.

---

[1] In Obinata [2002], while setting the matching concept as the core of the Revenue and Expense View, he confirms that the same concept is not required in the Asset

The third style is the "norms advocacy type survey" under which multiple norms that propose a certain vision for accounting are laid out to enable a demonstration comparing the merits of those norms based on the facts discovered through the empirical research survey. Tokuga [2011] establishes norms for two types of accounting standards setting, namely the accounting profit model and net asset book value model, and attempts to prove the appropriateness of those norms, as well as governmental policies on the establishment of accounting standards based thereon, through an empirical research survey.

The purpose of this Task Force is to clarify the original functions of accounting through historical research. When considering the significance of this paper in light of this purpose, it is believed that the expectation of resolving problems through historical research determining how fair value accounting affects modern accounting, or what problems fair value accounting faces, based on experiential knowledge acquired by employing an empirical approach is in line with the purpose of the Task Force. Therefore, in this paper, a "status and issues clarification type survey" is conducted.

3-3. Accounting Functions and Hardness of Fair Value

(1) Accounting functions and fair value accounting

Basic functions fulfilled by financial accounting information are known to aid in the decision-making process of investors and the coordination of interests among stakeholders. Suda [2000] calls the former the "information role," defining it as the "function that provides accounting information useful for the decision-making of investors to promote effective transactions on securities markets" (pp.16-17), whereas the latter is labeled as the "contract role", defined as the "function that promotes the supervision and performance of contracts to reduce conflicts of interest among the parties thereto thus lowering agency costs" (pp.21-22). Of these

---

and Liability View and then establishes the hypothesis "if accounting standards based on the Asset and Liability View became dominant, then there should be few standards explained in the matching/allocation concept" thus confirming the wording of enormous standards. As a result, he indicates that the Asset and Liability View, which negates matching and allocation, is not well-rooted.

two basic functions, the primary objective of IFRS, which aggressively pushes forward the progression of fair value accounting, is the fulfillment of the information role. If this occurs, fair value accounting (or accounting standards that proactively incorporate fair value accounting) should, at the very least, be evaluated from the viewpoint of whether its main objective is being fulfilled, that is to say whether fair value accounting is useful in the fulfillment of the information role. Moreover, because accounting figures are used in contracts that require the coordination of interests, fair value accounting should be examined to the greatest extent possible also in terms of its effect on the (subordinated) contract role.

(2) Fair value accounting and hardness of measured values

When evaluating fair value accounting, a factor that cannot be ignored is the level of hardness[2] of fair value measurements. The Revenue and Expense View, formerly the basis of conventional accounting standard formulation, made net income, which indicates how well a company is performing, the linchpin of accounting system formulation. Specifically, income was calculated by evaluating assets based on historical cost followed by the allocation of the costs thereof after setting multiple allocation rules. However, it has been pointed out that the sheer number of allocation and matching rules presented opportunities for earnings management by managers. Meanwhile, the central player in the Asset and Liability View, the basis for recent accounting standard formulation, is the direct presentation of corporate value through the measurement of net assets as the difference between assets and liabilities after evaluating future economic benefits and sacrifices that would engender assets and liabilities. Because of this, there is no need for the formulation of meticulous rules that provide for allocation and therefore no abuse in earnings management on the part of managers. However, regarding the measured values of account items, there is another view that the estimated values have problems such as the lack of visibility of estimation processes.

This section introduces typical empirical results regarding the hardness of fair value measurements. The interference of personal

---

[2] Ijiri [1975] defined the lack of room for disputes over measurement as the hardness of the measurement. For instance, A *"hard"* measure is one constructed in such a way that it is difficult for people to disagree, and *"soft"* measurement is one that can easily be pushed in one direction or the other (p. 36).

discretion on the part of managers in fair value measurements is spotlighted in prior surveys. Obinata [2011] shows that discretionary fair value estimation of low hardness are made for tangible fixed assets, goodwill, stock options, financial instruments and other account items. Shuto [2011] states that the discretionary nature of fair value measurements is divided into two levels, "opportunities for discretion" and "motive for exercising discretion," arguing based on experiential evidence that fair value accounting provides new opportunities to managers to use their own personal discretion not proffered by conventional historical cost-based accounting and thus showing that the act of earnings management by managers is based on opportunistic motivation. Moreover, Tokuga [2011] points his finger at three factors that affect the hardness of accounting values, namely accounting actor, measured object and measurement method and, while quoting empirical results, states that fair value measurement hardness is biased by these three factors[3].

In relation to subsequent discussions on the matter, typical items were taken from researcehes quoted in the aforementioned survey papers to confirm the hardness of fair value measurements (for details, refer to Obinata [2011], Shuto [2011] and Tokuga [2011], respectively).

Juettner-Nauroth [2004] points to problems with financial instruments such as derivatives that are traded on inactive markets when estimating pseudo-fair values for an active market. Results of simulations using models reveal that, even if estimates are based on a single evaluation model, any change in the scenario, conditions or other fundamentals for measurement will result in

---

[3] The accounting actor bias is brought in by the estimating actor when forecasting forward-looking economic benefits and sacrifices of account items. For example, measurement values tend to vary depending on the experience of the estimating actor (whether that person has a technical or management background, etc.), the existence of incentives relating to accounting measurements (performance-linked compensation, etc.), among others. Next is the measured object bias that presents itself when there is a discrepancy in the amount of effort expended on estimation depending on the relative ease of forecasting. For example, forecasting the value of intangible fixed assets and the value-in-use of tangible fixed assets is quite complex compared with other account items. Lastly, the measurement method bias affects measurements depending on which calculation model and variables are selected when measuring items based on any estimation model, for example, selecting the Discounted Cash Flow Method, Binomial Model or Black-Scholes Model and difference variables such as discount rate, among others (Tokuga [2011], pp. 28-29).

fair values with no value relevant. Carlin and Finch [2009] found that, in their survey of goodwill impairment accounting practices by Australian companies, (1) fair value measurements vary significantly depending on the discount rate, and (2) the act of choosing a discount rate presents opportunities to maneuver periods of impairment loss accounting. As indicated by the aforementioned research, fair value measurements greatly fluctuate depending on the conditions and input variables selected at the time of estimation.

Next, the following four literatures may be provided here as examples of research on accounting actor that effectuate discretionary fair value estimations and the motive therefore. Zhang and Zhang [2007] stated that during business combination efforts, managers dislike burdening their entities with amortization expenses from assets succeeded from the acquired firm and tend to overestimate the fair value of goodwill. Under U.S. GAAP, acquiring firms allocate costs (depreciation and amortization) after a reevaluation of the debt on the acquired firm's tangible fixed assets and recognizable intangible assets based on fair value measurements subsequent to the business combination. Further, the difference between the value paid at the time of acquisition and the fair value of recognizable assets is recognized as goodwill, which then undergoes the impairment test. It was discovered that, with this system as a backdrop, managers can avoid amortization costs of indistinguishable assets by overestimating the proportion of the acquired firm's indistinguishable assets to post a more significant amount of goodwill. Shalev *et al.* [2010] reported that the higher the proportion of bonuses paid out on an annual profit base in total management remunerations, the greater the amount of goodwill recorded (or the greater the fair value measurement of goodwill). The bonus plan determined based on annual income as part of a CEO's compensation package is more likely to motivate people to present their entity's performance in a better light, compared with stock options and other equity-based compensation, thus leading to the ballooning of goodwill, an un-amortizable asset, leaving behind amortizable assets that are charged to income (or the overstating of goodwill fair value). Dechow *et al.* [2010] found that, when managers evaluate the fair value of retained interests after having securitized claims, the discretionary selection of the discount rate, which is an input variable in fair value estimation models, the setting of a personally desirable fair value is the outcome. Coundhary [2011] indicates that stock options given to employees are understated by companies that account for them as expenses on their income statement in comparison to companies that disclose stock option fair value measurements in the notes to financial statements.

As illuminated by the aforementioned prior research, fair value measurements may be leveraged as a tool when opportunistically reporting performance. The next Section and beyond is an examination of the impact of fair value accounting, which is saddled with the issue of hardness, on the fundamental functions of accounting.

3-4. The Information Role and Fair Value Accounting

This Section examines whether fair value accounting improves the information role by dividing empirical research results into several perspectives, the first of which is the comparison of the usefulness of net income and comprehensive income with apparent disparities in views of income. If calculating net income, conventionally based on an accounting system that espouses the Revenue and Expense View, using the Asset and Liability View based on fair value accounting, income would be labeled as comprehensive income computed as the difference between beginning-of-term and end-of-term net asset valuation. Considering its relation to net income, comprehensive income is presented as "net income + other comprehensive income," the latter of which includes value measurements of land not necessarily traded on active markets, such as land valuation difference, as well as measurements based on estimation models (not mark-to-market values but mark-to-model values), such as additional minimum liability. Therefore, by comparing the usefulness of net income and comprehensive income, we can see whether fair value accounting improved the usefulness of investment decisions.

The second perspective deals with comparing the usefulness of account figures compiled under IFRS, which strongly advocates fair value accounting, with those calculated under national standards[4].

---

[4] In this comparison, this is a somewhat strong assumption that the number of account items measured based on fair value is greater under IFRS than under national accounting standards prior to the former's introduction.

As the number of countries and regions requiring the adoption of IFRS increased initially from the state level, so did the quantity of companies disclosing two parallel sets of accounting information during the transition period towards full IFRS adoption, one IFRS-based set and one national accounting standards-based set. With these conditions, usefulness of the IFRS-based "income information + net assets information" and the national standards-based "income information + net assets information" can be compared[5].

The third perspective is the comparison of the usefulness of categorical fair value measurements, an example of which is the practice of classifying financial instruments into categories when measuring their fair value specifying the measurement attribute to be applied thereto according to category.

In concrete terms, "Level 1" instruments, for which there exists an active market, are measured according to market values, "Level 2" instruments, whose published prices are not made available, are measured based on the market value of similar assets or liabilities, and "Level 3" instruments, which have an inactive market and no similar assets or liabilities exist, are measured based on optimum estimations utilizing the company's own data and models. For Levels 1 and 2, any measurement based on a market price (mark-to-market) will retain its objectivity, but for Level 3, the hardness of measurements decreases when the estimation is made by the manager (mark-to-model).

The following examines whether fair value accounting improved the investment decision-making function based on the aforementioned three perspectives.

(1) Value relevance comparison of net income and comprehensive income

First, research that compared the usefulness of net income with comprehensive income is examined[6].

---

[5] Collins *et al.* [1997] shows that the importance of the value relevance of accounting information is shifted from income information to net assets information, meaning that a comparison based on the secondary view point enables not only a comparison of income information but also of usefulness including net assets information thus lifting expectations for a more significant comparison.

[6] Incremental information content study and relative information content study are commonly known as means to examine the content of accounting information A and

Dhaliwal et al. [1999] confirms with regard to the value relevance of income information that, at the very least the fact that comprehensive income is not lesser than net income. Dhaliwal et al. [1999] examines the interpretability of net income, comprehensive income and other comprehensive income with respect to the stock price rate of change. As a result, although net income and comprehensive income possess value relevance, the Vuong test showed that comprehensive income is not clearly superior in terms of usefulness to investor decision-making, with no disparity in the significance of the strength of their respective value relevance. Moreover, that test revealed that, among other comprehensive income account items, the existence of incremental information content in net income is only for valuation differences of available-for-sale securities based on market prices, suggesting that comprehensive income includes a great amount of noise. O'Hanlonm and Pope [1999], when attempting to prove the interpretability of ordinary profit with respect to the rate of change of U.K. companies' stock prices and the incremental information content of dirty surplus account items that consist of purchased goodwill impairment loss, fixed asset revaluation reserves and foreign currency translation adjustment, saw that dirty surplus account items generally lack stock price interpretability and comprehensive income does not have a higher degree of usefulness in

---

B. Incremental information content study evaluates whether, in the event of two types of accounting information, there is any additional information content present in one type when the other accounting information type is given. The other, relative information content study, compares the magnitude of the information content of two types of accounting information and evaluates whether one type provides more information than the other. In terms of relation to value relevance-themed research, such could be relabeled as research that compares whether either type consists of accounting information that can provide estimates close to the stock price (Biddle et al [1995], Suda [2001], Ota and Matsuo [2004]).

For example, if either of components A and B that make up information content is greater than the other, then that component (either A or B) can be emphasized as having incremental information content. This is expressed as a formula as either [information content (A,B) >information content (B)] or [information content (A,B) >information content (A)]. Relative information content is compared in terms of size difference between information A and B, which is expressed as a formula as either [information content (A) >information content (B)] or [information content (B) >information content (A)]. Please note that the Vuong test is known as an effective method to prove relative information content.

investment decision-making. Chambers *et al.* [2007] revealed that, although supplemental stock price interpretability of other comprehensive income information was detected, results are limited and although the other comprehensive income information provided in the statement of shareholders' equity has statistically significant incremental information content, the other comprehensive income information appearing in the income statement does not possess any usefulness for investment decision-making.

There is other research on the same theme that analyzed Japanese companies. Suda [2008] utilized data on Japanese companies over a period from 1999 to 2004 and compared the information content of net income and comprehensive income to show that net income is superior to comprehensive income in terms of relative information content. However, he pointed out that "net income + valuation difference on available-for-sale securities" exceeds "net income" in terms of relative information content. Also indicated was that, although there are some other comprehensive income account items with a higher value relevance than net income, "net income + all other comprehensive incomes" did not win over net income in terms of value relevance. Wakabayashi [2009] calculates the comprehensive income of Japanese companies between FY2002 and FY2006 and compares the value relevance of net income and comprehensive income revealing that the former has relative information content with respect to comprehensive income. However, she states that, after verifying the existence of some other comprehensive income account items with incremental information content with respect to net income, other comprehensive income information is also useful in forming stock prices despite the fact that, as an indicator of corporate performance, net income is superior to comprehensive income.

Contrastingly, there is research that shows that comprehensive income is more useful than net income. Biddle and Choi [2006], effecting the same study as Dhaliwal *et al.* [1999], broadened the sample period and increased the quantity of data to prove that comprehensive income has relative information content[7]. Kanaga-

---

[7] "Other comprehensive income account items" that constitute comprehensive income may be understood to have the same properties as the "special items" making up net income. However, Jones and Smith [2011] point out that, compared to special items, which may or may not be accounted for depending on changes in the economic climate, other comprehensive income account items have persistence

retnam *et al.* [2009] also obtained results showing that comprehensive income has relative information content compared to net income[8].

In light of results of the overview provided up to this point, regarding the usefulness of comprehensive income information, although no clear conclusion can be drawn, it seems that the sheer number of empirical results show that net income information has usefulness in terms of relative information. Moreover, regarding other comprehensive income account item information, despite the indication of value relevance in available-for-sale securities, foreign currency translation adjustments and other account items with a market price, this research stops at confirming the existence of incremental information content with very little research pointing to predominance with respect to net income in terms of relative information content.

(2) Value relevance comparison between national standards and IFRS

Next is a summary of research comparing the usefulness of the "income + net assets" information under national standards to that of the "income + net assets" information under IFRS.

Hung and Subramanyam [2007] studied the volatility and value relevance of accounting figures posted by German companies applying IAS between 1998 and 2002. As a result, they found that the volatility of both net assets and net income was greater under IAS than German GAAP. In addition, analytical results showed a relative decrease in the value relevance of accounting figures under IAS vis-à-vis that of accounting figures under German GAAP. Schiebel [2007] juxtaposed IFRS, which is a set of accounting standards geared toward investors, and German GAAP, which is for the benefit of creditors, to confirm that both IFRS' net assets and German GAAP's net assets provide positive stock

---

and exceed in their capacity to forecast future cash flows. Although other comprehensive income account items are highly volatile, they differ in nature from special items.

[8] Shuto [2008] state that, among the dirty surplus account items posted directly in the net assets portion of the balance sheet without going through the income statement (whose bottom line is net income), some possess a significant level of interpretability with respect to debt cost, and fair value accounting may provide useful information to investors when deciding on bonds and other financial instruments.

price interpretability. Furthermore, it was shown that value relevance is greater in accounting information compiled under German GAAP.

Morricone et al. [2009] attempted to identify how the value relevance of net income, net assets and intangible assets posted by listed companies in Italy was impacted by that country's conversion of applicable accounting standards from its GAAP to IFRS. Results indicate that the conversion to IFRS decreased the value relevance of net income, net assets, goodwill and other accounting items. Jarva and Lantto [2012] made a comparison of the usefulness of accounting information under Finnish standards and that of accounting information under IFRS subsequent to Finland's forced application of that set of accounting standards. First, an analysis from the perspective of finding to what extent income information is reflected in information embedded in stock prices was effected unearthing signs of a strong relativity of income figures compiled under Finnish standards with stock yields compared with income figures under IFRS signifying that the former is a corporate performance indicator with more usable information embedded. Moreover, results show that stock price interpretability of IFRS' net asset account item does not surpass that of Finnish standards.

As in the aforementioned, analytical results from European sources provide experiential evidence that suggests the failure of IFRS to deliver accounting information with value relevance relative to national standards[9]. On the other hand, there are analytical

---

[9] In addition to value relevance-themed research, there are also studies on the impact of IFRS' application to the expansion/contraction of information asymmetry among investors. Platikanova and Nobes [2006] look at fluctuations in bid-ask spread of European listed companies before and after IFRS introduction and confirm a significant decrease in bid-ask spread in France and Germany, while the same indicator increased in the U.K. and Austria.

In cases that assume markets with market makers, Stoll [1978] shows that bid-ask spread can be divided into three elements: (1) information asymmetry, (2) costs necessary for dealers to run their business and (3) inventory costs from the purchase of securities. Platikanova and Nobes [2006] presume only the "information asymmetry items" (IAC: Information Asymmetry Components) in the bid-ask spread during extraction. As a result, the period before and after IFRS introduction saw a sharp IAC increase in both the U.K. and German companies, an insignificant IAC increase in the French companies and an insignificant IAC decrease in Scandinavian companies. In other words, this study shows that, although some

results that denote the possibility that IFRS constitutes accounting standards that provide a richer abundance of information content than national standards[10].

Capkun et al. [2008] study (a) the value relevance indicated by the "income + net assets under national standards" information and (b) the ["income + net assets under national standards" + "income (difference between national standards and IFRS)" + "net assets (difference between national standards and IFRS)"] information in European countries that have introduced IFRS. A statistical analysis of (a) and (b) showed that (1) income and net assets information under national standards has value relevance and (2) income (both under national standards and IFRS) differential information possess incremental information content (net assets differential information did not indicate value relevance). However, Capkun et al. [2008] did not study the relative information content of "income + net

---

countries witnessed their pre-IFRS bid-ask spread go down post-IFRS, if excluding only the element indicating "information asymmetry" in bid-ask spread, the information asymmetry among investors may broaden after IFRS is introduced.

[10] Horton and Serafeim [2010] is known as a study on the super-rapid information content generated in IFRS conversion fiscal years. In the U.K., when switching from national standards to IFRS, authorities require the release of IFRS-based financial statements first and then the disclosure of a reconciliation statement that shows the differences between the last financial statements prepared under the U.K.'s standards and what they would be under IFRS. Horton and Serafeim [2010] conducts an event study and value relevance research that focuses on the reaction of securities markets to the disclosure of these reconciliation statements. Results showed that, in response to negative monetary amounts appearing in released IFRS reconciliation statements, (1) stock prices trended downward and (2) information on differences between U.K.-based and IFRS-based net asset and income reporting possesses very positive value relevance.

There is other research that shows identical results. Chalmers et al. [2011] analyzed Australian companies that disclosed national standards and IFRS reconciliation statements after mandatory application of the latter in fiscal 2005 revealing that such statements reconciling Australian GAAP and IFRS possess value relevance. Comier et al. [2009] confirmed the presence of additional stock price interpretability in national standards/IFRS reconciliation statements by French companies.

However, this research does not target relative information content of accounting figures compiled under national standards and those under IFRS, and care must be taken in the study of incremental information content added to information possessed by national standards-based accounting figures when converting to IFRS.

assets under national standards information" and "income + net assets under IFRS information".

Prather-Kinsey et al. [2008] implements an event study and value relevance research targeting companies in European countries over the period prior to and after mandatory IFRS adoption. The event study detected information content generated by IFRS-based accounts settlement releases. Moreover, a survey of the value relevance of "income + net assets under national standards" information as of 2004 and the value relevance of "income + net assets under IFRS" information as of 2006 revealed an increase in the interpretability of income and net assets with respect to stock prices in code-law countries despite no clear change at all in common-law countries. However, this research is a comparison of accounting information compiled at different pre- and post-IFRS times and not a comparison of value relevance of "national standards-based accounting information" and "IFRS-based accounting information" compiled at the same time. Because of this, even though it can be said that "IFRS-based accounting information includes information that is useful to investment decision-making," it cannot be claimed that "IFRS-based accounting information is superior to national standards-based accounting information in terms of value relevance".

Chalmers et al. [2011] survey the chronological transition of the value relevance of income and net assets over the period from 1990 to 2008 after mandatory IFRS adoption in 2005 indicating that value relevance of income and net asset increase over time.

This research shows that the switch from national standards to IFRS resulted in (1) an improvement in value relevance over time and (2) the discovery of incremental information content in national standards and IFRS differential information. However, if only looking at research on relative information content, some results show a deterioration of value relevance due to IFRS introduction, with no empirical results purporting to an improvement or any indication of any clear predominance of IFRS over national standards.

On the other hand, there are some literatures to use cross-country data. Atwood et al. [2011], by using 33 countries data, made a comparison among the earnings quality under IFRS, U.S. GAAP, and non- U.S. GAAP. As a result, it shows that earnings reported under U.S. GAAP are more closely associated with future cash flows than earnings reported under IFRS. In addition, Ahmed *et al.* [2013] implemented a comparison of 20 IFRS adopting countries and 15 non-IFRS adopting countries. It finds evidence of a significant increase in income smoothing and accrual aggressiveness as well as a significant decrease in timeliness of loss recognition from firms in IFRS adopting countries relative to benchmark firms in non-IFRS adopting countries. Therefore, Accounting quality declines after mandatory IFRS adoption.

Research results comparing the usefulness of "national standards-based accounting information" and "IFRS-based accounting information" depend on multiple factors, such as whether IFRS introduction at sample companies was mandatory or voluntary, whether analyzed countries were code-law or common-law or industrialized or emerging, and whether there exists any discrepancy in the level of adoption of IFRS (whether IFRS adoption was partial or full), etc., and are therefore difficult to interpret. For this reason, it is believed that this field should have more empirical results accumulated by researchers going forward.

(3) Comparison of value relevance of stratified fair value measurements of financial instruments

This Section is a summary of research on the value relevance of stratified fair value measurements of financial instruments. Kolev [2008] attempts to identify the correlation between fair value measurements and stock prices at every Level in the banking industry between the first and second quarters of fiscal 2008 finding that (1) despite having confirmed the value relevance of fair value measurements at Levels 1, 2 and 3, (2) the regression coefficient becomes smaller as the level decreases from 1 to 2 to 3 and there is a significant difference between the magnitude of Level 1 and Level 3's regression coefficient (or the scale of interpretability with respect to stock price). In other words, this research shows that investors do not trust Level 3 fair value measurements relative to the other levels. Goh *et al.* [2009], as a result of surveying the relativity with stock price regarding bank-held assets, like in Kolev [2008], indicates that (1) fair value measurements at Levels 1, 2 and 3 have value relevance and (2) interpretability with respect to stock price deteriorates as you move down the ladder from Level 1 to Level 3. Moreover, as the target period goes from the first quarter to the second, analysis results show that the stock price interpretability of the fair value measurements of assets in the Level 2 and 3 categories deteriorates over the passage of time on a quarterly basis. In addition, in cases where banks are audited by leading auditing firms, the stock price interpretability of Level 3 fair value measurements increase.

Song et al. [2010] shows that, although Levels 1 and 2 fair value measurements have value relevance, Level 3 measurements do not, and even if a case involves financial instruments for which fair value measurements are easy to determine, Level 3 information with an enormous discretionary component provided by managers will not be of any use to investors in their decision-making process. In addition, this research conducted additional analyses on the strengths and weaknesses of sample company corporate governance concluding that measured values for Level 3 account items of companies with strong corporate governance have value relevance.

Riedl and Serafeim [2011] surveys the relativity of data that indicates capital costs with stratified fair value measurements by American financial institutions with results showing that (1) fair value measurements at Levels 1, 2 and 3 all have significant interpretability with respect to capital cost and (2) the lower the category of the assets' fair value measurements, the larger their regression coefficient becomes. In other words, the lower the level of fair value measurements, the less they are trusted by investors, suggesting that they are a factor in bringing up capital procurement costs.

Based on these research results, we understand that, compared with measurements of Level 1 and 2 account items, measurement value information on Level 3 account items are unreliable to investors and have relatively low usefulness. Further, there are some cases where Level 3 measurement values have statistically significant interpretability, however, these are strictly situated cases where (1) samples are limited to commercial banks and (2) audits by large leading audit firms and a strong corporate governance framework buttress the reliability of measurement values.

Results of the surveys outlined in this Section clarify that (1) for comprehensive income and net income, although there is some research confirming the usefulness of comprehensive income, there is a lot of research supporting the relatively high level of usefulness of net income, (2) there is a mix of analytical results purporting that, after having introduced IFRS, the value relevance of accounting figures both improved and deteriorated compared with those disclosed under national standards prior to IFRS introduction, and the relative information content within these results did not confirm any predominance of IFRS vis-à-vis national standards, and (3) despite finding value relevance in Level 1 and 2 market price-based measurement values in financial instrument accounting geared toward stratified fair value measurement, only relatively low value relevance (or no value relevance) was detected in measurements of Level 3 account items to be estimated. Moreover, as a backdrop, the loss of reliability of measurements was also confirmed. From these results, we know that fair value accounting does not necessarily heighten the usefulness of investor decision-making and may not play a role in improving the information role.

3-5. The Contract Role and Fair Value Accounting

Also studied was the effect on the contract role, another basic function of accounting, of the increase in the number of fair value accounting account items in an accounting system. Companies are composed of "nexus of contracts" whose interest oppositions are alleviated with accounting figures. These agreements deal with management appointments and dismissals, management compensation, monetary obligation contracts, government regulations (taxes, business licenses, grants, price determinations), examinations for listings on securities exchanges, and more. This Section investigates the impact on contractual relations of fair value measurements if they are of low hardness and high volatility.

Among all empirical research analyzing the effect of fair value accounting on various types of agreements, only a few relating to debt covenants were found (to the extent known by the author), therefore, without testing agreements in other fields, a clear conclusion cannot be made regarding the overall impact on the contract role. In light of this constraint, the following is an overview of empirical results relating to debt covenants.

As research on the effect of fair value accounting on debt covenants, Demerjian [2011] is a good example. Demerjian [2011] indicates the possibility that the progress of the adoption of accounting standards based on the Asset and Liability View has rendered useless the accounting information of balance sheet items in debt covenants. Specifically, after verifying the adoption rate of account items used as debt covenants over a period between 1996 and 2007, results showed that balance sheet items (current ratio, etc.) decreased from 82.8% to 31.5%. On the other hand, income statement account items (interest coverage ratio, etc.) hovered between 80.7% and 73.9%, a high level indeed.

Moreover, Demerjian [2011] switched the core of accounting standards formulation to the Asset and Liability View and calculated the "VR indicator[11]", which measures effects appearing in financial statements, revealing an increase in the VR indicator over the passage of time. As propounded in Footnote 12, the increase in the VR indicator indicates that fluctuations in net assets (numerator) intensify as the years go by.

In addition, this research observed a significant negative correlation between as to whether to embed balance sheet items into debt covenants and increases/ decreases of the VR indicator. Contrastingly, no significant correlation was found between as to whether to embed income statement items into debt covenants and increases/decreases of the VR indicator. In other words, due to the advent of Asset and Liability View-based accounting standards formulation, borrowing companies may avoid highly volatile balance sheet items when establishing debt covenants[12].

Christensen *et al.* [2009] analyzed U.K. companies and found that the adoption of IFRS increases the risk of violating debt covenants and therefore has a negative effect on stock prices. When applicable accounting standards are converted from U.K. GAAP to IFRS, the reaction of stock prices in the face of released IFRS-based income figures may include (1) altered expectations with respect to future cash flows brought upon by the change in income calculation method and (2) effects on contractual clauses akin to debt covenants brought upon by IFRS (risk of infringement of debt covenants). In this survey, the analysis of interpretability with respect to stock price reaction showed that such does exist in the case of (2), but does not in the case of (1). From these results, Christensen *et al.* state that the higher the possibility of the risk of

---

[11] The VR indicator is the result of dividing the "net assets fluctuation amplitude" by the "adjusted net income fluctuation amplitude". "Adjusted net income" is calculated as the value resulting from deducting special items and other comprehensive income account items from net income. In other words, the VR indicator is the ratio of the "net assets fluctuation amplitude" including dirty surplus account items and the "income fluctuation amplitude" excluding special items.

[12] In the event of a conflict with respect to the ratio requirements of indicators provided for in debt covenants, companies saddled with debt are penalized by additional interest payments, additional collateral pledges or the early redemption or reimbursement of borrowed capital.

violation of existing debt covenants, the more likely will wealth be transferred between shareholders and creditors, and therefore the news of the adoption of IFRS is not necessarily good news to shareholders. Further, additional analyses revealed that the smaller the company, the lower the interest coverage and the longer the term of the debt, then the higher the possibility of conflict in debt covenants. The stronger these attributes are within a company, the stronger its first accounts settlement release after IFRS introduction will affect its stock price.

Looking at the aforementioned empirical results, we see the possibility that, by introducing fair value accounting to a far extent in accounting standards will increase the volatility of measurements and (1) may render them difficult to leverage as indicators for debt covenants and (2) an increase in the risk of conflict in debt covenants will be reflected in stock prices and, albeit only in the case of debt covenants, fair value accounting negatively impacts the contract role.

3-6. Conclusion

The purpose of this paper was to shed light on the current status and issues facing fair value accounting by summarizing empirical results relating to the economic consequences engendered by fair value accounting.

First, regarding the hardness of fair value measurements, it was confirmed that such hardness is low and that fair value measurements may be used in discretionary income reporting. In addition, a survey of their usefulness for investment decision-making revealed that (1) comprehensive income is not necessarily superior to net income, (2) in terms of relative information content, value relevance surpassing that of national standards was not necessarily confirmed, although there exists much research pointing to the presence of incremental information content after the adoption of IFRS compared with national standards-based accounting figures, and (3) in financial instruments accounting, measurement value information on Level 3 account items are unreliable to investors and have relatively low usefulness. Therefore, it can be said that few facts whatsoever came to light proving any significant improvement in the information role by the practice of fair value accounting.

Furthermore, a look at its effect on the contract role showed that, in debt covenants, an increase in the quantity of fair value measurement account items, particularly assets, liabilities, net assets and other account items, lead to their removal from contractual clauses by the borrowing company, suggesting that fair value accounting may undermine the contract role.

In other words, there is little improvement in the information role and the contract role is deteriorated (albeit in a limited scope). The cause of this was found as possibly including the broad range of discretion in fair value measurements, the low reliability and high volatility thereof and other factors.

[References in English]
Ahmed, A. S., M. Neel, and D. Wang [2013], "Does Mandatory Adoption of IFRS Improve Accounting Quality? Preliminary Evidence", *Contemporary Accounting Research*, Forthcoming.

Atwood, T. J., M. S. Drake, J. N. Myers, and L. A. Myers. [2011], "Do earnings reported under IFRS tell us more about future earnings and cash flows ?", *Journal of Accounting and Public Policy*, Vol. 30, No. 2, pp. 103-121.

Biddle, G. C., and J. Choi [2006], "Is comprehensive income useful ?", *Journal of Contemporary Accounting and Economics*, Vol. 2, No. 1, pp. 1-32.

Biddle, G, G.Seow and A.Siegel. [1995] "Relative versus incremental information content", *Contemporary Accounting Research*,Vol. 12, No. 1, pp. 1-23.

Capukun, V., A. Cazavan-Jeny, T. Jeanjean, and L. A. Weiss [2008], "Earnings management and value relevance during the mandatory transition from local GAAPs to IFRS in Europe", SSRN Working Paper (id: 1125716).

Carlin, T. M. and N. Finch [2009], "Discount rates in disarray: evidence on flawed goodwill impairment testing", *Australian Accounting Review*, Vol. 19, No. 4, pp. 326-336.

Chalmers, K., G. Clinch, and J. M. Godfrey [2011], "Changes in value relevance of accounting information upon IFRS adoption: evidence from Australia", *Australian Journal of Management*, Vol. 36, No. 2, pp. 151-173.

Chambers, D., T.J. Linsmeier, C. Shakespeare, and T. Sougiannis [2007], "An evaluation of SFAS No. 130 comprehensive income disclosure", *Review of Accounting Studies*, Vol. 12, No. 4, pp. 557-593.

Choudhary, P. [2011], "Evidence on differences between recognition and disclosure: a comparison of inputs to estimate fair values of employee stock options." *Journal of Accounting and Economics*, Vol. 51, No. 1-2, pp. 77-94.

Christensen, H. B., E. Lee, and M. Walker [2009], "Do IFRS reconciliation convey information?; The effect of debt contracting", SSRN Working Paper (id: 997 800).

Collins, D. W., E. L. Maydew, and I.S.Weiss [1997], "Changes in the value-relevance of earnings and book value over the past forty years", *Journal of Accounting and Economics*, Vol. 24, No. 1, pp. 39-67.

Comier, D., S. Demaria, P. Lapointe-Antunes, and R. Teller [2009], "First-Time adoption of IFRS managerial incentives, and value relevance: some French evidence", *Journal of International Accounting Research*, Vol. 8, No. 2, pp. 1-22.

Dechow, P. M., L. A. Myers, and C. Shakespeare [2010], "Fair value accounting and gains from asset securitizations: a convenient earnings management tool with compensation side-benefits", *Journal of Accounting and Economics*, Vol. 49, No. 1-2, pp. 2-25.

Demerjian, P. [2011], "Accounting standards and debt covenants; has the "balance sheet approach"led to a decline in the use of balance sheet covenants?", *Journal of Accounting and Economics*, Vol. 52, No. 2-3, pp. 178-202.

Dhaliwal, D., K. R. Subramanyam, R. Trezevant [1999], "Is comprehensive income superior to net income as a measure of firm performance?", *Journal of Accounting and Economics*, Vol. 26, No. 1, pp. 43-67.

Goh, B. W., J. Ng, and K. O. Yong [2009], "Market pricing of bank's fair value assets reported under SFAS 157 during the 2008 economic crisis", Working Paper, Singapore Management University.

Goodwin, J., K. Ahmed, and R. Heaney [2008], "The effects of international financial reporting standards on the accounts and accounting quality of Australian firms ; a retrospective study", *The Journal of Contemporary Accounting and Economics*, Vol. 4, No. 2, pp. 89-119.

Horton, J. and G. Serafeim [2010], "Market reaction to and valuation of IFRS reconciliation adjustments: first evidence from the UK", *Review of Accounting Studies*, Vol. 15, No. 4, pp. 725-751.

Hung, M., and K. R. Subramanyam [2007], "Financial statement effects of adopting international accounting standards; the case of Germany", *Review of Accounting Studies*, Vol. 12, No. 4, pp. 623-657.

Ijiri, Y. [1975], *Theory of accounting measurement*, American Accounting Association.

Jarva, H. and A, Lantto [2012], "Information content of IFRS versus domestic accounting standards: evidence from Finland", *The Finnish Journal of Business Economics*, Vol. 2, pp. 141-177.

Jones, D. A. and K. J. Smith [2011], "Comparing the value relevance, predictive value, and persistence of other comprehensive income and special items", *The Accounting Review*, Vol. 86, No. 6, pp. 2047-2073.

Juettner-Nauroth, B. [2004], "Problems associated with the value-relevance of financial derivatives according to IAS 39", Working Paper Series in Business Administration No. 2003-2, Stockholm School of Economics.

Kanagaretnam, K., R.Mathieu, and M. Shehata [2009], "Usefulness of comprehensive income reporting in Canada", *Journal of Accounting and Public Policy*, Vol. 28, No. 4, pp. 349-365.

Kolev, K. [2008], "Do investors perceive marking-to-model as marking-to-myth? early evidence from FAS 157 disclosure", SSRN Working Paper (id: 1336368).

Morricone, S., R. Oriani, and M. Sobrero [2009], "The value relevance of intangible assets and the mandatory adoption of IFRS", SSRN Working Paper (id: 1600725).

O'Hanlonm, J. F., and P. F. Pope [1999]," The value relevance of UK dirty surplus accounting flows", *British Accounting Review*.Vol. 31, No. 4, pp 459-482.

Platikanova, P. and C. Nobes [2006], "Was the introduction of IFRS in Europe value -relevant ?", SSRN Working Paper (id: 949160).

Prather-Kinsey, J., E. K. Jermakowicz, and T. Vongphanith [2008], "Capital market consequences of European firm's mandatory adoption of IFRS", Working Paper, University of Missouri.

Riedl, E. J. and G. Serafeim [2011] "Information risk and fair values: an examination of equity beta", *Journal of Accounting Research*, Vol. 49, No. 4, pp. 1083-1122.

Schiebel, A. [2007], "Empirical value relevance of German GAAP and IFRS", *Journal of Economic and Financial Sciences*, Vol. 1, No. 2, pp. 141-170.

Shalev, R., I. Zhang, and Y. Zhang [2010], "CEO compensation and fair value accounting; Evidence from purchase price allocation", *SSRN Working Paper* (id: 600903).

Song, C. J., W. B. Thomas, and H. Yi [2010], "Value relevance of FAS No. 157 fair value hierarchy information and the impact of corporate governance. mechanisms", *The Accounting Review*, Vol. 85, No. 4, pp. 1375-1410.

Stoll, H, R. [1978], "The pricing of security dealer services: an empirical study of NASDAQ stocks", *Journal of Finance*, Vol. 33, No. 4, pp. 1153-1172.

Zhang, I. and Y. Zhang [2007], "Accounting discretion and purchase price allocation after acquisitions", SSRN Working Paper (id: 930725).

[References in Japanese]

Obinata, Takashi [2002], "Allocation and evaluation of cash flow" in S. Saito ed., *Basic Concept of Accounting Standards* 2003, Chuokeizai-sha, Inc., pp. 185-259.

Obinata, Takashi [2011], "Abuse of fair value accounting and financial crisis", Tokyo University, CARF Working Paper J-073.

Ota, Koji and Akihiko Matsuo [2004], "The Vuong (1989) Test and its application", *The Journal of Musashi University*, Vol. 52, No. 1, pp. 39-75.

Shuto, Akinobu [2008], "The role of dirty-surplus items in debt contract", in K. Suda ed.,*Design of Accounting System* 2008, Hakuto-shobo Publishing Company, pp. 249-274.

Shuto, Akinobu [2011], "Empirical evaluation of fair value information", in K. Kitamura ed., *Significance and limitation of fair value accounting*, Final Report by Special Committee of Japanese Accounting Association, pp. 305-324.

Suda, Kazuyuki [2001], "Usefulness of cash flow information and income information -Part 1-", *Kaikei (Accounting)*, Vol. 162, No. 1, pp 39-50.

Suda, Kazuyuki [2008], "Net income and comprehensive income", in K. Suda ed., *Design of Accounting System* 2008, Hakuto-shobo Publishing Company, pp. 212-232.

Tokuga, Yoshihiro [2011], "Examination of mixed accounting model in accounting standard", Discussion Paper No. 2011-J-19, Nihon-Ginko KinyuKenkyusho.

Wakabayashi, Hiromi. [2009], "Value relevance of comprehensive income and net income", K. Wakabayashi, *Empirical Research on Comprehensive Income*, 2009, Chuokeizai-sha, Inc., pp. 141-152.

Chapter 4

Conflict in
Fair Value Accounting
— The Spell of Realization Principle —

Norio Takasu
The University of Hyogo

Abstract

In this Chapter, I considered first the switch in views of financial accounting (views of earnings) from the revenue and expense view to the asset and liability view that brought upon the advent of fair value accounting, and the problems involved in selecting the measurement attributes in the latter view, based on my awareness of the issue of clarifying the significance of the criticism regarding the so-called "paradox of the liability" that gains are posted as a result of measurement of financial liabilities based on fair value when a reporting company's credit standing deteriorates. In light of the above, I examined the essence of that criticism and its appropriateness.

As a result, the current accounting practices are conducted from the perspective of a "restricted asset and liability view" and an "expanded revenue and expense view", in which the concept (accounting mind) under which unrealized losses are recognized but unrealized gains are not forms the basis thereof. Also, I found that, the asymmetrical handling of unrealized gains and unrealized losses comes from the fact that there are many shareholders who do not meet the criteria for allowing an external transfer of shareholder limited liability and, therefore, the ability to exercise freely such external transfer of shareholder limited liability is restricted to short-term investors (speculators).

However, risks generated by shareholders unable to exercise such transfer owing to the posting of unrealized gains can be eliminated by prohibiting dividends based thereon (external outflow). But, if posting unrealized gains the released accounting information draws speculators to the reporting company, then conflicts may result between the long-term viewing company on the side of production and the short-term viewing speculator on the side of investment.

Keywords

fair value accounting, asset and liability view, revenue and expense view, measurement attribute, realization principle, accounting mind, economics mind

4-1. Introduction

The Financial Accounting Standards Board (FASB) and the International Accounting Standards Board (IASB) have been working on the convergence of financial instrument accounting with the long-term objective of measuring all financial instruments based on fair value and recognizing realized and unrealized gains at the time of occurrence. The IASB published in December 2003 the IAS39 *"Financial Instruments, Recognition and Measurement (revised 2003)"* which approves the fair value option (par. 9) of measuring all financial assets and liabilities upon initial recognition under fair value and recognizing fair value differences as profits or losses. However, because of concerns abound with regard to this treatment, it published in June 2005 the IAS39 *"Financial Instruments, Recognition and Measurement"* stating that only after meeting certain conditions can the fair value option be applied (pars.9, 11A, 12). Meanwhile, the FASB published in February 2007 the SFAS No.159 *"The Fair Value Option for Financial Assets and Financial Liabilities, Including an amendment of FASB Statement No.115"* in which it approved the application of the fair value option for financial assets and liabilities. But because these include financial liabilities in the scope of applicability of the fair value option, there is the possibility that, if the reporting company's credit standing deteriorates and the reporting company measures financial liabilities at fair value, the result may be the posting of a gain (the so-called "paradox of the liability"). Concerns regarding this treatment are followed on the fact that Citigroup and other financial institutions posted valuation gains on financial liabilities as profits as they plunged into an operational crisis in the wake of the Lehman collapse in 2008.

In this Chapter, with an awareness of the issue of attempting to shed light on the significance of the criticism spawned by this "paradox of the liability", first I considered the switch from the revenue and expense view to the asset and liability view that brought on the advent of the fair value accounting and the issues regarding the selection of measurement attributes in the asset and liability view. Based on this, I then examined the essence and appropriateness of that criticism.

4-2. Switch of Views of Financial Accounting from the Revenue and Expense View to the Asset and Liability View

The FASB published in December 1976 the Discussion Memorandum *"An analysis of issues related to Conceptual Framework for Financial Accounting and Reporting: Elements of Financial Statements and Their Measurement"* (hereinafter "the 1976 Discussion Memorandum"), in which it carefully examined the "asset and liability view" and the "revenue and expense view", that assume the articulation of financial statements, and the "non-articulation view", that does not assume such articulation.

However, if looking at the way by which the views of financial accounting were examined in this Discussion Memorandum, the focus thereof was a comparison of the asset and liability view and the revenue and expense view as a view of financial accounting based on articulation, and that comparison was not a purely conceptual pairing of these views but rather the FASB's weighing of the pros and cons of its new income calculation model, the asset and liability view, and of the conventional accounting practice, the revenue and expense view (Takasu [1995], p.30).

(1) **Comparative analysis of the asset and liability view with the revenue and expense view**
The FASB describes, in the 1976 Discussion Memorandum, the

asset and liability view and the revenue and expense view as follows.

Some people (=proponents of the asset and liability view) view earnings as a measure of increase in net resources of a business enterprise during a period. Thus, they define earnings primarily in terms of increases and decreases in assets and liabilities. The positive element in earnings — revenues — is defined in terms of increases in assets and decreases in liabilities during the period; the negative element in earnings — expenses — is defined in terms of decreases in assets and increases in liabilities during the period. Assets and liabilities — financial representations of economic resources of an enterprise and its obligations to transfer resources to other entities (including individuals) in the future — are the key concepts in that view. According to its proponents, measuring attributes of assets and liabilities and changes in them is the fundamental measurement process in financial accounting. All other elements of financial statements — owners' equity or capital, earnings, revenues, expenses, gains, and losses — are measured as differences between or as changes in measures of attributes of assets and liabilities (par. 34).

Meanwhile, some people (=proponents of the revenue and expense view) view earnings as a measure of the effectiveness of an enterprise in using its inputs to obtain and sell output at a profit. They define earnings primarily in terms of the difference between revenues and expenses for a period. Revenues and expenses — financial representations of outputs from and inputs to enterprise earning activities — are the key concepts in that view (par. 38). According to proponents, measuring revenues and expenses and timing their recognition to relate effort (expenses) and accomplishment (revenues) for a period is the fundamental measurement process in financial accounting (par. 39). As a result of the above, measures of assets and liabilities are generally determined by the requirements of the earnings measurement process. Thus, a balance sheet reflecting the revenue and expense view may include, as assets and liabilities or as other elements, items that do not represent economic resources of the enterprise or obligations to transfer resources to other entities (par. 42).

Based on the above, this Memorandum considers the disparities between the asset and liability view and the revenue and expense view basically in terms of earnings as the net result of certain changes in assets and liabilities which bring increases of wealth (par. 48) or as a measure of effectiveness of performance of the enterprise during a period (par. 49), thus returning to the disparities in views of financial accounting that these views possess (Takasu [1994], p. 46). However, the Memorandum specifically states here that (1) balance sheet items include thereto fictitious items which do not represent economic resources of an enterprise or its obligations to transfer resources to other entities, namely deferred charges, deferred credits and reserves (pars. 51, 54), and (2) the basis for recognition of revenues and expenses in earnings measurement is unclear (par. 61), thus criticizing the characteristics of the revenue and expense view.

(2) Income measurement model as the basis for the asset and liability view and the revenue and expense view

To demonstrate the income measurement model, on which both the asset and liability view and the revenue and expense view of financial accounting are based, I provide below a mathematical formula to express the income measurement process expounded in these views. This formula provides the product of quantity Q and price P for each individual transaction because the views recognize transactions based on asset and liability fluctuations (or occurrence of revenues and expenses) and these are measured as fluctuations in the attribute measurement values. Expressing this in a general formula yields $Q_i P_{iti}$ (ith transaction; note that P_{iti} expresses the measurement attribute at the time of the relevant transaction) whereby earnings based on the asset and liability view and that based on the revenue and expense view would be calculated together as follows: $Q_1 P_{1t1} + Q_2 P_{2t2} + \cdots\cdots + Q_n P_{ntn}$

In addition, for the above earnings to provide results with theoretical significance, since the above formula takes the form of a linear aggregation of quantity and price, for each term to have additivity (or homogeneity), the following two methods may be considered. One of these, the First Income Measurement Model, focuses on the time aspect of each individual transaction. In other words, because each term is stipulated in the attribute measurement value at the time of transaction (t_i), it can be corrected to the attribute measurement value at any specified time (ex. accounts settlement date). In this case, some measurement value at that time is utilized as its measurement attribute. The other method, the Second Income Measurement Model, ignores the time aspect of each individual transaction. In other words, because each term is stipulated in the attribute measurement value at the time of transaction (t_i), it is interpreted from a different perspective. Put another way, each is interpreted as cash receipts and outlays. Therefore, in this case, the transaction price (historical cost) at the time of each individual transaction is used as the measurement attribute (Takasu [1995], pp. 32-33).

From the above, we can surmise that in the First Model, the wealth dynamics is assumed as the fundamental concept, whereas that of the Second Model is assumed as the money dynamics (Takasu [1996a], pp. 71-72). Therefore, these income measurement models not only create disparities in the measurement attributes selected in their measurement processes but also have disparities in the fundamental recognition and measurement structure. In other words, the First Model based on wealth dynamics possesses a recognition and measurement structure under which the quantitative changes (Q) in individual wealth are recognized as recognition subjects and then they are converted to currency (QP) as the common scale from the perspective of income calculation. Put another way, the process by which all wealth is converted to currency as the common scale — the valuation process —, is necessary causing problems in the selection of measurement attributes to arise. Meanwhile, the Second Model based on money dynamics possesses a recognition and measurement structure under which the quantitative fluctuations (QP) of cash receipts and outlays are recognized as recognition subjects and they are simultaneously measured based thereon. Put another way, under this model, recognition and measurement are inseparable and there is no problem of valuation.

Also, the disparities of recognition and measurement structure in transaction bring about disparities in transactions identified using these income measurement models. In other words, the First Model allows for the recognition of not only wealth quantity fluctuations but also measurement attribute fluctuations. On the other hand, in the Second Model, because only fluctuations in cash receipts and outlays are recognized as transactions, they are identified discontinuously based on asset and liability (cash) fluctuations. Because of this, the recognition of conversions (singular point) of money from investment to collection is necessary. Put another way, the recognition criteria for revenues and expenses — the realization and matching rules — need to be established (Takasu [1996a], pp.71-72). Also, in this case, the First Model models the asset and liability view as a new income calculation model which the FASB developed (Takasu [1997a], p. 47), and the Second Model models the revenue and expense view as the conventional accounting practice (Takasu [1996c], p. 41).

(3) The asset and liability view propounded by the 1976 Discussion Memorandum

The asset and liability view came in criticism of specifically two areas of the revenue and expense view, namely (1) the extension of balance sheet items to include fictitious items that do not represent economic resources of an enterprise or its obligations to transfer resources, and (2) the obscure recognition criteria for revenues and expenses in the income measurement. In addition, the application thereof allows for the elimination of criticism (1), but the elimination of criticism (2) will necessitate the selection of specified measurement attributes upon its application, which presents the problem of multiple objects on recognition, particularly the handling of both property and currency in parallel.

In other words, the calculated currency, obtained by converting the property recognized under this view into currency as the common scale using measurement attributes, coexists with real currency as the means of payment. Therefore, the selection of measurement attributes is required to make the coexistence of calculated currency and real currency logically consistent, however, when doing so, there exists two ways to interpret all wealth, as calculated currency or as real currency (Takasu [1997b], p. 45). But, because the asset and liability view is based on the wealth dynamics, here the method of interpreting all wealth as calculated currency is selected[1].

In such a case, because all wealth is interpreted as calculated currency, not only is the sameness of time demanded as a precondition when converting to currency as the common scale, but a condition (first condition) is imposed in that when converting real currency (cash) to calculated currency, the amounts have to match. Also, because the property expressed in calculated currency is ultimately exchanged into real currency, to eliminate criticism (2) above, another condition (second condition) is imposed in that the process mapped out here must be continuously comprehended

---

[1] When interpreting all wealth in terms of real currency in kind, such is based on the money dynamics.

without any singular points.

The FASB provides five measurement attributes in the 1976 Discussion Memorandum, namely the historical cost/historical proceeds, the current cost/current proceeds, the current exit value in orderly liquidation (current market value), the expected exit value in due course of business (net realizable value) and the present value of expected cash flows (FASB [1976],p.189)[2]. However, those that coincide at different past and future points in time, namely the historical cost/historical proceeds and the expected exit value in due course of business (net realizable value) cannot be selected as they do not meet the precondition of sameness of time. Regarding the current cost/current proceeds, because of a discontinuous conversion from assumed cash outlays (assumed cash receipts) to real cash receipts (real cash outlays) under the recognition and measurement process and therefore violating the second condition thus its selection is impossible. From this we see two possibilities for measurement attributes, the method to determine the current exit value in orderly liquidation (current market value) and the method to determine the present value of expected cash flows (Takasu [2001a], pp. 6-7). Put another way, there are two asset and liability views. However, this Discussion Memorandum uses a definition

---

[2] The FASB, in the 1976 Discussion Memorandum, explained these measurement attributes as follows (FASB [1976], p. 193).

The historical cost (historical proceeds) is the amount of cash (or its equivalent) paid to acquire an asset (the amount of cash (or its equivalent) received when an obligation was incurred).

The current cost (current proceeds) is the amount of cash (or its equivalent) that would have to be paid if the same asset were acquired currently (the amount of proceeds that would be obtained if the same obligation were incurred currently).

The current exit value in orderly liquidation is the amount of cash that could be obtained currently by selling the asset in orderly liquidation (the cash outlay that would be required currently to eliminate the liability).

The expected exit value in due course of business is the amount of cash (or its equivalent) into which asset is expected to be converted in due course of business less the direct costs necessary to make that conversion (the amount of cash (or its equivalent) expected to be paid to eliminate liability in due course of business including the direct costs necessary to make those payments).

The present value of expected cash flows is the present value of future cash inflows into which asset is expected to be converted in due course of business less the present value of cash outflows necessary to obtain those inflows (the present value of future cash outflows to eliminate liability in due course of business including the cash outflows necessary to make those payments).

based on future cash flow as the definition of assets and liabilities complying with the asset and liability view (FASB [1976], pars. 91 A-1, 149 L-1) and from this we can surmise that the FASB assumed the latter asset and liability view.

4-3. Problems involved in the Selection of Measurement Attributes in the Asset and Liability View

The FASB originated in the 1976 Discussion Memorandum the asset and liability view wherein the present value of expected cash flows is the measurement attribute. It published six Statements of Financial Accounting Concepts (SFACs) between 1978 and 1985 in which the asset and liability view is used and the elements of financial statements based thereon are defined, however, regarding measurement attributes, it is stated that "rather than attempt to select a single attribute and force changes in practice so that all classes of assets and liabilities use that attribute, this concepts Statement suggests that use of different attributes will continue" (FASB [1984], par. 70).

Subsequently, the FASB published in June 1997 the Proposed Statement of Financial Accounting Concepts (Exposure Draft) *"Using Cash Flow Information in Accounting Measurements"* (hereinafter "the Proposed SFAC"), whose main theme is measurement issues, and in March 1999, the Proposed Statement of Financial Accounting Concepts (Exposure Draft (Revised)) *"Using Cash Flow Information and Present Value in Accounting Measurements"* (hereinafter "the Proposed SFAC (Revised)"), further the Statement of Financial Accounting Concepts No. 7 *"Using Cash Flow Information and Present Value in Accounting Measurements"* (hereinafter "the SFAC No. 7") in February 2000.

(1) The basic concept propounded in the Proposed SFAC

The FASB, in the Proposed SFAC, includes the writings, (1) whether to require fair value or entity-specific measurement at initial recognition and fresh-start measurements[3] and (2) the Board expects to decide whether a particular situation requires fresh-

---

[3] The FASB, in the Proposed SFAC, described these measurement attributes as follows.

start measurement or some other accounting response on a project-by-project basis (FASB [1997], pars. 12, 42), and avoided going further. However, because the FASB offers two measurement attributes, namely the fair value and the entity-specific measurement in initial recognition and fresh-start measurements, it is likely that it planned to use them for assets and liabilities according to the respective objects thereof. In addition, the FASB seemingly assumed the application of the fair value to items that do not engender discrepancies between the fair value and the entity-specific measurement (i.e.: monetary items), while assuming the application of the entity-specific measurement to items that bring out discrepancies to both (i.e.: non-monetary items). This is because, in any other case, there would be no need to offer the entity-specific measurement as a measurement attribute because only the fair value would be sufficient (Takasu [2001b], p. 26). This means that the entity-specific measurement is applied to all assets and liabilities as a measurement attribute.

Further, on the selection of the fresh-start measurement and other accounting response, the FASB states that accountants frequently face situations in which a change in an asset can be recognized by either a fresh-start measurement or an adjustment to the existing amortization convention (FASB [1997], par. 12), changes from the original estimate of cash flows, in either timing or amount, can be (1) accommodated in the interest amortization scheme or (2) reflected in a fresh-start measurement of the asset or liability, moreover, if the amount or timing of estimated cash flows changes and the item is not remeasured, the interest amortization scheme must be altered to reflect the new estimate of cash flows (FASB [1997], par. 61).

From these fragments, I extracted the FASB's fundamental concept which states that, in the event of a change in the amount or timing of estimated cash flows, a fresh-start measurement is to be conducted in principle, however, if not effecting this, a correction

---

The fair value of an asset (or liability) is the amount at which an asset (or liability) could be bought (or incurred) or sold (or settled) in a current transaction between willing parties (FASB [1997], par. 46).

The entity-specific measurement of an asset (or liability) is the present value of the future cash flows that the entity expects to realize (or pay) through the use (or settlement) and eventual disposition of the item over its economic life (FASB [1997], par. 43).

of the interest amortization scheme is allowed exceptionally. I can therefore conclude that the FASB assumes amortization based on the interest methods without any fresh-start measurement of assets and liabilities on a measurement of fluctuations in assets and liabilities for each accounting period when there should be no changes in the amount or timing of estimated cash flows (Takasu [2001b], p. 26).

(2) The basic concept articulated in the Proposed SFAC (Revised) and the SFAC No.7

Both in the Proposed SFAC (Revised) and the SFAC No. 7, the framework of the FASB's basic concept are the same as before the adjustment except for the exclusion of the entity-specific measurement at initial recognition and fresh-start measurements (FASB [1999], par. 105)[4].

In other words, the FASB is using the following measurement mechanism in the Proposed SFAC (Revised) and the SFAC No. 7, that is, it assumes the application of the fair value to all assets and liabilities upon initial recognition or fresh-start measurements. When changes in the amount or timing occur in estimated cash flows, conducting a fresh-start measurement is the general rule, but if such is not effected, an adjustment of the interest amortization scheme is allowed exceptionally. On the other hand, if there is no change in the amount or timing of estimated cash flows, amortization based on the interest methods is effected without a fresh-start measurement of assets and liabilities on a measurement of fluctuations for assets and liabilities in the accounting period. Also, regarding the latter part of the mechanism, the SFAC No. 7 provides additional clarity by shedding light on the application of the expected cash flow approach on amortization technique based on future cash flows, or the interest methods (FASB [2000], pars. 15, 45; Takasu [2001b], p. 28).

---

[4] The Proposed SFAC states that measurement of liabilities based on the fair value in settlement should exclude any adjustment for the chance that the entity might default, however, the Proposed SFAC (Revised) states that the most relevant measurement of an entity's obligation at initial recognition or in fresh-start measurements should include the effect of the entity's credit standing (FASB [1999], par. 111).

(3) Change of FASBs' basic concept and transformation of the asset and liability view

The FASB put forth in the Proposed SFAC the utilization of the asset and liability view which sets the entity-specific measurement, or the present value of expected cash flows, as the measurement attribute, however, in the Proposed SFAC (Revised) and the SFAC No. 7, it propounds the use of the asset and liability view with the fair value, or the current exit value in orderly liquidation (current market value), as the measurement attribute.

In addition, in the Proposed SFAC (Revised), the FASB states that an internally generated intangible asset (self-created goodwill) that demonstrates an entity's advantage or disadvantage relative to others in the marketplace creates differences between the fair value and the entity-specific measurement, therefore, while recognizing the intangible assets as earnings in the initial recognition when the entity measures an asset and liability using the entity-specific measurement, if the entity measures an asset or liability at the fair value, its comparative advantage or disadvantage will appear in earnings as it realizes assets or settles liabilities for amounts different than the fair value (FASB [1999], pars. 106-110; Takasu [2001b], p. 28).

Moreover, the FASB concluded that the most relevant measurement of an entity's obligation at initial recognition or in fresh-start measurements should include the effect of the entity's credit standing, in such a case, the fair value in settlement of an entity's liability should assume settlement with an entity of comparable, rather than superior, credit standing (FASB [1999], pars. 111, 117).

I can deduce from the above that the FASB utilized the asset and liability view with the fair value as the measurement attribute with the goal of eliminating the posting of unrealized gains exceeding the fair value in assets. However, with regard to liability, in the event of deterioration in the entity's credit standing, the above would be about a counter-effect. Moreover, consistently, (1) the use of the expected cash flow approach (FASB [1997], par. 35) and (2) the recommendation of the catch-up approach as a means of adjusting the interest amortization scheme (FASB [1997], par. 62) are imbedded as mechanisms and then the cost allocation method based on the interest methods is substituted for the measurement of assets and liabilities. This was initially to avoid the problem of arbitrariness on information preparers, when having to estimate the present value of expected cash flows because of a lack of a complete market, by using the cost allocation method based on the interest methods. This means that the use of the interest methods in this case can position the simplified method for measurement under the asset and liability view (Takasu [2003a], pp. 136-138).

Then, because the fair value in the initial recognition used after changing measurement attributes is actual exchange price (FASB [1999], par. 21; FASB [2000], par. 27) or the historical cost, thus differing from the initial attempt, the asset and liability view here is transformed into the revenue and expense view within its framework. Here the use of the interest methods as a cost allocation method caused the basic mechanism comprising the core components in measurement to change (Takasu [2003a], p. 138).

4-4. Development of the Revenue and Expense View and the Realization Principle

The revenue and expense view recognizes only the movements of cash receipts and outlays as transactions and does not have a time restriction on such transactions, therefore, an entity can manipulate without limitation both past cash receipts and outlays and future cash receipts and outlays by deferral or accrual when calculating earnings.

From this, we see that, under the revenue and expense view, both the realization principle and matching principle are used as criteria for the recognition of revenues and expenses from which operability (or arbitrariness) should be eliminated. This consequently gives way to an enormous dilemma as to how to stipulate the realization principle in the recognition of revenues.

(1) Transition of the realization concept

Paton and Littleton [1940], which formularized the requirements for realization and determined the conceptualization thereof (Fujii [1999], p. 115), provided two requirements therein, namely the conversion through legal sale or similar process and the validation through the acquisition of liquid assets (Paton and Littleton [1940], p. 49). The traditional realization concept was defined operationally through a series of activities and events, namely (1) the transfer of ownership rights through the delivery of wealth, followed by (2) the completion of a transaction, and then lastly (3) the acquisition of cash or its equivalent (receivable). (Harada [2005], p. 398) However, the American Accounting Association (AAA) published in 1957 *"Accounting and Reporting Standards for Corporate Financial Statements, 1957 Revision"* stating the following regarding the realization concept.

The essential meaning of realization is that a change in an asset or liability has become sufficiently definite and objective to warrant recognition in the accounts. This recognition may rest on an exchange transaction between independent parties, or on established trade practices, or on the terms of a contract performance of which is considered to be virtually certain. It may depend on the stability of a banking system, the enforceability of commercial agreements, or the ability of a highly organized market to facilitate the conversion of an asset into another form (AAA [1957], p. 538).

Here, the conventional realization requirement of "reality of transaction" has been paired with "virtual certainty of contract performance" thus relaxing the restrictions on the traditional realization concept in aims of expanding it. But, as a precondition to the expansion of that realization requirement, the stability of the "system, contract and market" is articulated.

Subsequent to the above publication, the AAA in 1965, with the goal of amending in part this 1957 Revised Accounting Standards (AAA [1965], p. 312) released "The Realization Concept", in which it set three criteria very similar to the two requirements of the traditional realization concept, namely (1) the nature of the asset received, (2) the presence of a market transaction and (3) the extent to which services have been performed (AAA [1965], p. 314; Fujii [1999], p. 121). This does not indicate a mere return to the traditional realization concept, but rather lies on the lineage of an alleviation of the restrictions imposed by the traditional realization concept and its expansion. This is also remarkable in the recognition of expenses and losses and signifies the implicit exhortation of the use of the lower of cost or market method (Fujii [1999], pp. 121 -122).

With the passage of time, the FASB subsequently published the SFAC No. 5 in December 1984 in which the term "realizable" was added to the term "realized" as a guidance of recognition of revenues and gains, which are the components of earnings (FASB [1984], par. 83). It also states that revenues and gains are realized when products (goods or services), merchandise, or other assets are exchanged for cash or claims to cash, revenues and gains are realizable when related assets received or held are readily convertible to known amounts of cash or claims to cash (FASB [1984], par.83). This is one of the milestones on road to an alleviation of the restrictions in the traditional realization concept and its expansion.

(2) Possible development of the revenue and expense view

In the revenue and expense view, first the past, present and future cash receipts are recognized as revenues under the realization principle, thereafter, the past, present and future cash outlays effected to earn those revenues based on the matching principle are recognized as expenses. This occurs by recognizing and measuring revenues and expenses by deferring cash receipts and outlays of previous fiscal years, treating cash receipts and outlays of current fiscal year as revenues and expenses, and accruing cash receipts and outlays of future fiscal years.

This tells us that, with the revenue and expense view, among asset account items, (1) revenue and yet non-cash-receipts accounts are accounted for based on future cash receipts, (2) cash-outlays and yet non cash-receipts accounts are accounted for based on past cash outlays or future cash receipts, and (3) cash-outlays and yet non-expense accounts are accounted for based on past cash outlays, however, among liability account items, (4) cash-receipts and yet non-revenue accounts are accounted for based on past cash receipts, (5) cash-receipts and yet non-cash-outlays accounts are accounted for based on past cash receipts or future cash outlays, and (6) expense and yet non-cash-outlays accounts are accounted for based on future cash outlays (Takasu [2005a], pp. 5–7).

Namely, under the revenue and expense view, before and after the point in time of realization asset valuations are overturned from past cash outlays to future cash receipts, meaning that assets are valued based on past cash outlays prior to the point in time of realization and by future cash receipts after the point in time of realization. From this, by relaxing restrictions of realization concept the scope of assets valuated based on future cash receipts is expanded. But it has limitations.

In order to expand the scope of assets valuated based on future cash receipts, the realization principle is discarded as the basis for revenue recognition and in its stead the accrual principle is employed. In this case, all assets are valuated based on future cash receipts, or the expected exit value in due course of business (net realizable value). Moreover, in this case, because the recognition process entails a continuous conversion from future cash receipts to actual cash receipts, criticism (2) of the 1976 Discussion Memorandum can be avoided (Takasu [2001a], p. 7).

4-5. Corporate Risk and Accounting Measurement

Although the asset and liability view offers two possibilities, the 1976 Discussion Memorandum assumes the asset and liability view with the present value of expected cash flows (the entity-specific measurement) as the measurement attribute. However, the SFAC No.7 uses the asset and liability view with the current exit value in orderly liquidation (current market value) (the fair value) as the measurement attribute. Meanwhile, the revenue and expense view also allows for the assumption thereof with the expected exit value in due course of business (net realizable value) as the measurement attribute. However, it persists the realization principle when recognizing revenues and a relaxing of its restrictions results only in a partial expansion of the scope.

Current accounting practices are being conducted now under both a "restricted asset and liability view" and an "expanded revenue and expense view". Also, what is characteristic here is the permission to account for unrealized losses while restricting the accounting for unrealized gains.

(1) Corporate risk and its transferability

Under the current stock company system, shareholder liability is limited; therefore, shareholders may bear liability up to the amount invested thereby. The shareholders of a listed company can transfer their limited liability externally by disposing of their shares on a securities exchange.

Because of this, with regard to shareholders of a listed company, there is no need to asymmetrically handle unrealized gains and unrealized losses even if uncertainty would ensue thereby. This means that such shareholders can sell their shares at any time after accepting equally the benefits from unrealized gains and the costs from unrealized losses during their investment periods. This is mostly applicable to short-term investors (speculators) among them.

Put another way, the above does not apply to shareholders who do not meet these requirements. Shareholders who are at the opposite pole of the above bear unlimited liability and cannot transfer it externally. Because they cannot avert corporate risk (for example, the risk of bankruptcy), there is no symmetry between the benefits from the posting of unrealized gains and the costs from the posting of unrealized losses[5]. Moreover, there are many variations in between these two extremes, a multitude of which result in the handling of unrealized gains and unrealized losses that vary depending on the circumstances.

(2) Corporate risk transferability and the accounting mind

The current accounting system was formed hundreds of years prior to the stock company system, meaning that the establishment of the accounting system now being practiced precedes creation of the stock company system. And it was formed based on the condition that shareholder liability is unlimited and non-transferable externally. With the passage of time, the stock company system took shape based on the shareholder limited liability system. But this came at a time when securities markets were not yet fully developed and so shareholders could not transfer their limited liability externally.

At the turn of the 20th Century, securities exchanges progressed sufficiently enough to allow for the external transfer of limited liability by shareholders. This did not change the role of the shareholder as the "ultimate risk taker" despite institutionally limited liability in the stock company, however, it became applicable only in certain instances like bankruptcy and not applicable in other cases, therefore, it was gradually stripped of its essence.

It is clear from the above that the accounting mind upon which the current accounting system was formed came to be well before the stock company system was ever conceived. Further, because the benefits from posting unrealized gains and the costs from posting unrealized losses are not symmetrical with respect to the shareholder, thus it results in asymmetry between the handling of unrealized gains and unrealized losses. In other words, the posting of unrealized losses is allowed but that of unrealized gains is not.

However, the accounting system formed on the basis of the accounting mind which came to be in this aforementioned way, was forced to transform with changes in the shareholder unlimited

---

[5] This is suitable for creditors and employees.

liability and the impossibility for external transfer thereof, which was a precondition for its advent. Then in the revenue and expense view the alleviation and expansion of the realization concept in the recognition of revenues came about as a result.

Moreover, this trend did not stop there. The next development was the conversion from the revenue and expense view which is limited to the realization principle, to the asset and liability view that does not require adherence to thereto. This development ousted the backbone of current accounting system, the "accounting mind", and replaced it with the "economics mind", which precedes the former.

This move has not made any traction despite the changes in the requirements. From this we can see that there is presently some power preventing the trend from happening. And the factor that moves this obstruction force may be restrictions on shareholders who meet the requirements for limited liability and transferability thereof. This means that even if the shareholders of listed companies meet the requirements, only short-term investors (speculators) are able to actually transfer their limited liability externally and there are multitudes of shareholders (capital contributors) of unlisted stock companies and companies structured in legal formats other than stock company that do not meet the requirements.

4-6. Conclusion

In this Chapter, I examined first the switch in views of financial accounting (views of earnings) from the revenue and expense view to the asset and liability view that brought upon the advent of fair value accounting, and the problems involved in selecting the measurement attributes in the latter view, based on my awareness of the issue of clarifying the significance of the criticism regarding the so-called "paradox of the liability" that gains are posted as a result of measurement of financial liabilities based on fair value when a reporting company's credit standing deteriorates.

As a result, I found the following. Although the asset and liability view offers two possibilities, the 1976 Discussion Memorandum assumes the asset and liability view with the present value of expected cash flows (the entity-specific measurement) as the measurement attribute. However, the SFAC No. 7 uses the asset and liability view with the current exit value in orderly liquidation (current market value) (the fair value) as the measurement attribute. Meanwhile, the revenue and expense view also allows for the assumption thereof with the expected exit value in due course of business (net realizable value) as the measurement attribute, but clings to the realization principle at revenue recognition and stops short at a partial expansion by alleviating the restrictions of the realization concept.

Current accounting practices are being conducted now under both a "restricted asset and liability view" and an "expanded revenue and expense view", and the "accounting mind" that allows the posting of unrealized losses but not unrealized gains is the basis thereof. Moreover, what is demanding the asymmetrical handling of unrealized gains and unrealized losses is the existence of many shareholders who do not meet the requirements for external transferability of shareholder limited liability. This is suitable for many shareholders of listed companies, only short-term investors (speculators) are allowed to exercise freely external transferability of shareholder limited liability.

But, by prohibiting dividends of unrealized gains (external outflow) the risk generated by shareholders unable to transfer their liability externally whenever unrealized gains are posted is eliminated. However, in the event of accounting for unrealized gains, that news brings in speculators whose involvement leads to conflicts between the company, whose perspective is long-term production, and the speculators, whose perspective is short-term investment.

[References in English]

AAA [1957], Committee on Accounting Concepts and Standards, "Accounting and Reporting Standards for Corporate Financial Statements — 1957 Revision", *The Accounting Review*, Vol. 32, No. 4, pp. 536–546.

——— [1965], 1964 Concepts and Standards Research Study Committee — The Realization Concept, "The Realization Concept", *The Accounting Review*, Vol.40, No. 2, pp. 312–322.

FASB [1976], *An analysis of issues related to Conceptual Framework for Financial Accounting and Reporting: Elements of Financial Statements and Their Measurement*, FASB Discussion Memorandum, FASB.

——— [1984], *Recognition and Measurement in Financial Statements of Business Enterprises*, Statement of Financial Accounting Concepts No. 5, FASB.

——— [1997], *Using Cash Flow Information in Accounting Measurements*, Proposed Statement of Financial Accounting Concepts, Exposure Draft, FASB.

——— [1999], *Using Cash Flow Information and Present Value in Accounting Measurements*, Proposed Statement of Financial Accounting Concepts,

Exposure Draft (Revised), FASB.

―――― [2000],*Using Cash Flow Information and Present Value in Accounting Measurements*, Statement of Financial Accounting Concepts No. 7, FASB.

―――― [2007], *The Fair Value Option for Financial Assets and Financial Liabilities, Including an amendment of FASB Statement No. 115*, Statement of Financial Accounting Standards No. 159, FASB.

IASB [2003], *Financial Instruments, Recognition and Measurement*, IAS39 (revised 2003), IASB.

―――― [2005], *Financial Instruments, Recognition and Measurement*, IAS39, IASB.

Ijiri, Y. [1967], *The Foundations of Accounting Measurement: A Mathematical, Economic, and Behavioral Inquiry*, Englewood Cliffs, New Jersey.

Paton, W.A. and A.C. Littleton [1940], *An Introduction to Corporate Accounting Standards*, AAA Monograph No. 3, AAA.

〔References in Japanese〕

Fujii, Hideki [1993],"The Model Analysis of Accounting Measurement", The Research Association for Accounting Frontier (ed.), *The Frontier of Financial Accounting*, Chuokeizai-sha, Inc., pp. 80-103.

―――― [1999],"The Down of Financial Accounting in America ― With a Transition of Realization Principle until 1960s as a Clue ― ", Okitsu, H. (ed.), *The Study of Financial Accounting System*, Zeimukeiri-kyokai, pp. 114-125.

Fukushima, Takao [1978],*The Theory of Revenue Recognition in Accounting*, the Faculty of Economics, Osaka Prefecture University.

Harada, Mitsunori [2005],"The Trace and Development of Decision Making Usefulness Approach", Toda, H., Okitsu, H., and T. Nakano (eds.), *The Trace of Japanese Accounting Research in the 20th Century*, Hakuto-shobo Publishing Co., pp. 391-416.

Takasu, Norio [1994],"Views of Earnings in FASB's Conceptual Framework ― The Asset and Liability View and the Revenue and Expense View ― ", *Kaikei (Accounting)*, Vol .145, No. 1, pp. 42-56.

―――― [1995],"The Asset and Liability View in FASB's Conceptual Framework", *Kaikei (Accounting)*, Vol. 148, No. 3, pp. 27-39.

―――― [1996a]," The Bookkeeping System of the Asset and Liability View in FASB's Conceptual Framework", *Sangyokeiri (Industrial Management and Accounting)*, Vol. 56, No. 2, pp. 68-74.

―――― [1996b],"The Development around Views of Earnings in FASB's Conceptual Framework ― The Asset and Liability View and the Revenue and Expense View ― ", The Study Group of Japan Accounting Association (chairman: Tsumori, T.), *The Synthetic Study concerning Theoretical Framework of Accounting (Interim Report)*, Japan Accounting Association, pp. 47-57.

―――― [1996c],"Some Considerations on the Characteristics of the Current Accounting System", *Kaikei (Accounting)*, Vol. 150, No. 5, pp. 33-46.

―――― [1997a],"The Trends of Accounting in America ― The Development around Views of Earnings in FASB's Conceptual Framework ― ", Kuroda,

M. (ed.), *International Trends of Accounting*, Dobunkan Shuppan Co., Ltd., pp. 39-52.

―――― [1997b],"The Problem around Views of Earnings in FASB's Conceptual Framework ― The Possibility of Integration ― ", The Study Group of Japan Accounting Association (chairman: Tsumori, T.), *The Synthetic Study concerning Theoretical Framework of Accounting* (*Final Report*), Japan Accounting Association, pp. 39-51.

―――― [2001a],"The Starting Point of FASB's Conceptual Framework Project and Its Arrival Point", *Shodai Ronshu* (*Journal of Kobe University of Commerce*), Vol. 52, No. 5, pp. 1-14.

―――― [2001b],"New Development of FASB's Conceptual Framework Project", *Sangyokeiri* (*Industrial Management and Accounting*), Vol. 61, No. 2, pp. 22-30.

―――― [2003a],"Accounting Framework of FASB ― A Contemporary Significance of the SFAC No.7 ― ", Hijikata, H. (ed.), *Modern Accounting and Double-entry Bookkeeping*, Zeimukeiri-kyokai, pp. 128-141.

―――― [2003b],"FASB's Conceptual Framework and Structure of Modern Accounting ― The Asset and Liability View and the Revenue and Expense View ― ", The Study Group of Japan Accounting Association (chairman: Gunji, T.), *The Study on Structure of Modern Accounting ― For an Construction of New Accounting System ―* (*Final Report*), Japan Accounting Association, pp. 9-15.

―――― [2005a],"Change of Views of Financial Accounting and Transformation of Property Management Function", *Research Paper* (the University of Hyogo), No. 193, pp. 1-11.

―――― [2005b],"Two Types of the Asset and Liability View ― Theoretical Model and Practical Model ― ", *Sangyokeiri* (*Industrial Management and Accounting*), Vol. 65, No. 3, pp. 19-28.

―――― [2011],"Conflict in Fair Value Accounting ― The Spell of Realization Principle ― ", The Committee on Theme Study of Japan Accounting Association (chairman: Watanabe,I.), *Fair Value Accounting in Historical Perspective ― An Inquiry into the Original Functions of Accounting ―* (*Interim Report*), Japan Accounting Association, pp. 105-120.

―――― [2012a],"Establishment of Decision Making Usefulness Approach and Formation of Conceptual Framework ― From a Viewpoint of Accounting Regulation in America ― ", Chiba, J. and T. Nakano (eds.), *History of Accounts and Accounting*, Chuokeizai-sha, Inc., pp. 373-409.

―――― [2012b] ,"Conflict in Fair Value Accounting ― The Accounting Mind and the Economics Mind ― ", The Committee on Theme Study of Japan Accounting Association (chairman: Watanabe, I.), *Fair Value Accounting in Historical Perspective ― An Inquiry into the Original Functions of Accounting ―* (*Final Report*), Japan Accounting Association, pp. 63-79.

Section II

Verification of Fair Value Accounting from the Historical Perspective

― From Current Value to Fair Value Measurement ―

Chapter 5

The British East India Company's Market Valuation in the Second Half of the Seventeenth Century (1664-1694)

Takeshi Sugita
Osaka University of Economics

Abstract

The history of market valuation in Joint stock company accounting can be traced back to the 17th Century. One of the oldest Joint stock companies in the world, The London East India Company (Governor and Company of Merchants of London trading into the East Indies,) use sale price or other value equivalent to market value for its inventory assets.

In this Chapter, the specifics of inventory asset valuation by The East India Company are provided to examine the significance of market valuation as a means to valuate assets as practiced by early Joint stock company accountants. This information is available in "Books of Account" held at The British Library, specifically the "General Ledgers" of 1664 to 1694 and other old documents and material related to that company.

Firstly, the imported commodity accounts, particularly those of pepper, spices and calico, arranged separately by item at the settlement dates of each ledger revealed the measurement method of each respective unsalable commodity. Also, a look at the company's treatment of valuation differences occurring as a result of unsalable commodity market valuation in parallel with its internal regulations regarding imported goods and the content of its board of directors' announcements revealed details on its market valuation practices.

Keywords
The British East India Company, valuation of assets, inventory, unsalable commodities, market value, valuation differences, weighted average method

5-1. Introduction

In studying the history of market valuation, one may ask from when was it utilized to measure assets and what was its implication with respect to such measurements. Previous research on the issue of inventory valuation examine handbooks and other accounting essays published both overseas and in Japan mainly between the 16th and 20th Centuries that present double-entry bookkeeping techniques to observe the valuation method for unsalable commodities at ledger closing dates. This is where the advent of market valuation comes to light[1].

Unfortunately, there is little research on accounting practices themselves, particularly dealing with the valuation method of unsalable commodities by early Joint stock companies in the U.K., the Governor and Company of Merchants of London trading into the East Indies (1600-1709; hereinafter, "The East India Company", "The Company" or "EIC")[2] established over 4 centuries ago in the year 1600, did practice market valuation for its inventories.

In this Chapter, I examine the significance of market value as a basis for asset valuation at early stock companies using the example of market valuation accounting practices with respect to inventories at that time with the knowledge that not only the economic and social backdrop but also the attribution of assets differed from the present debate, which is centered squarely on the market valuation

---

[1] Vanes [1967] and Watanabe [2000] and other major research.
[2] Governor and Company of Merchants of London trading into the East Indies merged with its rival the English Company trading into the East Indies (1698-1709; hereinafter, "The English Company") and later became the United Company of Merchants of England trading into the East Indies (1709-1874; hereinafter, "The United Company"). In this thesis, these three entities are referred to collectively as the "The British East India Company."

of financial instruments[3]. Specifically, my approach is an observation of the measurement method and treatment of valuation differences by EIC to show the market valuation practices of The Company and reveal the background market valuation application.

5-2. Overview of EIC and its Method of Selling Imported Commodities

In 1600, EIC was established to acquire pepper and spice through eastward maritime navigation. Some 60 years later, it was changed to a limited liability company, but before that, it had been formed as a regulated company under the old guild system and established limited or separate joint stock each time a voyage was undertaken[4]. In 1613, that structure was replaced with a joint-stock company[5]. In 1657, an effort to establish a permanent entity with the eradication of demand deposits, the Company switched to a limited liability company structure to curtail the liability of all its employees based on "An act declaratory concerning Bankrupts" enacted in 1662[6]. The East India Company then merged with its rival The English Company becoming The United Company. These three companies, known as the The British East India Company, survived for over 200 years.

The East India Company was also a chartered company by Elizabeth I with exclusive rights to trade in the East Indies from the Cape of Good Hope to the Straits of Magellan[7]. That explains why it was famous at that time in the East-Indian trade.

The main business activity of EIC was the procurement of pepper and spices by ship from the East Indies and transport it to England for sale[8]. The Company built Factories in various cities of India making them hubs of activity and hired representatives to

---

[3] Winjum [1970], Yamey [1959/1970/1977], Baladouni [1983/1986a/1986b], Motegi [1994], Bryer [2000] and other early research did not delve into The Company's inventory valuation.
[4] Otsuka [1969], pp. 184–186, p. 449.
[5] Otsuka [1969], pp. 470–471.
[6] Otsuka [1969], p. 184, pp. 500–501.
[7] Nishimura [1960], pp. 26–27.
[8] Chaudhuri [1978], p. 135.

bear the brunt of their procurement tasks[9].

EIC's general method of selling imported commodities was by auction. The rules of the General Court and *The Lawes or Standing Orders of the East India Company* (hereinafter, "*The Lawes or Standing Orders*") formulated in 1621[10], and the rules regarding the establishment of the New General Stock of 1657 all stipulate the auction sale of goods "by the light of a candle[11]". In addition, the oldest ledger in existence "Ledger B" (1664-1669) has the "at the candle" annotation and the Court of Committees' Court Minutes provides opinions handed down by that Court on the need to moderate the auctioning of certain commodities[12], therefore, it seems that at that time auctioning was the general method of sales.

From its incorporation to the mid-18th Century, trading commodities was the Company's core competency, however, from the mid-18th Century, it underwent a transformation. In 1757, the British faced the French in the Battle of Plassey fought in an attempt to break the former's hegemony over trading in the East Indies. The East India Company came out of this conflict victorious resulting in its de-facto control over India and acquisition of the right to levy taxes in India, or *Diwani*. The acquisition of *Diwani* transformed the Company from a merchant to military occupier[13]. Until its dissolution in 1874, the Company had not only undertaken trading but also greatly facilitated British rule in India.

5-3. Unsold Goods Valuation Method at Closing of Ledger

(1) Overview of commodity

Presently, the records, books of account and other massive amount of historical documents on The British East India Company are stored at London's British Library[14]. We have the Court

---

[9] Chaudhuri [1978], p. 148, pp. 208-211.
[10] Governor and Company of Merchants of London trading into the East Indies (hereinafter Governor and Company) [1621], p. 59.
[11] Sainsbury [1916], pp. 197-198.
[12] Sainsbury [1925], p. 31, p. 37.
[13] Nishimura [1966], p.170, pp.177-178.
[14] There are over 300,000 volumes of related historical documents. Recording relating to the Company's accounting are classified mostly by British Library, IOR/L/AG numbering over 8,200 volumes (Moir [1988], pp. 127-130, pp. 156-163).

Minutes of the Company's Court of Committees[15], the records of each regional Factory overseas and other piles of old papers, however, those regarding accounting include the General Ledgers, General Cash Journals, General Commerce Journals and others dating from 1664 to 1874. These manuscripts contain mainly the Company's oldest "Ledger B" (Aug. 1664 to Mar. 1669) all the way to its "Ledger K" (Sept. 1703 to Jun. 1703), as well as the corresponding General Cash Journals and General Commerce Journals.

Factory accounts were set up in the ledgers by type, or lot-specific[16]. Although goods for export and imported goods make up the bulk of its inventory, records show that the sale of the latter was the main source of revenue for the Company. These were set apart initially from goods bound for export in the ledgers and a manager was clearly annotated for each respective commodity account[17].

I mentioned earlier here that commodities imported from East India included pepper and spice as well as calico and Indian textiles. Specifically, there was a black pepper, a green ginger, a turmerick and other pepper accounts, a chints, a sallampores, a ginghams and other spice accounts, and accounts for textiles. These were all brought in by ship from overseas and warehoused after arriving at London's port. Note that, according to *The Lawes or Standing Orders* and the Court of Committees' Court Minutes of 1621, a separate person in charge was assigned responsibility over respective merchandise[18].

Meanwhile, goods for export included items to be sold at their destination, consumed by the Company such as on voyages, or bartered on site. Specifically, the Company used "Reales of Eight" silver and gold to pay for goods purchased in East India, as well as other tender such as lead, broad cloth, corrall and copper plate. Before their lading on ships, goods for export were managed by

---

[15] The Court of Committees comprised of the Governor, the Deputy-Governor and 24 Committees and exercised executive control over the Company (Otsuka [1969], pp. 184–186.

[16] Ledger H (Jul. 1682-Jun. 1694) shows comprehensive accounts for some imported goods such as "Silke and Callicoe Books a/c".

[17] Upon introduction of double-entry bookkeeping in August 1664, the name of persons in charge for both imported and exported goods is demanded by the Accounts Committee (British Library,IOR/H/15, p. 3). However, such were only annotated for imported goods and only in Ledger B. From C onward, there are no manager names for accounts.

[18] Governor and Company [1621], p. 14.

the "Clarke of the Stores in London[19]".

In this thesis, I separated imported goods from those for export by the Company and focused on the former to examine its valuation of unsalables, or balance. In doing so, I extracted imported goods accounts with balances at ledger closing and made an analysis.

(2) Entries in goods accounts

An example of entries in imported goods accounts in provided in Table 1 as "Ledger G's Peeper white a/c". These accounts had balances itemized from the old ledger to the General Joint Stock Account by debtors to which entries for purchases were made. There is a total amount entry in the amount field and the name of the Factory, quantity and ship name entered in the remarks field, however, there is no cost for unit[20]. Profit on goods is entered at the last debtor.

Meanwhile, the amount field for creditors in goods accounts had the sale price (total) for each transaction log and the remarks field had the ship's name, purchaser name, price (unit) and volume at the time of the transaction. The ledger method was similar to the total cost accounting method. Note that these accounts were closed about once a year, for a total of 4 times a year. From F onward, ledgers had multiple new accounts introduced that were closed multiple times during those periods.

Therefore, why is it that the sale prices (unit) are logged at the sale of goods but not the purchase prices (unit) of goods upon their purchase? This is because the record sent from the procurement location only includes the quantity and total purchase amount provided by local "factors" (representatives) onsite.

This is also reflected in the Court of Committees' Court Minutes and the Company's internal rules. Its systematic *The Lawes or Standing Orders* formulated in 1621 contain the detailed tasks undertaken by each person in charge. A rule for the "Warehouses" where

---

[19] Governor and Company [1621], p. 14, p. 57.

[20] For exported goods, for purchased items to be entered in customer accounts, the names of the opposing parties and personal account names were annotated and the remarks field showed quantity and, although not in all cases, the unit cost depending on the commodity. The East India Company used the volume unit "1 hundredweight" (= cwt. = 50.848kg; hereinafter, "cwt") = 4qtr. = 112 pounds, as shown in Table 1. They used not the Gregorian but the Julian calendar, therefore, their year started on March 25. In addition, the currency unit was £1 = 20s = 240d.

[Table 5-1] Ledger G's pepper white account (154) example entry

		Pepper white			Dr		
			Cwt.q.1b				£.s.d.
1678.6.1	2	To the General Joint Stock	190.-.-		Brought from Ledger F fol.157	1	1330.-.-
7.31	7	to Owners of the Loyal Subject			for freight	34	283.1.2
		to ditto for freight of the wants					3.5.1
	7	to Factory at Bantam for	55	83.2.21	Per Ann	9	177.10.-
8.31	14	to Owners of the East India Merchant			for freight	30	82.10.2
		to ditto			for freight	34	0.10.3
1679.3.31	68	to Factory at Bantam for	78	124.3.23	Expectation	9	251.15.11
			Omission				
1682.6.30	423	to Profit and Loss advanced				496	4346.8.4
				1566.-4			8321.16.7

		Pepper white			Cr		
				Cwt.q.1b			£.s.d.
1678.7.31	7	By Owners of the Loyal Subject for		3.2.25	want	34	27.3.1
8.31	14	by Owners of the East India Merchant for		-.2.10	want	30	4.5.11
10.31	47	John Langham	14	42.-.4	at 7.16 Loyal Subject	357	327.17.6
12.31	50	John Langham	11	33.-.7	at 7.16 ditto	357	257.17.10
12.31	51	Anthony Deprement	31	94.-.16	at 8.12 East India Merchant	391	808.17.2
1.31	56	John Legandre	31	80.1.-	at 8.10	415	682.2.6
		John Langham	9	27.-.18	at 7.16 Loyal Subject	357	211.17.-
			Omission				
1682.6.30	429	by balanced carried to new		974.2.8	Ledger H		5000
				1566.-.4			8321.16.7

Source: The author based on British Library, IOR/L/AG/1/1/8, fol. 154.

imported goods were stored tell manages to "Let the Warehouses for Merchandize bee charged with a Booke for that purpose, wherein every particular Commodity is set downe by number, waight or measure, as it received out of each Ship severall[21]".

Also, another rule for the "Clarkes of the Ware-house" (individuals who managed storage) stipulate that "They shall received all the said Ware carefully and justly, by number, waight, or measure, as the Merchandize it selfe shall require, and thereof make true entry in a Booke of purpose...[22]", therefore, when receiving goods, there is no specific requirement for logging prices. This is the same as the explanation provided by the "Committees of Ware-houses" that oversee the Warehouses requiring the following cautions when receiving imported goods landing in London: "...they shall see all the Merchandize whatsoever for this Company, safely and orderly lodged in the Warehouses, taking a true accompt of every Ships lading, concerning the quality and quantity of the Wares severally, and so shall they compare all things by the Accompts from the *Indies*, to see that the Company be not wronged in their waight, number, measure, false packing, or other defects[23]". Therefore, even when receiving imported goods and taking them to warehouse, the logging of quantities was required but their prices, specifically unit prices, are absent. Although there are no rules for the recording commodity prices, that doesn't mean not one of these persons in charge ever dealt with prices. I found this amongst the rules on goods sales by the so-called *Clarkes of the Ware-houses*: "...noting downe in a faire Booke every particular thing delivered, thetime, the parties name, his sureties, tare, trets, price, and every other circumstance, to make the parcel plaine and perfect[24]".

This indicates the price when selling imported goods. As already mentioned, sales prices were normally based on auctions taking place in London and the prices set when procuring in India are separate. From this, we can also see that the recording of prices at reception of imported goods was secondary after the more important quantity, weight and scale entries. At the same time in the series of *The Lawes or Standing Orders*, it is suggested that, when forwarding imported goods to some destination, the

---

[21] Governor and Company [1621], p. 81.
[22] Governor and Company [1621], p. 57, CCLIX.
[23] Governor and Company [1621], p. 58, CCLXII.
[24] Governor and Company [1621], p. 58, CCLXL.

indication of purchase prices by type of commodity was not necessarily required. Actually, as the above shows, for about a half century of records, I found directives regarding the non-recording of purchase cost at importation.

The Court of Committees stated on November 27, 1678, "Accounts Committee to consider and report their opinion of paper delivered in by Beyer touching the more orderly keeping of the Company's accounts in India...,to be sent home yearly without fail and an exact diary to be kept by the Chief and Council and all the factors in the Bay of all goods bought for the Company, with their prime cost, also what the Company's goods are sold for, no imaginary prices to be put, as the Company understand has been the practice formerly[25]".

This report states that no record of purchase price was made regarding goods received from the procurement site and requests a remedy. From the above, we can see that the records themselves sent to head office from local onsite Factory only provided quantities per imported goods and purchase prices (total) based on local currency because no one ever demanded the recording of prices. The creditor's remarks field for "goods or merchandize a/c" has a sale (unit) price logged, but because the sale of goods was generally by auction in London by the Company, not all sale prices (unit) are clear.

(3) Calculation of valuation method of unsalable goods

As mentioned above, commodity accounts were set up by type and the same were closed periodically whether or not inventory was completely sold off. In the event of unsalable inventory, a trading profit or loss is calculated by commodity for each account and, in hopes of preventing dead stock, some valuation was made and the same was carried over to the new ledger[26]. They did not wait for a certain type of commodity to be sold off before closing the account. The Table shows each account as subject to a valuation on each respective unsalable commodity at ledger closing with the result was carried over to the new ledger. Let's look at the valuation method for unsalable portions.

When analyzing their valuation method, one should note the

---

[25] Sainsbury [1938], p. 229.
[26] However, Ledgers B, C and D are not necessarily transferred to the balance account.

118   Fair Value Accounting in Historical Perspective

ambiguity of the relationship between the flow of goods with the process by which values are accounted in each of the ledger's merchandise accounts[27]. In light of the characteristics of such merchandise accounts, when considering whether cost allocation is possible, it may be adequate to use the weighted average method to estimate the inventory balance and unit value of unsalables at ledger closing. Therefore, I hypothetically examined the valuation method of unsalable goods by estimating the inventory balance and unit value of unsalable merchandise based on the weighted average method and compared results with the values and unit values for unsalables entered in merchandise accounts. If, when doing so, the valuation of the unsalables hypothetically does not recognize historical cost, then the price is, for example, compared to the sale price. To highlight the discrepancies between the two, a comparison is made of the cost allocation-based unit value of those unsalables with the unit value thereof as actually recorded. Results are shown in Table 2 below.

Within the subject of this Chapter's analysis, namely the imported goods accounts of the Company's Ledgers B to K, I examined the valuation method of unsalables focusing on those accounts with balances at ledger closing[28] In the commodity accounts, I first calculated the total purchase amount of goods logged in the debtor field, based on the weighted average method, and the cost (weighted average unit price) calculated by dividing the total incidental expenses by the quantity received[29]. When calcu-

---

[27] Sugita [2010], pp. 35-36.

From the General Ledger and General Commerce Journals, nothing was found that would indicate that the outflow of the merchandise from warehouse was governed by a set of rules such as a set average or an organization resembling "FIFO" or "LIFO" under which cost would be assumed.

Conversely, the flow of merchandise and the process by which value is accounted do not necessarily match. Some accounts have creditor entries on sales made prior to debtor entries on purchases. This means that, regardless of whether goods were purchased, a sale is logged. This can be seen in multiple accounts in each of the ledgers providing further proof that the flow of goods does not necessarily correspond with the value accounting process.

[28] For this research, I wasn't able to specify the valuation method from the information in Ledgers J and K, therefore, the title of this Chapter was not decided in consideration of the periods thereof.

[29] Here, I checked whether quantities or volumes are used for unit measurements and which of these units is used as a multiplier when estimating values for entry at the

lating the weighted average unit price, in the event of multiple ledger closings, I deducted both the transfer amount to the gain or loss account occurring as a trading gain or loss and the carried-off and carried-in balance. This is because the total purchase amount and the purchased quantity, or the total sales amount and the sold quantity, are treated accurately.

Even when estimating average sales price (unit), the balance annotated in the creditor field is deducted meaning that only the merchandise quantity and total price are extracted and the hypothetical cost allocation is conducted accurately. Then, although a comparison is made of the unit value of unsalables based on hypothetical cost allocation vis-a-vis the actually logged unit value of unsalables, both were compared as unit prices to shed light on their discrepancies. If by chance both prices are the same, then this would be recognized as a valuation based on "cost".

On the other hand, if such is not recognized as cost-based valuation, then a sale price-based valuation is provided as follows. As mentioned above, sales price is basically the value at the time of the sale of goods recorded in unit form in the remarks field of the creditor in the merchandise account, with the quantity entered along side the total sales amount in the amount field. However, the merchandise sales amount is not necessarily fixed throughout the ledger period. I recognized the unsalable unit values as corresponding to the values between the lowest sale value (unit) and highest sale value (unit) logged during the ledger period as sale price-based valuation. Note that in sale price-based valuation, the sale price (unit) itself may be lower than the cost and the value of unsalables also may be valuated lower than the cost. The reason for this is, depending on the type of goods, the sale price itself may invariably be lower than the cost. In such a case, a price that is lower that the original cost may be recognized as one type of sale price. Therefore, unsalables evaluated as lower than cost may be considered to have been evaluated based on a sale price that is lower than cost and therefore included in sale price.

Where the valuation method is based neither on cost nor sale price, I categorized it as either "valuation lower than cost", "valua-

---

time of a purchase or other outflow of merchandise in each account. When volume is the unit, the unit price is 1cwt., when quantity is the unit, 1bag, 1piece and 1quilt is the unit price. These units were actually logged in each account and used discriminately depending on the type of merchandise.

tion higher than cost" or "valuation higher than sale price".

(4) Unsalable merchandise valuation method

As stated above, when confirming the value of unsalables, many of the unit values thereof in Ledgers B to H at closing were as shows in Table 2[30], which indicates sale price, or unit price-based valuations such as "valuation lower than cost", "valuation higher than cost" and "valuation higher than sale price".

[Table 5-2] Unsalable Unit Value Valuation Analysi Results

Ledger \ Unit price	Valuation lower than cost	Cost	Valuation higher than cost	Sale price	Valuation higher than sale price	Unknown	No outflow	Account total
Ledger D (1664.8-1669.3)	1	0	2	3	0	0	0	0
Ledger C (1669.4-1671.4)	2	2	2	19	0	0	2	27
Ledger D (1671.5-1673.7)	2	3	4	40	2	0	3	54
Ledger E (1673.8-1675.12)	6	0	8	29	2	2	3	50
Ledger F (1676.1-1678.5)	7	0	6	21	1	0	5	40
Ledger G (1678.6-1682.6)	4	1	7	11	0	0	1	24
Ledger H (1682.7-1694.6)	1	0	1	1	1	0	0	4
Ledger J (1694.7-1703.8)	0	0	0	0	0	32	0	32
Ledger K (1703.8-1713.6)	0	0	0	0	0	0	0	0
Total	23	6	28	126	6	34	14	239

Source: The author based on British Library, IOR/L/AG/1/1/2-11.

---

[30] I plan to present detailed tabulation results for this Table in a separate manuscript. The lowest sale price (unit), highest sale price (unit) and average sale price for each type of goods during the ledger period. The latter was calculated by dividing the total sale amount by the quantity.

Specifically, there are 207 types of commodity accounts with unsalables at closing in Ledgers B to K and 126 of them feature valuations based sale price. Meanwhile, there are only 6 types whose valuations are based on cost calculated based on the weighted average method.

After merchandise valuated based on sale price was carried-over to a new ledger, a revaluation by a method resembling the lower of cost or market method occurred in the current accounting treatment thus resulting in the problem of whether valuation was based on original historical cost.

However, in the new ledger, the value carried-over from the old ledger was logged as is, therefore, in the new ledger, no revaluation occurred. Note that, in Ledger J (Jul. 1694 to Aug. 1703), commodity accounts were not closed and no balance was recognized, but in Ledger K (Sep. 1703 to Jul. 1713), although the opening entry in the General Commerce Journals shows a carried-over balance for each type of merchandise logged in Ledger J, specifying the valuation method was difficult. This is because, despite being able to differentiate only value amounts, because values relating to carry-over quantities and sales are not always entered, calculations by cost allocation-based weighted average method is also a daunting task. In addition, because of the many accounts not closed in Ledger K, I wasn't able to recognize the balance of commodity accounts.

5-4. Sale Price-Based Estimation

(1) Selection of sale price

So, why is it that, while many unsalables were valuated based on cost, others were measured using other values namely sale price or something close to it. In examining this point, let's verify what values were actually used. As mentioned above, merchandise sale entries were made in the creditor field of each merchandise account and, when doing so, quantities and sale prices (unit) were logged in the remarks field and General Commerce Journals and then sale prices (total) were entered in the amount field. When carrying over unsalables, entries were made in the creditor's last item and the carried-over quantities and amounts (valuation) were generally entered in the remarks field. In addition, although not always, the General Commerce Journals included the unit value and quantities of unsalables as carried-over entries.

Therefore, in light of the above, the ledgers show that, when calculating the value of unsalables, the unit price was multiplied by the quantity of unsalables. In the previous section, I pointed out that the unit cost to which the quantity of unsalables logged in each account was multiplied was mainly the sale price or another value close to it. There were very few goods evaluated based on the lowest or highest sale price (unit) or most recent sale price (unit). This number was only 10 out of 127 types and 2 of which were valuated by the same average sale price calculated by the author. In other words, there were only 8 types simply interpretable as sale price at ledger closing.

I will now provide specific examples of unsalable valuations, unsalable quantities and unsalable unit values appearing in Ledgers B to F (1664–1678). The Turmerick account of fol.457 in Ledger B has an entry of £320 (= 80cwt × @£4.00) and Baftaes Narrow white's entry in fol. 516 is £38 (= 19cwt × @£2.00). In Ledger C, the Tea account of fol. 55 is £29 (= 29cwt × @£1.00), Long Cloth blew of fol. 305 is £775 (= 500 pecees × @£1.55) and Narrow Bafts of fol. 354 is £15 (= 10 pecees × @£1.50). In Ledger D, Hane Clouts of fol. 37 is £540 (= 5,400pieces × @2s), Ginghams white of fol.62 is £2,993 (= 2,993pieces × @20s). In Ledger E, Bafts broad blew of fol. 134 is £300 (= 600 pieces × @10s). In Ledger F, Saltpeter of fol. 150 is £33,920 (= 13,568cwt × @£2.50), Green Ginger of fol.152 £3,450 (= 1150cwt × @3.00) and Pepper white of fol. 157 is £1,330 (= 190cwt × @£7.00)[31].

As shown above, in the unit price in the valuation of unsalables, there are differences in pound sterling and shilling entries in that, although not in all cases, figures were stated in relatively simple terms such as "@£1.00," "@£1.50," "@£2.00" and "@20s." Also, many of them used a sale price in the range between lowest and highest values during the ledger period, as stated above, or the value nearest to the sale price. Actually, sale prices (unit) were not constant throughout the ledger period and, despite the use of multiple sale prices, these accountants did not select the lowest or highest sale price (unit) and those closest to the account closing date in their valuations but rather tended to choose rounded unit prices that were easy to calculate.

---

[31] In Ledger D, unit prices were recorded with any fractions of 1 shilling truncated.

(2) Reason for lack of cost allocation and estimated value of unsalables

Why is it that in the valuation of unsalables, no cost allocation was conducted and a single sale price (unit) was selected instead? There are two reasons for this. First, there is one factor leading to entries in accounts. The number of sales of goods during a ledger period were great. Depending on the type of merchandise, there were over 100 transactions during a given ledger period that spanned several years. In such cases, entries to commodity accounts would involve logs of over 100 items for purchases and sales, respectively, and although sometimes the purchase unit price is entered for merchandise export accounts, for merchandise import accounts which are the subject of this Chapter, logs at the time of purchase did not always reflect cost and neither was a cost allocation always done for incidentals such as freight charged when purchases occurred depending on the type of merchandise.

Meanwhile, generally, when a sale would occur, not only would the sale price (total) be entered in the amount field of the account whenever a transaction took place, but also the sale price (unit) in the remarks field. From this, we can surmise that one sales price (unit) entered in the remarks field of the ledger accounts used to measure the unsalable merchandise value was simpler than attempting to measure the unsalable merchandise value by cost allocation based on a regulated outflow thereof such as LIFO or FIFO, even though such methods do not provide the purchase unit cost for each purchased goods.

In addition, many of the unsalable goods unit values had fractions of 1 pence truncated, whereas for pounds sterling conversions, fractions of 1 shilling were truncated, in other words, for shilling conversions, rounded figures were entered to have unit prices without pences.

Considering the above, rather than measure the unsalable merchandise value based on some kind of cost allocation, the accountants chose the obviously simpler path of basing valuations on already logged, rounded unit prices, particularly for valuations, to calculate unsalabale merchandise values.

In addition, another factor may be to find out what is the price of unsalables using sale price, or the ability to approximately estimate the market value of this merchandise. Specifically, Ledger G shows a trend differing from all prior ledgers that demonstrate the aforementioned reasons. A look at the unsalable merchandise values logged in Ledger G shows that they differ from those in all previous ledgers with many entries in units of £10 and £100, therefore, valuations resulting in £10 or £100 unit amounts with fractions of 1 pound truncated are evident.

Specifically, unsalable merchandise values included £300 (21bag, 74cwt) for Cowries in fol. 152, £700 (400 bag, 260cwt) for Green Ginger in fol. 161, £2,000 (39bales, 3666pounds) for Silk Raw in fol. 185, £29,410 (16,731bag, 19,618cwt.2qr.4lb) for Saltpeter in fol. 189, £20,000 (1,052,318lb) for Pepper black in fol. 190 and £1,400 (992peeces) for Black Silk in fol. 204 all entered in Ledger G. Among 24 types, 18 unsalable merchandise values were counted in terms of truncated units of £10 or £100.

As mentioned above, this unsalable merchandise valuation method is generally based on the sale price or some other value close to it. However, note that, for Ledgers B to F, unsalable value is calculated by multiplying the unit price by the quantity, however, in Ledger G, values divisible by £10 and £100 are prevalent and, while truncated to the nearest £10 or £100, most values are not rounded by quantity.

In Ledger G, unsalable merchandise valuations are not necessarily the result of multiplying the quantity by the unit price, as in ledgers up to F. Rather, Ledger G tends to prioritize the estimation of unsalable merchandise valuation whereby sale price or the like is used as a computation base and the unsalable merchandise values themselves are estimated and logged after truncating not fractions of 1 pound, but rather £10 or £100.

Here, we can see that simplicity and convenience were prioritized in the computation of values, but this lax calculation method shown in ledgers up to F, is different from simply using a unit price-based valuation system, and in Ledger G, values themselves were estimated pointing to a different concept of simplicity and convenience for these accountants. Therefore, they used sale price or the like for unsalable merchandise valuation to estimate the approximate market value of unsalable merchandise. Even in Ledger B to F, a method was employed whereby a conveniently truncated sale price or the like, neither the lowest nor the highest value, was multiplied by the quantity to compute the unsalable merchandise value, however, Ledger G employed a simpler and more convenient method whereby sale price or the like was used to estimate the unsalable merchandise. There wasn't any apparent problem with the approximate estimation of prices for unsalables.

Note that, as indicated in section 3 herein, no records were being sent from India, the origin country of all goods, regarding the purchase cost of merchandise, until a report calling for a remedy thereof was released by the Court of Committees in 1678. However, as far as the time period-concordant Ledger G (Jun. 1678 to Jun. 1682) entries are concerned, there is no indication of purchase cost, and particularly unit prices, as demanded by the report. The demands of the Court of Committees are neither reflected in the actual ledger entries nor in any account of Ledger H and beyond.

5-5. Treatment of Valuation Differences Based on Sale Price, etc.

Behind unsalable merchandise valuation based on sale price, etc. is the possibility or assumption of expected earnings due to the occurrence of gains or losses from revaluations of unsalables. An examination of this point is provided below to find out how gains from revaluations are treated in terms of their relation with dividends due to the large number unsalables being valuated based on sale price.

However, in those days (around 1670) there were never any relation between gains calculated based on these ledger entries and dividends. The EIC's monopoly in the spice trade meant that as long as ships arrived safely to London from the East, their business was profitable. In other words, the arrival of those ships was the point in time on which the acquisition of gains could be recognized and was therefore one of the factors in declaring a dividend[32].

This is represented in the profit and dividend entries of the Valuation of the General Joint Stock[33] (hereinafter "Stock Valuation") prepared on the same date as the 1671 closing of Ledger C (April

---

[32] Winjum [1970], pp. 348-350; Sainsbury [1925], p. vii.
[33] In December 1664, the first "The Valuation of The Company's Estate" was submitted to the general meeting of adventures (=shareholders). This Stock Valuation was stipulated in 1657's New General Stock prospectus as enabling the calculation of each adventures's equity in the Company and the free participation by adventures and withdrawal therefrom (Sainsbury [1925], pp. 115-116; Winjum [1972], pp. 352-353). The first "The Valuation of The Company's Estate" did not include any entries relating to profit. (Sainsbury [1925], pp. 113-114).

30th). The profit values entered in the Stock Valuation were not brought over from the profit-and-loss account but rather estimated individually based on an expectation of acquired gains through future sales of merchandise[34]. This was indicated by the Company's Court of Committees on August 18, 1671, prior to the holding of The General Court. The Court of Committees ordered the accounting committee to estimate the total gains from merchandise sold for the second Stock Valuation. Thereafter, the Court of Committees on August 23rd of that same year decided on the estimation of a 10% profit on goods for export and approx. 40 to 50% on goods imported to England[35]. Although this estimate called for the accounting of an estimated monetary amount based on some account entries, this was for purchased merchandise with no relation to amounts calculated based on the profit-and-loss account for sales.

In addition, the amount of dividends entered in the Stock Valuation itself was merely a calculation based on the amount of capital[36], and the profit-and-loss account to which gains and losses were transferred from commodity accounts was not related whatsoever to the profit available for dividend calculation made by the Company[37].

In light of this, it seems that in the EIC's "Profit-and-Loss" account, the comprehensive calculation of profit and loss was not that important. At that time, the calculation of trade profits and losses for each merchandise account was done based on accounts set up for each type of merchandise. Of course, the above unsalable valuation method mingles in gains or losses based on revaluations other than trading gains or losses. However, expected earnings were estimated separately from merchandise trades and, assuming expected earnings and other values, there is little possibility that unsalables were valuated based on sale price.

---

[34] The Stock Valuation has the statement: "By the profit on £98,569 5s. 9d. cost of the cargoes of four ships sent to Surat in 1669, and arrived there and part of them sold, which we hope will produce 10 percent" (British Library, IOR/B/31, pp. 310–311; Sainsbury [1932], pp. 69–70).

[35] Sainsbury [1932], p. 66.

[36] Sainsbury [1916], p. 174.

[37] Perhaps symbolic of this practice, although Ledger B and C's profit-and-loss accounts were closed, those of Ledger D, E and J were not and no tabulated calculations were made.

5-6. Conclusion

The purpose of this Chapter was to examine the significance of market valuation in early Joint stock company accounting by showing the inventory valuation method practiced by EIC. Specifically, I looked at the unsalable merchandise (inventory asset) valuation method employed in the Company's General Ledger (1664–1694) to find out what measurement method they used. An analysis of the unsalable valuation method based on its ledger accounts and other records revealed that its accountants, while not valuating based on cost, they calculated unsalable merchandise value using a simplified sale price without fractions or the like and the resulting values were logged as estimated valuations.

Moreover, such valuations came about probably when they attempted to valuate unsalables and, instead of basing themselves on some cost allocation, using the sale price (unit) already entered in merchandise accounts was simpler and more convenient. Although purchased merchandise quantities were entered at the time of purchase, the purchase cost was not logged meaning that not only the cost allocation of incidentals is unknown, the relation between the flow of merchandise and the process by which value is accounted is also unknown. Meanwhile, when selling merchandise, the sale price (unit) was entered in the relevant account at the time thereof. Therefore, to valuate unsalables, they did not take the effort to use some kind of cost allocation, but rather they simply and conveniently took the sale price (unit) appearing in ledger accounts or the like and multiplied it by the quantity.

In other words, because the purchase cost of goods is unknown, instead of calculating the value of unsalables by cost allocation based on the regulated outflow of goods such as FIFO and LIFO, without considering that purchases of merchandise that consist of unsalables is a different thing, as already mentioned, the simple multiplication of a single cost value among sale prices is a much less taxing job.

This simplicity of task is represented by the application of a single sale price (unit) for most values used to determined the unit value of unsalables, and not the average sale price, the lowest or the highest or the closest value to the sale price at ledger closing. In other words, they used a sale price value picked from between the lowest and highest values and truncated shillings (in case of pounds sterling) and pences (in case of shillings). From this, we can surmise that they wanted to use the simplest unit value, not only one, to calculate the value of unsalables.

In addition, an examination of Ledger G (1678-1682) revealed that, while referring to sale price or the like, without multiplying the quantity thereof by the unit price, they used a method whereby the value of unsalables is estimated so that the resulting value is divisible by £10 or £100. Therefore, in Ledger G, and not in all others up to Ledger F, calculations were not based on a simple unit value but rather on an estimated value that was posted in the ledger and then used to enable an approximation of the merchandise's market value, which was not done from the standpoint of simplicity.

Note that, from the relation between earnings and dividends, expected earnings were maybe assumed when valuating based on unsalable sale price. However, because of the lack of any relation between the tabulated Profit-and-Loss accounts and dividends, and because of the estimated values of individual export merchandise for expected profit, this possibility is low.

【References in English】
British Library, IOR/B/31, Court Minutes, London.
British Library, IOR/ H/4, Home Miscellaneous Series, London.
British Library, IOR/L/AG/1/1/2−11, General Ledgers, 1664−1713, London.
British Library, IOR/L/AG/1/5/1−9, General Cash Journals, General Commerce Journal, 1664-1713, London.
British Library, IOR/L/AG/1/6/1, 4−5, General Commerce Journal, 1671−1673, 1694−1713, London.
Baladouni, V. [1981] "The Accounting Records of The East India Company," *The Accounting Historians Journal*, Vol. 8, No. 1.
─── [1986a], "Financial Reporting in the Early Years of the East India company," *The Accounting Historians Journal*, Vol. 13, No. 1.
─── [1986b], "East India Company's 1783 Balance of Accounts," *Abacus*, Vol. 22, No. 2.
Bryer, R. A. [1997], "Accounting for the 'Bourgeois Revolution' in the English East India Company 1600-1657" The Fifth Interdisciplinary Perspectives on Accounting Conference, UMIST/University of Manchester, 7−9 July 1997, Conference Proceedings.
─── [2000], "The history of Accounting and the transition to capitalism in England. Part two : evidence," *Accounting, Organizations & Society*, Vol. 25, No. 4/5.
Chaudhuri, K. N. [1978], *The Trading World of Asia and The English East India Company 1660−1760*, Cambridge.
Gardner, B. [1971], *The East India Company*, London.

Governor and Company of Merchants of London trading into the East Indies [1621], *The Lawes or Standing Orders of the East India Company*, England, (reprinted ed., Germany, 1968).

Learmount, B. [1985], *A History of the Auction*, London.

Moir, M. [1988], *A General Guide to The India Office Records*, London.

Sainsbury, E. B. [1907/1909/1912/1913/1916/1922/1935/1938] *A Calendar of the Court Minutes etc. of the East India Company 1635–1679*, Oxford.

Vanes, B. A. [1967], "Sixteenth-century Accounting; The Ledger of John Smythe, Merchant of Bristol" *The Accountant*, Vol. CLVII, No. 4829.

Winjum, J. O. [1970], *The Role of Accounting in the Economic Development of England: 1500 to 1750*, Urbana, Illinois.

Yamey, B. S. [1940], "The Functional Development of Double-Entry Bookkeeping" *The Accountant*, Vol. CIII, No. 3439.

——— [1959] "Some Seventeeth and Eighteenth Century Double-Entry Ledgers," *The Accounting Review*, Vol. 34, No. 4.

———, Edey, H. C. and Thomson, H. W. [1963], *Accounting in England and Scotland: 1543–1800*, London.

——— [1970] "Closing the Ledger," *Accounting and Business Research*, Vol. 1.

——— [1977] "Some Topics in the History of Financial Accounting in England, 1500–1900," in *Studies in Accounting*.

[References in Japanese]

Nakano, Tsuneo [1978] "A Genealogy of Asset Valuation," *Kokumin Keizai Zassi (Journal of Economics & Business Administration)*, Vol. 137, No. 3.

——— [2002] "The British East India Company and its Corporate Governance," *Kokumin Keizai Zassi (Journal of Economics & Business Administration)*, Vol. 186, No. 4.

Nishimura, Takao [1960] *History of British East India Company*, Keibunsha.

Otsuka, Hisao [1969] *History of Corporation*, Iwanami Shoten.

Sugita, Takeshi [2010] "Inventory Valuation of The British East India Company in the 17th Century," *Kaikei (Accounting)*, Vol. 178, No. 1.

Watanabe, Izumi [2000] "The Valuation Methods of Goods Remaining Unsold in theBookkeeping Textbooks in 16th–18th Century Great Britain," *Osaka Keidai Ronshu (Journal of Osaka University of Economics)*, Vol. 50, No. 6.

——— [2011], "The Standpoint of Fair Value from the Viewpoint of History — Historical Cost and Market Value as the Transaction-price-based Accounting—" *Kaikei (Accounting)*, Vol.180, No.5.

——— [2012], "A Warning Bell from History on The Excessive Usefulness Approach of Decision Making," Working Paper of Osaka University of Economics, No. 2012–1, April.

Chapter 6

Appearance of Current Valuation in Seventeenth and Eighteenth Century Britain

— Ledger Entries of Monteage, Malcolm, Hayes and Hamilton[1] —

Izumi Watanabe

Osaka University of Economics

Abstract

Double-entry bookkeeping started in the beginning of thirteenth century Italy and appeared on the stage of history as a memorandum of receivables and debts. The role of double entry bookkeeping at its birth was not to calculate the gross income of businesses but to record receivables and debts. Profit and loss accounts were not formed at that time. In consequence, if the merchants of those days wanted to know the income of businesses, it was necessary for them to calculate it by *Bilanzio* through physical inventory, which is a sort of statement of appropriation of income with inventory. In order to prove the correctness of the income which was calculated by *Bilanzio*, reliability of the account entries was required. This reliability of price evidence was achieved by using the price generated in continuos records, as in double-entry bookkeeping, at the moment of the

---

[1] The Author expresses much gratitude to J. Roger Mace, who is a former senior lecturer in Accounting and Finance at the University of Lancaster, for his perceptive and helpful comments and modifications of my English. And the Author also appreciate Alma Topen, who is an archivist in Glasgow University Archive, for her contribution in collection of historical records.

transaction. The factual transaction price is the measurement attribute for profit and loss calculations that provides the most reliability. Accounting was developed on the inherent basis of historical cost, or transaction price.

In this Chapter, we review the methods of valuing assets by market value in seventeenth and eighteenth century English publications for the revision of historical cost, which had already appeared in thirteenth century Italy. The current valuation of accounts receivable can be found in the oldest account ledger dated 1211 and the current valuation of fixed assets was already being used by bookkeepers in Italy in the fourteenth century. Therefore, inherent in accounting is the coexistence of historical cost and market value, and the differences between these two depend only upon their timing, that is both of them are essentially the same. Such valuations based on market value greatly expanded during seventeenth and eighteenth centuries England. The current valuation of fixed assets came in the latter half of the seventeenth century, and that of inventory assets in the first half of the eighteenth century. Current value was market value and it was used in two different ways depending on the case, namely as sales value and replacement cost. Profits or losses from valuation were transferred to the profit and loss account as realised loss and gain.

Keywords
Valuation of fixed assets, valuation of inventory assets, bad debts, Monteage, Malcolm, Hayes, Hamilton

6-1. Introduction

Double-entry bookkeeping first appeared in history in the northern city-states of Italy at the beginning of the thirteenth century as a memorandum on receivables and debts. At its conception, double-entry bookkeeping did not have profit and loss accounts, but even if it did, it wasn't calculating the gross income of businesses as a whole. Because of this, accountants could only calculate gross income of an overall enterprise using the *Bilanzio* (profit allocation statement and statement of assets and liabilities) based on actual inventories and not by continuous ledger entries[2].

However, if doubt arose on the reliability of the income computed by *Bilanzio*, it became necessary to prove the correctness of the calculated income by using some alternative method. In order to meet this demand, double-entry bookkeeping evolved completely from a simple memorandum of receivables and debts to a means by which to calculate gross income of a business partnership or company. From the daily transaction facts recorded up to then, revenues and expenses were collected in a profit and loss account to find the gross income of a business applying both of the above methods in an attempt to prove the correctness of the income on the *Bilanzio* by calculating gains from continuous accounting records.

This means that double-entry bookkeeping was developed in order to prove the distributable profits calculated by actual inventories using continuous records. The essence of double-entry bookkeeping is to prove the world of "things" (i.e.: real phenomena as a result of the trading of money, land, houses and other assets) using the world of "occurrences" (i.e.: abstract phenomena as a cause of the dealings in money, land, houses and other assets)[3]. This was in the first half of the fourteenth Century.

Thus, double-entry bookkeeping which based on continuous records developed into a tool to prove income arrived at as a result of amounts of net assets in hand. The inevitable result thereof is the focus on reliability above all else. Double-entry bookkeeping as supporter of accounting's income calculation structure inherently possessed reliability from its very onset. Because of this, priority No. 1 is the recording of transactions based on fact as a value proving method with high evidentiality, and assigning historical cost as the basis for proving the above as the original records of transaction price at the time of occurrence thereof is the natural consequence. Merchants created a profit and loss calculation recording system within the tenets of Judaism and Christianity for the sublimation of their customs and conventions applied in commercial transactions that were independently fostered over a etemal history[4]. This is double-entry bookkeeping.

Accounting was developed from its beginning as the basis for

---

[2] Regarding circumstances during that time, refer to Watanabe [2008a], pp. 40-42.

[3] Refer to Kimura [1982], Part 1 "Time of the Occurrence".

[4] At that time, under the Statute Against Usury in Christian society (The Book of Deuteronomy in the Old Testament orders believers not to "charge your fellow Israelites interest — whether on money, provisions, or anything one might loan" Iwai [1992], p. 24), the interpretation of interest charged on monetary loans in arrears was made by scholastics and Thomas Aquinas (circa 1225-1274). Aquinas

proving historical cost which is the market value at the time of the moment in transactions, that is historical cost is the same thing as market value in the respect of transaction price. In this Chapter, I identify the approximate period in history when the method of valuing assets by current value came to be a part of double-entry bookkeeping development based on transaction price from its onset, and I examine how seventeenth and eighteenth century English publications explained current valuation.

6-2. Advent of Current Valuation

The oldest surviving accounting ledger is a vertically continuous log with two folios, or four pages, recorded at a Bologna Fair by a Florentine banker in 1211. Because of the mere 4 pages in length, there is no way to verify whether any loss from bad debt account was included among the items. However, we can easily surmise from the wording in the ledger of the accountant's full awareness of the risk of default as a result of bankruptcy of debtors. It states the following: "1211. Orlandino Galigaio from Santa Trinita must give us 26 pounds for mid-May, for <u>buolongnini</u> which we gave him in Bologna for the San Brocoli market; if they stay longer [the interest] is 4 denari per pound each month. Should he fail to pay,

---

thought that the portion of loss may be demanded only for the period in arrears because of the "loss of anticipated earnings" that arose from settlements in arrears. In the latter half of the thirteenth Century, this way of thinking slowly spread. At first, usury was strictly prohibited as stipulated by Christ in the Gospel of Luke as "lend, expecting nothing in return," however, at the dawn of the thirteenth Century, what is prohibited by the Bible began to be seen as applicable only to cash loans for consumption and not with respect to investment loans, or interest charged on normal commercial transactions thus introducing a rational basis for demonstrating the justification of usury. This was started by Pope Gregorius IX's edict Naviganti (circa 1230), which led to the separation of interest charged on investment loans or commercial transactions and usury on cash loans thus gradually leading to the formulation of a theory that allowed usury (Oguro [2006], pp. 40-50). It goes without saying that gains from commercial transactions generate from differences between one value system and another value system (Iwai [1992], p. 58), or more specifically, spatial differences (differences in exchange rates according to regional disparities) and time differences (price disparities between acquisition cost and present value), therefore, it was not seen as an unlawful practice that necessarily violated the teachings of Christ.

Angiolino Bolongnini Galigaio promised to pay us. Witnesses, Compangno Avanelle and Bellacalza. Item, he must have 43 soldi for Mikele, son of Gallacalza: we posted them from the account of Scilinquato Mainetti[5]". In other words, to guard against default, guarantors are provided by debtors in support of their obligations. This expression tells us that the account receivable was revalued by present value. The interest on loans here was as much as 40% and if no payment was made in violation of contract up to the end of the term, an additional 20% late penalty fee was imposed. The interest, as mentioned above, was charged on the portion of loss of anticipated earnings and was the average rate in the usual trades at that time[6].

We can find an example of an actual bad debt expense account in the ledger of the Barcelona Branch in Datini Company in the fourteenth century[7]. This example in the ledger is the entry of a bad debt expense as an "irrecoverable account" after a revaluation of receivables based on present value. Also, in 1404, Florence Branch in Datini Company posted irrecoverable portions of receivables as "cattivo debitore[8]".

Pacioli's *Summa* states in Chapter 3 "Example of an Inventory with All its Formal Requirements," Paragraph 14 "In total I have so many ducats to collect, you will say, of good money, if the money is due from good people, otherwise you will say of bad money[9]". Moreover, in *Summa*, all the accounts except assets, liabilities and capital were transferred to profit and loss account, after then the balance of profit and loss account was carried over to a new ledger when a ledger is closed and the differences of debitor and creditor are posted to capital account.

"The profit-loss-account served the purpose, at balancing time, of collecting all account balances not required in the new ledger, and of closing these in an orderly manner into the capital account, which appeared in the balance account and so maintained the equality of debts and credits.... The profit-and-loss account therefore contained a hotch-potch of entries besides those of business gains and losses[10]". Because of this, the concept of

---

[5] Alvaro [1974], part 1, p.329.
[6] Alvaro [1974], part 1, p.322.
[7] De Roover [1974], p. 149.
[8] Penndorf [1933], S. 37-38.
[9] Geijsbeek [1914], p. 37.

calculating income using a profit and loss account was mostly rarified as late as the first half of the fourteenth century. The same can be said about closing balance accounts and in Nicolo and Alvise Barbarigo's balance accounts at the end of February in 1483, not only items relating to assets and liabilities but also all revenue and expense items were transferred[11]. Though the balance of this account is not added up yet, it played the same role as a trial balance.

In Peele's second book published in London in 1569 entitled *The Pathe waye to perfectness, in th' accomptes of Debitour, and Creditour*, the item of "doubtfull detters.&c[12]" was entered in the last part of inventory. According to Yamey, Peele "advises that the entry for debtors should distinguish between the amount of good debts and that of bad. ...But he does not indicate whether they should be treated differently in the accounts[13]" in his second book.

Current valuation of fixed assets was also discovered in the furniture and fixtures account of del Bene Trading House's settlement in the beginning of the fourteenth century. Entries show that because of wear and tear, 163 fir wood planks purchased on March 5, 1318 for 48 fiorino, 5 soldi and 8 denari were revaluated on September 1, 1321 for 35 fiorino, 3 soldi and 1 denari and a loss of 13 fiorino, 2 soldi and 7 denari was posted[14]. At the turn of the 1400s, Datini Trading House's Florence Branch was revaluing forest produce based on current value in their inventory charts[15].

The practice of revaluing based on merchandise inventory has appeared on the books of those merchants at the first half of the fifteenth century. We can find the practice of revaluations on merchandise inventory in Florence Branch of Datini Company, in which the merchandise were bought at 84 fiorino and 15 soldi on December 31, 1404,, were revalued at 80 fiorino, and the revaluation loss of 15 soldi 4 fiorino was allocated to profit and loss account[16].

---

[10] The use of a profit and loss account as a "hotch-potch" account was found in Pacioli's *Summa* (Yamey [1978], "Scientific Bookkeeping and The Rise of Capitalism," p.109).
[11] Watanabe [1993], p. 31.
[12] Peele [1569], The Inuennnntorie, the fifth page.
[13] Yamey [1982], pp. 96–97.
[14] Alvaro [1974], part 2, pp. 535–536.
[15] Penndorf [1933], S. 36.

The practice of evalution by current cost of inventory goods was also seen in Ledgers B to D in the London East India Company from August 1664 to July 1673. Because of the simplicity of this operation, it was used to value merchandise inventory by market value. At the time of purchase of merchandise, the purchase unit value and the allocation of incidental expenses consequential thereto were not necessarily logged[17]. Moreover, in Jacques Savary's *La Parfait Negociant* published in 1675, when textiles dropped 5% in value, an explanation was provided of the treatment of the decrease[18].

Thus the practice of revising historical cost by present value came into being at the same time as appearance of double-entry bookkeeping. Therefore, the practice of measurement based upon the transaction price (historical cost) and measurement by revaluation of current value (market value) coexisted at the time of the advent of double-entry bookkeeping in the thirteenth century. In light of the above, I will examine in the next section how current value accounting, which coexisted with double-entry bookkeeping at its origin in Italy in the Middle Ages, was incorporated into many works published in eighteenth century England. I will give examples describing the treatment method for revising historical cost based on market value and an analysis of the current value measurement treatment method at that time in an effort to explain the essence of double-entry bookkeeping measurements, which not only support accounting but also its calculation structure.

6-3. Current Valuation of Fixed Assets up to the Eighteenth Century

Generally, in the works published in Great Britain up to the middle of the eighteenth century, the valuation of fixed assets was based on historical cost. However, by the latter half of the seventeenth century, examples of book entries showing market value-based revaluation procedures appeared for the first time not only in the actual books of tradesmen but also in published works.

---

[16] Penndorf [1933], S. 37.
[17] Sugita [2010], p. 40.
[18] Kishi [1975], pp. 263-264.

(1) Monteage's fixed asset valuation

Stephen Monteage, who authored *Debitor and Creditor Made Easier* in London in 1675, described asset account items including farmland with leasehold rights, horses, cows, sheep, ships, etc. (Table 6-1).

[Table 6-1] Grange-Farm Account

	Grange = Farm Account Debtor	fol	l.	s.	d.		Grange Farm Account Creditor	fol	l.	s.	d.
1675 Apr. 10.	To Stock valued my Lease	1	300	—	—	1675 Apr. 23.	By Cash reed for butter and cheese	2	22	—	—
20	To Cash pd for 60 load of Manure	2	1	10	—	25	By 100 load Hay valued at 35 s.	15	175	—	—
21	To Cash pd for Seed-Corn	2	24	3	—	May. 3.	By Calves No. 16. valued at 17s. 6d. pc.	11	14	—	—
24	To Cash paid *Besse Hobbs her* wages	2	2	10	—	1676 Apr. 9.	By ballance which I value my Lease	40	280	—	—
28	To Cash pd Taxes	2	1	10	—				491	—	—
May. 1.	To *John Broughton* Esq; 6 Mo. Rent	16	25	—	—						
1676 Apr. 9.	To loss and gain prosited	12	136	7	—						
			491	—	—						

(Monteage [1675], London, fol. 4)

This farmland with leasehold rights account starts with a entry of 300 pounds in the list of property at the beginning of the fiscal term on April 1, 1675, with the debitor side featuring fertilizer, seed, tax and proceeds entries that result from the maintenance and cultivation of the farmland. On the creditor side, we can see the entries depicting sales revenue from dairy products and hay produced from the use of the farmland, as well as a transfer of 14 pounds to the calf account for 16 heads born thereat, and other transactions. Upon closing the accounts, the farmland was revalued at a present value of 280 pounds at the end of term and transferred to the balance account. Monteage shows the journalising as follows: [Balance Debtor to *George* Farm, for its present value], this Lease was valued for 280*l*. and wrote directly below, "In the Account of Stock this Lease was valued at 300*l*. but now a year being elaps'd, it is fit it should be valued at less, which will make no difference in Account of Balance; but only lessen the Gain[19]". Upon settlement, it is favourable to revalue based on present value and transfer any resulting valuation loss to the profit and loss account. Similarly, the *"Ship Bonadventure"* account also had a revaluation from 250 pounds historical cost to 225 pounds at settlement. However, this valuation loss is transferred to the profit and loss account with other profit and loss as a mixed account (Table 6-2).

[Table 6-2] Ship Bonadventure Account

	Ship Bonadventure Debtor	fol	l.	s.	d.		Ship Bonadventure Creditor	fol	l.	s.	d.
1675 Apr. 10.	To Stock for 1/8 part thereof costs	1	250	—	—	1675 Nov. 25.	By Peter *Biggs* for my 1/8 Dividend of *the Profit of a Voyage*	21	75	—	—
Nov. 2.	To Cash pd *Premium* & ch of Insurance	19	7	11	6						
1676 Apr. 9.	To loss and gain prosited	35	42	8	6	1676 Apr. 9.	By ballance which I value my part	40	225	—	—
			300	—	—				300	—	—

(Monteage [1682], fol.9)

Up to the mid-1600s, in many works published in Britain, it is general that the standard procedures for asset valuation were described under treatments based on historical cost. Generally speaking, these works were published as textbooks for the academies and grammar schools of those days for instructing young scholars and children of merchants in the basic principles of the Italian methods of double-entry bookkeeping. Because the explanation of the journalising for adjustment at the end of a fiscal term by current value came to be rather complex, accountants provided only an explanation for students of simply carrying over procedures based on historical cost. However, in the latter half of the seventeenth century, some works explaining current value-based valuation were distributed. Then, from the end of the eighteenth century, a lot of textbooks entitled "Practical Bookkeeping" or "Improved Method" were being published one after the other to teach people how to directly apply principles to accounting practices without going through the conventional or traditional textbooks[20].

---

[19] Monteage [1675], 'Here followeth the Balance of the whole Leidger', L2. Monteage's book does not have through pages, a title and classification number is entered for each item.

[20] Watanabe [1993], pp. 111–115.

6-4. Eighteenth Century Fixed Asset Valuation Methods

(1) Malcolm's fixed asset valuation

Alexander Malcolm explains valuation in his work *A Treatise of Book-keeping, or Merchants Accounts* (London, 1731) in a way that shows that accounting practices based on market value had already started to be used.

Two examples of fixed assets entries are explained, that is "House *in* Castle-Street" account and "House *in* Broad-Street" account (Table 6-3)[21]. Of course, he did not use the concept of fixed assets yet.

[Table 6-3] House *in* Castle Street Account

1729	HOUSE in CASTLE-STREET	fol	*l.*	*s.*	*d.*	1729	HOUSE in CASTLE-STREET	fol	*l.*	*s.*	*d.*
Aug. 26	To *John* Campbel. 00		300	15	00	Aug. 16	By *William Devidson*... 1/2 Years Rent from *Whitsunday* Last	10	00	00	
Oct. 8	To *Profit* and *Loss*	17	10	00	00	Oct. 8	By *Ballance*.	17	300	15	00
	Sum		310	15	0		Sum		310	15	0

(Malcolm [1731], fol. 14)

In Table 6-3, Malcolm treats house accounts as mixed accounts just like general merchandise accounts. As mentioned above, when depreciation and amortization came in the first half of the 19th century, revaluations by present value posted in mixed accounts ceased. I assume that the recognition of the depreciated portion of fixed assets came about due to the advent of depreciation or amortization expense accounting.

The House in Castle Street was purchased on August 26th for 300 pounds from John Cambel, whereby 15 shillings, which is a quarter of the annuity, to borrow on Martinmas (St. Martin's Day), was paid prompting an entry of 300 pounds and 15 shillings total on the debit side of the house account, which was carried over to the closing balance account as is shown on the closing date. Note that this house is now owned by *William Davidson* and 20 pounds a year, 10 on Martinmas and 10 on Whit-Monday or The Day After Whit-Sunday (the 7th Sunday after Easter at end of May)[22]. The price of House in Castle Street was carried over to the next term by histor-

---

[21] Malcolm [1731], Leger Book No. 1, fol. 14.
[22] Malcolm [1731], p. 108.

ical cost without entering the valuation loss which was brought about by revaluation by reference to market value. The entry on debit side in House in Castle Street account, that is "profit and loss: 10 pounds", indicated rent that was transferred to the profit and loss account at closing.

The Entries are described as follows for the house and ship accounts, for which historical cost was carried over to the next term. "You may value them at the first Cost; and when that is stated on the Creditor — side, the Difference of the Debt and Credit is Gain or Loss, arising from the Difference of Reparations &c. and the Rents or Freights. ...And then in a new Inventory you enter it again, at what Value you think proper; and sometimes also you may appear to be a Loser, which must go to *Profit and Loss* but the first Method I think the best: And though these Subjects do not really keep up their Value, yet I would continue them at the first Value they were disposed of, or lost; or you may chuse to state them at another Value from Time to Time, as you think they are then really worth[23]". Upon valuation of assets at closing, because valuations at market value do not absolutely provide the real value of something, generally, it is favourable to use historical cost, but sometimes it is not. The choice is whether historical cost or current cost was adopted. However, the valuation of merchandise inventory is based on historical cost.

(2) Mair's fixed asset valuation

In one of the representative treatises of the eighteenth century, John Mair's (1702/3-1769) *Book-keeping Methodiz'd* (Edinburgh, 1736), an explanation of the valuation of inventory goods, ships, houses and other assets at year-end and some examples of ledger entry are provided.

The first examples of transactions are for the ships account, in which the debit side includes all costs incurred for the purchase price, the maintenance and improvement of ships, and all the revenues that is the price which set upon a sale and freight rental income and so on are entered on the credit side.

The method of closing the asset accounts such as ships, houses, etc. is described in Chapter 3 "Of balancing the Ledger". On the debit side, the explanation is based on three assumptions: (1) no entry is made, (2) only the sale or the adjusted amount is entered,

---

[23] Malcolm [1731], p. 90.

and (3) only the transportation fees and rental fees are entered[24]. However, there is no mention of whether valuations for carrying over figures to the next ledger at closing are based on historical cost or market value. Judging from the transaction cases provided in "Ship Britannia", we can see the transfers to the balance account are entered by historical cost at year-end[25].

The explanation of fixed asset valuation is a bit different in *Book-keeping Methodiz'ed* and its revised and enlarged edition *Book-keeping Moderniz'd* (1773). In *Book-keeping Methodiz'd*, the explanations of daily entries and closing of ledger of ships, houses and other assets are as follows: "...*3dly*, If the Cr. Side contain only the Freight or Rent, in this Case, first charge the Ship, House, &c. Dr. to *Profit and Loss*, for the Freight or Rent; and then close the Accompt with *Ballance*, No. 4[26].

Conversely, *Book-keeping Moderniz'd* says that "...*3dly*, If the Cr. Side contain the freight or rent, in this case, first give the account credit by *Balance*, for value of the ship or house, and then close the account with *Profit and Loss*, No. 10, 11, 53, 85[27]".

If we only look at the wording "value of the house", we can't tell whether he means historical cost or current value. However, as shown in the transaction examples (Table 6-4), the "Sloop, Unity" account[28] indicates a transfer to the proceeding term the amount of 235 pounds of historical cost on the settlement date of December 31. The "House in Fleetstreet" account also shows a transfer to the next term using historical cost[29].

[Table 6-4] Sloop, Unity Account

1793	Sloop Unity, Dr	fol	l.	s.	d.	1793	Contra, Cr	fol	l.	s.	d.
Jan. 1	To *Stock, for* my 1/2 freighted to Virginia, . .	1	470	—	—	Apr. 5	By *Cash, for* my 1/2 fright,	2	110	—	—
Apr. 17	To *Cash*, for repairs, To *Profit and Loss*, gained,	2 36	10 124	11 7	6 6	7	By *Sundries*, for 1/4 sold, By *Balance*, for prime cost of my 1/4.	— 35	260 235	— —	— —
			605	—	—				605	—	—

(Mair [1773], pp. 180–181)

---

[24] Mair [1736], p. 79.
[25] Mair [1736], pp. 126–127.
[26] Mair [1736], p. 79.
[27] Mair [1773], pp. 71–72.
[28] Sloop ship refers to a relatively light, single-mast fore-and-aft sail boat common used at the time.

(3) Hamilton's fixed asset valuation

In *An Introduction to Merchandise* (Edinburgh, 1777), written by another influential writer in eighteenth century England, Robert Hamilton (1743-1829), describes in its first transaction case two fixed assets namely the *House in Lawn-market* and *Share of Ship Hazard* in Edinburgh.

Hamilton states that, at balancing of ledger, "If the whole be still on hand, enter the present value on the Dr. of the balance sheet[30]; and if this be different from the prime cost, charges included, enter the difference in the proper side of the profit and loss sheet[31]". This description shows that present value is used for valuing assets regardless of whether they are inventories or fixed assets[32].

In the case of the *House* in *Lawn-market*, the price at the beginning of year is transferred to the next year using historical cost[33], however, judging from the aforementioned description, this is not valuation by historical cost but should rather be interpreted as a lack of change in the value at the beginning of year and four months after.

The *Ship Hazard* 1/4 share is the current valuation at settlement of a 150 pound entry on 25 March upon acquisition to 140 pounds

[Table 6-5] Share of Ship Hazard Acccount

Dr. 1774	Share of ship Hazard,	fol	l.	s.	d.		Contra Cr. 1774	fol	l.	s.	d.
Mar. 15	To William Ainslie, bought 1/2 share for	7	150	—	—	Apr. 25	By Cash, for share prof. of a Voyage to Rot.	1	33	—	—
Apr. 30	To Profit and Loss	1	23	—	—	30	By Balance-accompt	7	140	—	—
			173	—	—				173	—	—

(Hamilton [1788], pp. 314-315

---

[29] Mair [1773], pp. 198-199.

[30] Hamilton states that, prior to closing the ledger, in order to accurately close the accounts and estimate gains, the balance of assets, liabilities and capital is transferred to the balance statement, and the expenses and earnings to the profit and loss statement. These two tabulation statements, although differing in format, serve the working sheet of these days. This point is explained in Watanabe [1993], Chapter 3 and Mepham [1988], pp. 222-223.

[31] Hamilton [1788], p. 285.

[32] Unsalable valuation in Hamilton's "Introduction to Commerce" (1777) is explained in Watanabe [2005], pp. 89-39.

[33] Hamilton [1788], pp. 306-307.

on 30 April. In other words, the 150 pound historical cost was revalued to the current value of 140 pounds. The 10 pound valuation loss is transferred to the profit and loss account at settlement to offset the share of gains acquired from the ships (Table 6-5).

The second transaction case for two accounts *Share of Ship Diligence* and *House in Fleetstreet, London* as fixed assets[34]. Because both incurred a loss on sale during the term, there was no accounting treatment whereby a transfer would be made to the balance account at end of term, therefore, we cannot say whether the term-end valuation was based on historical cost or market value. The Fleet-street house account[35] received 500 pounds in insurance benefits on July 6 from an insurance provider due to a fire on June 8, and the building was sold for 200 pounds on July 8[36]. Finally, a 120 pound loss was incurred and transferred to the profit and loss account.

6-5. Advent of Current Valuation of Inventory Assets

(1) The valuation of merchandise inventory in the sixteenth and seventeenth centuries

Procedures of balancing accounts that involve the revaluation of term-end inventory merchandise based on current value was already practiced when double-entry bookkeeping first appeared in the thirteenth century, so we believe that it was already taking place among Florentine merchants.

For example, the inventory of December 31, 1404 of the Florence Branch in Datini company posts a valuation loss due to the decrease in value of merchandise at closing[37]. As mentioned above, in Ledger B to D of the London East India Company dating from August 1664 to July 1673, to simplify tasks, unsalables are valued at sale price. The present valuation of inventory goods at term-end in Datini, the deviation of the value thereof at accounts closing from the historical cost can be blamed on the different objectives sought at the different points in time, even if revaluing based on the same present value.

---

[34] Hamilton [1788], pp. 416-417
[35] Hamilton [1788], p. 418.
[36] Hamilton [1788], p. 356.
[37] Penndorf [1933], S. 37.

Chapter 6: Appearance of Current Valuation in Seventeenth and Eighteenth Century Britain

In Jacques Savary's *La Parfait Negociant* published in 1675, because the price of merchandise inventory of textiles at the year-end dropped 5%, a method to lower its price to market value is explained[38].

The first book to recognise unsold inventories and clearly explain the term profit and loss calculation method not based on revenue and purchase cost but costs of goods sold is Jan Ympyn Christofells' *Nieuwe Instructie*, published posthumously in 1543 in Antwerp[39]. In its transaction examples written in French, cases cover a period of roughly 8 months from 28 December, 1542 to 31 August, 1543, closing on August 31.

The sum total of the merchandise inventory, concretely Stones (i.e.jewelry), English Ostades (worsted cloths), Flanders Cloth, Grey Friezes, Ribbed Taffets and Holland Linen, 349 livres, 1 sous and 8 deniers was transferred to the balance account at year-end. For example, the Grey Friezes account[40] shows that, on 3 February, 1543, 48 boxes of Grey Friezes at a unit price of 18 sous, 6 deniers were purchased from the Thomas Grenfell company for a total of 44 livres, 8 sous[41]. The year-end inventory balance for the unsold merchandise account is 7 boxes for a total of 6 livres, 9 sous and 6 deniers. This is a unit price of 18 sous, 6 deniers, a figure that matches the historical cost on February 3, 1543. It goes without saying that the profit and loss account established at year-end[42] does not have a valuation profit and loss account regarding unsold merchandise.

In the first work on accounting by an Englishman, James Peele's *The maner and fourme how to kepe a perfecte reconyng*, (London, 1553), as with Ympyn, unsold merchandise is clearly recognised[43] in year-end and valued at historical cost. According to its transaction examples, 14 tons French wine of 112 pounds of total amounts is purchased at the unit price 8 pounds on 25 May,

---

[38] Kishi [1975], pp. 263–264.

[39] This work was published in 1543 in Dutch (*Nieuwe Instructie*) and then immediately afterwards in French (*Nouvelle Instruction*). The English version (*A notable and very excellente woorke*), which omitted over 4/5 of the ledger examples was published in 1547.

[40] Ympyn [1543], grant liure, fol. 10.

[41] Ympyn [1543], grant liure fol. 10 & Iournal.

[42] Ympyn [1543], grant liure, fol. 22.

[43] Peele [1553], The Quaterne or greate booke of accomptes, fol. 15. For Peele's first work, see Kojima [1971], Chapter 5 for details.

1553[44]. At balancing account the following year on 24 March, 1554, the cost of goods sold of the unsold 2 tons is calculated on the debit side at 16 pounds, that is 8 pounds per ton, or the same as the historical cost.

The Fustian weave account in John Weddington's *A Breffe Instruction, and Manner, howe to kepe, merchantes bokes of accomptes*, which was published fourteen years after Peele, the goods which were purchased by 260 pounds worth of from Thomas Lane on September 25 is carried over completely to the following term as is, meaning the 260 pound by historical cost, for all items which remained unsold until the date of settlement[45].

In Simon Stevin's *Vierde Stvck Der Wisconstighe Ghedachtnissen* published in Brugge from 1605 to 1608, and in Richard Dafforne's *The Merchant Mirror* published in 1635 in London, the valuation of unsold goods is based on historical cost. This trend continued generally until the eighteenth Century.

(2) The valuation of merchandise inventory in eighteenth century Britain

John Mair's accounting books published in Edinburgh, were some of the most widely read in the eighteenth century. His first work entitled *Book-keeping Methodiz'd* (1736) in which the accounting of inventory difference losses is recognised for each respective merchandise account established separately for all merchandise handled and, for each entry therein, he states, "Contains, upon the Dr. Side, the prime Cost and Charge; and upon the Cr. Side, the Sale or Disposal of them. ...When none of the Goods are disposed of, then it is closed by *Ballance* for the whole Sum on the Dr. Side. ...When only part of the Goods are disposed of, which will appear by the Inequality of the Quantity Columns[46]". It is clear that Mair treats year-end inventory merchandise valuation based on historical cost.

Daniel Dowling's *A Compleat System of Italian Book-keeping* published in Dublin in 1765 also describes the inventory of merchandise valued at historical cost[47].

---

[44] Peele [1553], The Quaterne or greate booke of accomptes, fol. 6.
[45] Weddington [1567], Lidger, fol. 29.
[46] Mair [1736], pp. 76–77.

(3) Hayes's assets valuation by present value

As some of the very few books published in England in the eighteenth century that advocate the valuation of unsold merchandises not by historical cost but by market value, Richard Hayes' *Modern Book-keeping: or, The Italian Method improved* published in London in 1731, and his enlarged and revised edition entitled *The Gentleman's complete book-keeper* published in London in 1741.

Regarding the closing of the ledger's accounts, he provides a detailed explanation spanning five chapters from Chap. 7 to 12[48]. An excerpt is as follows: CHAP.VIII: In *The Way to balance your Accounts, without shutting up your Ledger*, he states "Now you are to consider, that your Ledger contains various Sorts of Accounts, and those being of different Kinds, different Methods must be pursued in balancing the same. And, *First*, If it be Account of Goods, if the whole Quantity of those Goods do remain unsold, Dt. Balance on your Paper for the whole Quantity remaining unsold, valuing the same at the present Market Price, or at the Price they cost you. ...*N.B.* It is usual with Merchants, when they make a general Balance of their books, to value the Goods that they have by them at Market Price they then go at, at the Time of their balancing; but some do not so[49]".

According to Hayes the merchants of that time normally valued unsold merchandise at market value. His term "Present Market Price" refers to the salable Market Price they go on at, at the Time of their balancing at balancing of accounts, or the selling price. The essence of the difference between historical cost and realisable present value arising from Hayes's method for valuing year-end unsold goods at realisable present value is not valuation profit, but rather "anticipated gain" or "deemed sale[50]", that is this can also mean that an "advance on profit" is posted in the term under profit and loss calculation of this period.

---

[47] Dowling [1765], p. 33. The hops account established for separate consignments among handled merchandise is clearly carried over at acquisition cost (Ledger of Domestic Proper Accounts, No. 1, fol. 7).
[48] Hayes [1731], pp. 75–92. and Hayes [1741], pp. 75–92.
[49] Hayes [1731], pp. 78–79. For details, see Yamey, Edey and Thomsonm [1963], p. 116, and Takatera [1999], pp. 95–97.
[50] Takatera [1999], pp. 95–97.

(4) Hamilton's assets valuation by present value

Equal in importance to Mair's work in eighteenth century England is Robert Hamilton's *An Introduction to Merchandise* (Edinburgh, 1777), whose Part 4 "Italian Book-keeping[51]" and Part 5 "Practical Book-keeping[52]" are examinations of bookkeeping. Transaction examples in Part 2 Italian Bookkeeping show the valuation of unsold merchandise based on historical cost. For example, the clover seed account[53] indicates that 1,200 pounds were purchased on 12 March for 29 pounds 17 shillings, and the unsold portion of 300 pounds at accounts closing on 30 April was valued at 7 pounds 10 shillings, for a unit price of 6 pence. The nominal purchase unit cost per pound is 6 pence. It differs from the purchase price of 5.97 pence per a pound by a 0.5% discount, possibly related to the quantity purchased, so we can understand that Hamilton estimated inventory of merchandise not by historical cost but by present replacement cost without anticipating any future discount.

Note that the 10 pound inventory loss on difference appearing in the remarks field as the quantity difference on the debit side is not deducted as a separate account item as an accounting loss on difference, but rather automatically added to cost of goods sold. In textbooks of that time, the explanation of such an accounting method was commonplace.

However, the explanation provided states that "It is proper, before balancing, to settle as many personal accompts as possible,; to clear all arrears and small charges; to take an exact inventory of the goods on hand, as far as can be done; and affix a moderate value to each article, according to the current prices at that time; such a value as the owner would be willing at present buy for[54]." Thus Hamilton points out the adequacy of valuation based on current value. However, Hamilton's current prices are synonmous to Hayes' current realisable value and valued based on re-procurement cost. While current realisable value means "anticipated earnings" and sometimes "advances on earnings," valuation by re-procurement cost means the following term's "early recognition of purchase cost."

---

[51] Hamilton [1788], pp. 265-466.
[52] Hamilton [1788], pp. 467-495.
[53] Hamilton [1788], pp. 314-315.
[54] Hamilton [1788], p. 285.

In the Port-wine account of Part 5 "Practical Book-keeping" transaction examples, as shown in Table 6-6, the purchase unit cost of 32 pounds per a cask and 12 shillings per a dozen became 34 pounds per a cask, but 15 shillings per a dozen upon year-end revaluation of inventory merchandise, or valuation profit of 2 pounds per a cask and 3 shillings per a dozen. This appraisal profit is transferred to the profit and loss account as realised profit. Prior to the enactment of the Income Tax Act (1799), even if transferring valuation gains as unrealised profit to the profit and loss account, there was no risk that the payment of profit taxes would result in cash outflows.

[Table 6-6] Hamilton's Port-wine Account

1772	Dr. Port-wine,	P.	D.	B.	l.	s.	d.	1772	Contra	P.	D.	B.	l.	s.	d.
April 6.	To J. Hartley, at L. 32: 12s. 4 months credit	20	—	—	652	—	—	Apr. 10.	By J. Almond, at L. 34: 13s.	5	—	—	173	5	—
22	To Cash, pd. corks and char. at bottling, 2 pipes into	—	112	3	12	3	9	22	By 2 pipes bottled	2	—	—	—	—	—
								May 22.	By Sundries, per J.	—	87	—	67	14	6
Dec. 31	To Profit and loss, for gain	—	—	—	38	14	9	25	By Cash, at L. 35	2	—	—	70	—	—
								July 16.	By Cash, at L. 34	5	—	—	170	—	—
								Aug. 7.	By Cash, at L. 33: 10s. at 15s. 4d.	2	12	—	76	4	—
								25	By Cash, at L. 34	2	—	—	68	—	—
								Dec. 31.	By Balance-accompt, at L. 34, at 15 s.	2	13	—	77	15	—
									Broken	—	—	3	—	—	—
		20	112	3	702	18	6			20	112	3	702	18	6

(Hamilton [1788], pp. 430-431.)

However, there is no appraisal profit or loss account for unsold merchandise. Therefore, appraisal profit or losses for year-end inventory merchandises are automatically added to cost of goods sold regardless of whether there is justification of the costs incurred. The appearance of accounting methods for the current valuation of year-end inventory merchandise came in the last half of the eighteenth century.

6-6. Conclusion

The most important function in double-entry bookkeeping, which originated in the beginning of the thirteenth century and was fully developed by the mid-fourteenth century as a means to prove earnings computed by *Bilanzio* (a sort of Inventory with Appropriation of Income Statement), is the recording of original entries a means to prove transactions with a high level of evidentiality and a focus on reliability. Thus the role of historical cost as the original entry providing the basis for the above was the logical conclusion. Merchants created a system over a long period to log profit and loss calculations derived from commercial transactions. This is double-entry bookkeeping. Accounting was developed on the bedrock of historical cost, i. e. transaction price (market value).

However, the accounting of market valuations of receivables or losses on bad debt appears in the oldest account ledger which are the fragments of a book of Florentine banker dated 1211. Current valuation occurred simultaneously as the birth of double-entry bookkeeping. Revaluations of fixed assets based on market value are also seen here and there in the accounting ledgers of fourteenth century Italian merchants. It was only in the latter half of the seventeenth century that they appeared in English textbooks of bookkeeping and clear descriptions of inventory asset present valuations came only in the early eighteenth century.

In as such, double-entry bookkeeping, which came to be in the northern city-states of Italy in the beginning of the thirteenth century, saw a revision of historical cost based on market value from its onset. In other words, measurements by present value appeared at the same time as double-entry bookkeeping and, in many works published in seventeenth and eighteenth centuries Britain, accounting methods for revaluations based on present value are explained.

It goes without saying that historical cost is market value at the moment of the transaction and therefore "transaction price" is "market value". This transaction price morphed into historical cost indicating historical value at the time of closing. Therefore, market value and historical cost constitute the same transaction price only at a different point on the timeline. Market value is essentially identical to historical cost.

[References in English and other languages]

Alvaro, Martinelli [1974], *The Origination and Evolution of Double Entry Bookkeeping to 1440, Part1 and Part 2*, Denton.
Dowling, Daniel [1765], *A Compleat System of Italian Book-keeping*, Dublin.
de Roover, Reymond [1956], "The Development of Accounting Prior to Luca Pacioli According to The Account-books of Medieval Merchants", in Littleton, A.C. and B.S. Yamey eds., *Studies in the History of Accounting*, New York.
―――― [1974], *Business, Banking, and Economic Thought*, Chikago & London.
Geijsbeek, John B. [1914], *Ancient Double-Entry Bookkeeping*, Denber.
Hamilton, Robert [1788] 2_{nd} ed. (1_{st} ed. 1977), *An Introduction to Merchandise*, Edinburgh.
Hayes, Richard [1731], *Modern Book-keeping: or, The Italian Method improved*, London.
―――― [1741], *The Gentleman's Complete Book-keeper*, London.
Littleton, A.C. [1933], *Accounting Evolution to 1900*, New York.
Malcolm, Alexander [1731], *A Treatise of Bookkeep-ing, or Merchant Accounts*, London.
Mair, John [1736], *Book-keeping Methodiz'd*, Edinburgh.
―――― [1773], *Book-keeping Moderniz'd*, Edinburgh.
Mellis, Jhon [1588], *A Briefe Instruction and Manner hovv to keepe bookes of Accompts*, London.
Mepham, Michael [1988], *Acccounting in Eghteenth Century Scotland*, New York & London.
Monteage, Stephen [1682], *Debtor and Creditor made Easie: or A Short Balance of the whole Leidger*, 2nd ed., London.
Peele, James [1553], *The Manner and Fourme how to kepe a perfecte reconyng*, London.
―――― [1569], *The Pathe waye to perfectness, in th' accomptes Debitour, and Creditour*, London.
Penndorf, Balduin [1933], *Luca Pacioli Abhandlung über die Buchhaltung 1494*, Stuttgart.
Stevin, Simon [1605-8], *Vierde Stvck Der Wisconstighe Ghedachtnissen Vande Weeghconst*, Leyden.
Weddington, John [1567], *A Breffe Instruction, and Manner, howe to kepe, merchantes bokes of accomptes*, London.
Yamey, B. S., Edey, H. C. and Thomson, H. W. [1963], *Accounting in England and Scotland: 1543-1800*, London.
―――― [1978], *Essays on the History of Accounting*, New York.
―――― [1982], *A Further Essays on the History of Accounting*, New York & London.
Ympyn, Christofells Jan [1543], *Nouuelle Instruction*, Antwerpen.

[References in Japanese]

Izutani, Katsumi [1980], *Original History of Double-entry Bookkeeping*, Moriyama Shoten.
―――― [1997], *The Pathway to Summa*, Moriyama Shoten.

Iwai, Katsuto [1992], *The Capital of Venezian Merchants*, Kodansha Ltd.
Oguro, Shunji [2006], *A Lie and Greed−A View of Commerce and Merchants in Medival Europe*, Nagoya University Publisher.
Kishi, Etsuzo [1975], *Generative History of Accounting−A Study of Accounting Regulations of Ordonnance du Commerce*, Dobunkan Shuppan.
Kojima, Osamu [1971], *Historical Development of Bookkeeping in Britain*, Moriyama Shoten.
Saito, Hiromi [2002], *Commerce and Cities in The Latter Medieval Italy*, Chisen Shokan.
Sugita,Takeshi [2010], "Inventory Valuation of The British East India Company in theseventeenth Century." *Kaikei (Accounting)*, Vol. 178, No. 1.
Takatera, Sadao [1999], *The Evolution of Income Accounting System*, Showado.
―――― [2006], "Rethinking the Merit of Earnings Conservatism", *Oska Keidai Rancho (Journal of Osaka University of Economics)*, Vol. 57, No. 1.
Tamaki, Toshiaki [2008], *Commerce and Economy in Northern Europe 1550−1815*, Chisen-Shobo.
Watanabe, Izumi [1993], *A History of Accounting Procedures of Closing*, Moriyama Shoten.
―――― [2005], *The Evolution of Profit and Loss Accounting*, Moriyama Shoten.
―――― [2000], "The Valuation Methods of Goods Remaining Unsold in the Bookkeeping Textbooks in sixteenth and eighteenth Century Britain", *Osaka Keidai Ronshu (Journal of Osaka University of Economics)*, Vol. 50, No. 6.
―――― [2008a], *Accounting Learned from History*, Dobunkan Shuppan.
―――― [2008b], "The Pitfall of Modern Accounting−The Essence of Accounting from the View of History−", *Kaikeisigakkai Nenpo (Yearbook of Accounting History Association)*, No. 27.
―――― [2009], "Paradox of Accounting Purpose−Between Reliability and Usefulness−", *Kaikei (Accounting)*, Vol. 175 No. 5.
―――― [2011], "The Standpoint of Fair Value from the Viewpoint of History −Historical Cost and Market Value as the Transaction-price-based Accounting−", *Kaikei (Accounting)*, Vol. 180 No. 5.
Yamashita, Katsuji [1963], *General Theory of Accounting, New Edition*, Chikura Shobo Co, Ltd.

Chapter 7

Significance of Current Value Information in 19th Century England Corporate Accounting
— Statute Companies and General Registered Companies —

Shigeto Sasaki
Senshu University

Abstract

This Chapter will unveil the handling of current value information in 19th Century England corporate accounting, when modern accounting was in its infancy. Specifically, I will bring to light the significance of the current value information applied to the valuation of tangible fixed assets of Grand Junction Railway Co., a statute company, and Neuchatel Asphalte Co. and Natal Land and Colonization Co., both general registered companies. At that time when accounting principles had not been formulated, acquisition cost or current value, the measurement benchmarks of accounting information, were being selected flexibly to implement the corporate financial policies of company directors. They were attempting to meet the expectations of shareholders with respect to securing distributable earnings. On this basis, acquisition cost and current value were leveraged to mutually complement, rather than mutually exclude, one another.

Keywords

stock account, impairment costs, £5,000 fixed amount method, asset revaluation method, accounting complaint, Lee principle, land revaluation gains, bad debt offsetting

7-1. Introduction

In the international financial accounting system that presumes the calculation of comprehensive income, while current value (fair value) is used as a fundamental measurement attribute in the Asset and Liability Approach, a basis of accounting information preparation, it is also a means to point out the limitations[1] of the Revenue and Expense Approach (framework of accrual accounting based on the acquisition cost and realization basis). However, even if there were dominant accounting thoughts (in other words, an emphasis on fair value) that were expressed in laws and accounting standards at certain time periods (eras) in history and locations (countries and regions), their controlling or fixing power was essentially maintained by the acquiescence of stakeholders with interests in accounting with no aim to guarantee that such were to be in existence forever in the future.

A look at corporate accounting in 19th Century England when accounting standards were not yet in existence reveals that the acquisition cost or current value (fair value) was selected arbitrarily by a financial policy, particularly in the measurement of tangible fixed assets. This Chapter presents an analysis of the "Director's Report" on the status of current value information used in the accounting of fixed assets (rolling stock) of Grand Junction Railway Co. (a railway company) as a statute company of that era as well as accounting lawsuits relating to mining rights accounting of Neuchatel Asphalte Co. (a mining company) and land of Natal Land

---

[1] The predominance of fair value over acquisition cost as an accounting figure with a focus on the accounting of financial instruments and financial liabilities is exemplified below.
　① Because initial cost does not exist in derivatives, even if there is a change in fair value at end of fiscal term, it is not recognized and excluded from the ledgers;
　② Although business operators recognize the importance of managing financial risk so as not to incur excessive losses from drastic price fluctuations, there is almost no relevance of financial asset and financial liability acquisition cost with respect to financial risk managerial decision-making; and
　③ Measurements by mixed attribution recognizing the carrying over of acquisition cost or fair value to the next fiscal term depending on the type of financial instrument generates mismatches of gains and loss recognition. From the 1997 IASC Discussion Paper, *Accounting for Financial Assets and Financial Liabilities*.
Urasaki [2002], pp. 17−18.

and Colonization Co. (a real estate development and sales company) as general registered companies.

7-2. The Role of Current Value Information in the Accounting Practices of Grand Junction Railway Co.

Grand Junction Railway Co. (hereinafter, "GJ Railway"), established on May 6, 1833, didn't recognize the amount of the depreciation of fixed assets (rolling stock) up to the latter half of 1838, however, with the annual increase of total expenditures for fixed assets came the question of how to arrange for capital for new purchases of fixed assets (rolling stock) by the company's future directors, and of how much replacement capital is to be set aside. In the face of this problem, GJ Railway directors proposed two basic methods for measuring the amount of the depreciation of fixed assets as follows. The first concept is a method by which the amount of increase of the replacement price of fixed assets (rolling stock) due to an increase in current value (Market Price) is recognized as the amount of the depreciation of the value of the rolling stock and placed in the framework of accounting (installing/drawing) — dubbed the "£5,000 Fixed Amount Method". The other concept is a comparison of current valuation of fixed assets (rolling stock) at term end and that at previous term end (beginning of term) with the difference (valuation loss) thereof treated as the amount of the depreciation of rolling stock — dubbed the "Asset Revaluation Method."

How were these accounting methods selected at that time? Did the selection of accounting method reflect an integrated, comprehensive accounting concept? Ultimately, the selection of an accounting method was completely random whereby GJ Railway would select and apply an accounting method that suited the circumstances to secure dividend assets. Table 7-1 shows how the selection and application of the method for recognizing the amount of depreciation of rolling stock assets by GJ Railway greatly affects financial results. This is analyzed based on the company's income and expenditure statement and the "Director's Report", as follows.

Table 7-1 Close relationship with the dividend policy and the selection of depreciation methods in GJ Railway Co.

(£. s. d.)

Term	Period	Profits and dividends			Method of Depreciation for rolling stocks		
	First half = ① Latter half = ②	P Pre-Disposal Earning	D Determined Dividend	P − D Excess Earning	The £5,000 Fixed Amount Method Depreciation Expense	The Asset Revaluation Method Revaluation Loss	The Asset Revaluation Method Revaluation Gain
Term1	1837 ②	56,035. 10. 10	54,590. 0. 0.	1,445. 10. 10.	—	—	—
	1838 ①	55,444. 4. 10.	54,590. 0. 0.	854. 4. 10.	—	—	—
	1838 ②	78,714. 16. 9.	72,058. 1. 0.	6,656. 15. 9.	—	—	—
Term2	1839 ①	87,269. 6. 5.	78,609. 12. 0.	8,659. 14. 5.	5,000. 0. 0.	—	—
	1839 ②	115,216. 17. 4.	99,353. 16. 0.	15,863. 1. 4.	10,000. 0. 0.	—	730.14. 8.
	1840 ①	111,296. 6. 5.	109,998. 17. 0.	1,298. 9. 0.	—	1,855.17.7.	—
	1840 ②	137,481. 11. 9.	136,117. 16. 0.	1,363. 15. 9.	—	674. 1. 5.	—
	1841 ①	119,414. 10. 11.	132,198. 0. 0.	△12,783. 9. 1.	—	—	2,306.17. 7.
	1841 ②	145,829. 16. 0.	132,198. 0. 0.	13,631. 16. 0.	5,000. 0. 0.	—	—
	1842 ①	122,487. 13. 0.	110,165. 0. 0.	12,322. 13. 0.	5,000. 0. 0.	—	—
	1842 ②	125,082. 6. 3.	110,165. 0. 0.	14,917. 6. 3.	5,000. 0. 0.	—	—
	1843 ①	110,781. 7. 5.	110,165. 0. 0.	616. 7. 5.	—	—	—
	1843 ②	127,793. 1. 1.	110,165. 0. 0.	17,628. 1. 1.	5,000. 0. 0.	—	—
	1844 ①	121,141. 5. 10.	110,165. 0. 0.	10,976. 5. 10.	—	—	—
	1844 ②	140,442. 4. 9.	110,165. 0. 0.	30,277. 4. 9.	—	—	—

Source: Grand Junction Railway Company, *Minutes of Annual and Special General Meeting of the Proprietors,* 1837−1844.

Notes:
1. Term1 = Term before applying the depreciation practice
2. Term2 = Term after applying the depreciation practice
3. Pre-Disposal Earning = Dividable Income − Depreciation
4. Excess Earning = Maximum amount of depreciation allowed to ensure Determined Dividend

(1) £5,000 fixed amount method

A relatively clear concept for recognizing the amount of depreciation from the wear and tear of fixed assets (rolling stocks) was revealed by GJ Railway directors in the first half of 1840. The "Director's Report" of that time states the following.

The advantage of laying by a surplus fund to meet every contingency become every day more evident. We hold a very large amount to (→ of) property subject to variation in value. Locomotive Engines, for instance are not now of the value that were two years ago by ten percent, owing to the increased number of persons who now manufacture them, and the improvement constantly making. In a course like ours, continually requiring additional Engines, every reduction or improvement is advanta-

Chapter 7: Significance of Current Value Information in 19th Century England Corporate Accounting

geous, and particularly so when the surplus fund more than meets the apparent depreciation in value of our permanent stock[2].

The above "Director's Report" shows the benchmark amount of depreciation of rolling stocks as 10% decrease in value over two years (estimated based on the increase in the purchase price of rolling stock over six months). This standard on a single-term basis (six months) is 2.5%. Directors deemed essentially that, at the end of each fiscal term, depreciation occurred due to a purchase price increase in an amount resulting from multiplying the total amount expended for fixed assets by 2.5% and put aside that amount for future new purchases of fixed assets (rolling stock) as a result.

The average amount of fixed asset depreciation during the two-year period up to the first half of 1840 stated in the "Director's Report" (latter half of 1838 to first half 1840) is about £5,216. This amount, the estimated increase in rolling purchase price over six months, was deemed as the fixed asset depreciation and the average of the amount resulting from multiplying the total amount expended on fixed assets for each fiscal term by 2.5%. Broadening the calculation scope to eight fiscal periods since the start of operations of GJ Railway results in an average depreciation for rolling stock of £4,904 (Table 7-2). These average amounts almost perfectly coincide with £5,000, the amount of rolling stock depreciation for six months actually calculated by GJ Railway. In this Chapter, the practice of accounting for depreciation of fixed assets at £5,000 for a fiscal term, is named as the "£5,000 Fixed Amount Method". As suggested in the following statement found in the "Director's Report" of the latter half of 1839, at the extraordinary general shareholders' meeting held on January 31, 1840 to announce the operating results of the company for the latter half of 1839, the directors describe the purpose of deducting £5,000 from the profits as a partial reserve of capital for the future purchase of rolling stock, as follows.

The Sum of £5,000, which the proprietors will remember was laid aside from the profits of the Six Months ending June 30th to meet depreciation in value of Stock previously to that date, has enabled the Company to reduce the expenditure of Capital in the purchase of Stocks to that content[3].

---

[2] *Minutes of the Annual General Meeting of the Proprietors of the Grand Junction Railway Company etc.*, August 10th 1840, p. 58.

Table 7-2 Total Amount expended on Fixed Assets in GJ Railway Co. and Estimated Increase in Purchase Price of Rolling Stocks over Six Months

(£)

Period First half = ① Latter half = ②	Total Amount expended on Fixed Assets for each Fiscal Term a	Estimated Increase in Purchase Price of Rolling Stocks over Six Months a × 2.5%
1837 ②	123,178	3,079
1838 ①	132,469	3,311
1838 ②	174,762	4,369
1839 ①	216,498	5,412
1839 ②	217,227	5,430
1840 ①	226,221	5,655
1840 ②	228,094	5,702
1841 ①	250,852	6,271
Average	196,162	4,904

Source: Grand Junction Railway Company, *Minutes of Annual and Special General Meeting of the Proprietors,* 1837-1841.

(2) asset revaluation method

The issue facing the directors of GJ Railway, who were concerned about the increase of the market price of replacement assets, is how to calculate and accumulate the amount of capital equivalent to the increase in market price of replacement assets for the future purchase of rolling stock assets. The directors of GJ Railway, in the latter half of 1839, proposed a new method for recognizing the amount of depreciation of fixed assets. This method is based on the valuation difference (loss) generated by revaluating rolling stock assets at on the term-end market price. Because the revaluation of assets at term end was the basis for calculating the fixed asset value decrease, this method is called here the "Asset Revaluation Method".

Under what kind of concept, in addition to the "£5,000 Fixed Amount Method", was the "Asset Revaluation Method" adopted by GJ Railway? As they anticipated excess earnings, they exaggerated self-financing functions through the recognition of depreciation of rolling stock assets. In addition, to meet the changing business

---

[3] *Minutes of the Special General Meeting of the Proprietors of the Grand Junction Railway Company etc.*, January 31st 1840, p. 46.

climate, multiple accounting methods were made available that were advantageous to management to recognize depreciation based on the amount of excess earnings.

(3) Significance and problems of asset revaluation method

The Asset Revaluation Method enables the recognition of current impairment of fixed assets through the use of Stock Account. The purpose of this accounting procedure was to prepare and accumulate the capital fund for rolling stock replacement that would actually be needed in the future by charging the asset revaluation loss into the profit and loss calculation[4]. On the other hand, this method contained a significant problem. When a revaluation gain or loss is recognized and the amount thereof is less than £5,000, the self-financing function of the Asset Revaluation Method is greatly weakened compared to the £5,000 Fixed Amount Method. According to the Summary of Stock Account (rolling stock revaluation table)[5] prepared to report the results of rolling stock asset revaluation at the shareholders' meeting in the latter half of 1839, when the Asset Revaluation Method was first adopted, a £730.14. 8 valuation gain[6] was calculated instead of the valuation loss [Table 7-3].

---

[4] The market value of rolling stock assets at beginning of term of £1,000 and the end of term revaluation thereof based on market value of £900 would result in the following journalization of rolling stock depreciation.

        Stock Account 100 / Rolling stock 100
        Surplus 100 / Stock Account 100
    (Fixed assets revaluation loss)

The character of the Stock Account created in the first half of 1839 is assumed to be the same as the reserve account. However, in the latter half of 1839, after posting an asset revaluation difference, Stock Account immediately took on the character of the account meant for the transfer of that difference to the income account.

[5] Although the Rolling Stock Asset Revaluation Summary Table is not directly related to the revenue and expenditure statement, however, it was prepared as a part of the accounting report from the latter half of 1839 to the first half of 1841 and appears in the Director's Report.

[6] Applying the Asset Revaluation Method on December 31, 1839 reveals the following revaluation breakdown.

                                        (£. s. d.)
    Locomotives   95. 11. 9. / Stock Account   730. 14. 8.
    Freight cars   425. 9. 10.
    Passenger cars   209. 13. 1.

Table 7-3 Revaluation of Assets, Dec. 31st 1839 in GJ Railway Co.

(£ s. d.)

Period	Fixed Assets	Valuation of Dec.31st 1839 a	Valuation of June 30th 1839 b	New Assets purchased in 1839 ② c	d (=b+c)	e (=a−d)	Balance of Stock Account f
Latter Half of 1839	Locomotives (=Engines)	96,969 16. 0.	85,672 13. 2.	11,201 10. 11.	96,874 4. 3.	95 11. 9.	
	Fright Cars (= Waggons)	51,324 4. 4.	47,535 9. 9.	3,363 5. 6.	50,898 14. 6.	425 9.10.	
	Passenger Cars (= Carriages)	49,050 16. 5.	44,355 0. 1.	4,486 3. 3.	48,841 3. 4.	209 13. 1.	
	Total	197,344 16. 9.	177,563 2. 5.	19,050 19. 8.	196,614 2. 1.	730 14. 8.	730 14. 8.

Source: Grand Junction Railway Company, *Minutes of Special General Meeting of the Proprietors,* January 31st 1840, p. 49.

The fatal defect of this accounting method, as mentioned above, is when a valuation gain is obtained from the calculation, the replacement capital for new fixed assets is not self-financed. However, the concern of directors at that time was not the systematic accumulation of replacement capital for fixed assets but rather the securement of dividend asset source. Therefore, only if there is sufficient pre-disposal earnings (P) to cover the determined dividend (D) can enough replacement capital be accumulated from the excess earnings resulting therefrom (P-D). To put it another way, the amount of surplus to be carried over to the next term is reduced as much as possible. But, conversely, if there isn't excess earnings, the replacement capital amount that can be accumulated is constricted within that range and, if there is very little excess earnings or a negative figure, then the accumulation of replacement capital is stopped. Very random fixed asset accounting practices ensued. These complicated fixed asset accounting practices became prominent particularly in and after the latter half of 1839. See Table 7-1.

As mentioned above, GJ Railway started the Asset Revaluation Method in the latter half of 1839 as a means to recognize the depreciation amount of rolling stock assets. However, this resulted in a rolling stock revaluation gain of £730.14.8., the opposite of the initial intent of assigning the rolling stock depreciation amount to self-financing. Here, GJ Railway avoided the addition of rolling stock revaluation gain into current net income and carried it over to the first half of 1840 together with applying, as in the previous term, the £5,000 Fixed Amount

Chapter 7: Significance of Current Value Information in 19th Century
England Corporate Accounting 161

Method at the same time and actually posting a multiple thereof £10,000. Such a determination did not result in the self-financing function by the Asset Revaluation Method, although, excess earnings rose significantly from the first half of 1839 at £9,659 to the latter half of 1839 at £15,863. In the latter half of 1839, when a rolling stock revaluation gain of £730 was recognized, a contradiction arose with recognition of the depreciation of £10,000 in rolling stock. This proves that they were aware that the £5,000 Fixed Amount Method was convenient for a self-financing for the purpose of fixed asset replacement.

Under the £5,000 Fixed Amount Method framework, there was an account named the Reserve Fund for Contingencies[7] newly established to retain the current fund of £10,000 inside the enterprise. However, this accounting treatment[8] was not presented in the accounting report of GJ Railway in the latter half of 1839[9]. The reason therefor is likely because GJ Railway did not prepare the general balance sheet[10].

---

[7] Reserve Fund for Contingencies was used to invest the internally retained £10,000 current capital in various securities (Mortgages or other undeniable security). *Minutes of the Special General Meeting of the Proprietors of the Grand Junction Railway Company etc.*, January 31st 1840, p. 46.

[8] The following journalizing is assumed.
    December 31, 1839   (£. s. d.)
    Surplus 10,000.0.0. /Reserve Fund for Contingencies   10,000.0.0

[9] In the bottom line of the income account-the statement of receipts and expenditures for the latter half of 1839, the amount of £115,216. 17. 4. was presented as a balance. This balance minus the amount allocated for the payment of dividends (£99,353. 16. 0.; appearing in the marginal notes and footnotes of the same receipts and expenditure statement) is the surplus (£15,863. 1. 4.). However, the amount actually brought forward to the next term's receipts and expenditures statement is not £15,863. 1. 4. but £5,977. 18. 10. The balance being £9,885. 2. 6. represents the difference between the £10,000. 0. 0. treated as the aforementioned Reserve Fund for Contingencies and the £114. 17. 6. (the surplus issued with settlement of unsettled items of the first half of 1839). GJ Railway ledgers had a reserve fund for contingencies account in which the £10,000 was recorded. However, because the accounting report does not have a general balance sheet that shows this account item, the same was only indicated in the Receipts field of the statement of receipts and expenditures (the first half of 1840). *Minutes of the Special General Meeting of the Proprietors of the Grand Junction Railway Company etc.*, January 31st 1840, p. 45.

[10] The general balance sheet is one of the fundamental reports consisting of an accounting report format that is based on the double account system. An example of an accounting report format based on a double account system is provided by the

(4) Asset revaluation method as income control valve

The concurrent use of the £5,000 Fixed Amount Method and the Asset Revaluation Method relating to rolling stock in the latter half of 1839 was needed only because of the large excess earnings and, from the first half of 1840 to the first half of 1841, the recognition of a fixed asset depreciation was effected using the Asset Revaluation Method. The application of the £5,000 Fixed Amount Method was materially impossible due to insufficient surplus, which made directors decide that the Asset Revaluation Method is a proper means to calculate fixed asset depreciation. Although £5,000 was not far reaching, £1,855. 17. 7. (first half of 1840)[11] and £674. 1. 5. (latter half of 1840)[12] were retained for replacement capital for rolling stock assets and the explanation of the significance thereof to shareholders was not so difficult. The directors explained at the stockholder's meeting as follows regarding their ability to maintain sufficient effective value or value in use of fixed assets, although the depreciation of them had decreased significantly relative to the previous fiscal term.

In the Locomotive Stock, on the other hand, there is an apparent decrease of £2,184. 2. 1. in part arising from the generally

---

London Birmingham Railway in its first half of 1844 accounts. The basis of the double account system is the posting in the capital account of the procurement of fixed assets from long-term capital sources such as shares and fixed liabilities. The general balance sheet shows the payment of dividends from income earned and current assets that can be allocated towards the settlement of current liabilities. The balance of the revenue account shows income distributable as dividends. This balance is presented as the revenue accounts statement balance item in the general balance sheet and, as mentioned above, the balance of the capital account is also presented as the capital account balance item in the general balance sheet. In other words, the format of the accounting report based on the double account system ultimately integrates organically the revenue account and the capital account with them tied to the general balance sheet. Sasaki [2010], p. 52 and pp. 64–65.

[11] Rolling stock revaluation loss of £1,855. 17. 7. for in the first half of 1840 was offset with the rolling stock revaluation gain of £730. 14. 8. carried over from the latter half of 1839. As a result, the net amount of £1,125. 2. 11. was directly deducted from surplus earnings and thus securing capital for self-financing. For a verification of the figures, see Table 7-1.

[12] Looking at the rolling stock asset revaluation of the latter half of 1840 in the locomotive field of Table 7-4, there is a revaluation loss of £2,184. 2. 1. However, the revaluation (net) loss of all rolling stock assets was £674. 1. 5. This means that, for rolling stock assets other than locomotives, freight cars saw a revaluation gain of £785. 2. 8., with passenger cars similarly at £724. 18. 0. in revaluation gain.

Chapter 7: Significance of Current Value Information in 19th Century
England Corporate Accounting   163

Table 7-4 The Rolling Stock Asset Revaluation in GJ Railway Co.
(£ s. d.)

Period	Fixed Assets	Valuation at the end of the current period a	Valuation at the end of the previous period b	New Assets purchased in the current period c	d (= b+c)	e (= a−d)	Balance of Stock Account f
First Half of 1840 (1840①)	Locomotives	104,445 9. 11.	96,969 16. 0.	6,692 19. 10.	103,662 15. 10.	782 14. 1.	
	Fright Cars	50,492 4. 9.	51,324 4. 4.	577 1. 8.	51,901 6. 0.	△1,409 1. 3.	
	Passenger Cars	50,237 16. 3.	49,050 16. 5.	2,416 10. 3.	51,467 6. 8.	△1,229 10. 5.	
	Total	205,175 10. 11.	197,344 16. 9.	9,686 11. 9.	207,031 8. 6.	△1,855 17. 7.	0. 0. 0.
Latter Half of 1840 (1840②)	Locomotives	109,215 6. 8.	104,445 9.11.	6,953 18. 10.	111,399 8. 9.	△2,184 2. 1.	
	Fright Cars	53,457 7. 5.	50,492 4. 9.	2,174 0. 0.	52,666 4. 9.	785 2. 8.	
	Passenger Cars	51,842 14. 3.	50,237 16. 3.	880 0. 0.	51,117 16. 3.	724 18. 0.	
	Total	214,515 8. 4.	205,175 10. 11.	10,007 18. 10.	215,183 9. 9.	△674 1. 5.	0. 0. 0.
First Half of 1841 (1841①)	Locomotives	124,202 12. 10.	109,215 6. 8.	11,009 6. 2.	120,224 12. 10.	3,978 0. 0.	
	Fright Cars	53,807 1. 8.	53,451 7. 5.	576 17. 8.	53,968 5. 1.	△161 3. 5.	
	Passenger Cars	54,730 19. 0.	51,842 14. 3.	4,398 3. 9.	56,240 18. 0.	△1,509 19. 0.	
	Total	232,740 13. 6.	214,509 8. 4.	15,984 7. 7.	230,433 15. 11.	2,306 17. 7.	0. 0. 0.

Source: Grand Junction Railway Company, *Minutes of Annual and Special General Meeting of the Proprietors,* 1840–1841.

Table 7-5 Transfer of the Balance of Stock Account to the Dividable Income in GJ Railway Co.
(£ s. d.)

Period First half = ① Latter half = ②	Total Amount expended on the Rolling Stock	Pre-Disposal Earning	Determined Dividend	Amount transferred from Stock Account to Dividable Income	Amount transferred from Reserve Fund to Dividable Income	Income carried over the next Period
1840 ①	226,221. 2. 5.	111,296. 6. 5.	99,353.16. 0. 10,645._1. 0.	△1,125. 2. 11.	—	172. 6. 6.
1840 ②	228,094. 16. 0.	137,481. 11. 9	136,117.16. 0.	△674. 1. 5.	—	689. 14. 4.
1841 ①	250,852. 16. 7.	119,414.10.11.	132,198. 0. 0.	2,306. 17. 7.	10,570. 16. 5.	94. 4.11.

Source: Grand Junction Railway Company, *Minutes of Annual General Meeting of the Proprietors,* 10th August 1840, *Minutes of Special General Meeting of the Proprietors,* 29th January 1841 and *Minutes of Annual General Meeting of the Proprietors,* 6th August 1841.

reduced market price of Engines, to which reference has been made on the present occasion, the efficient value of the Stock there is reason to believe is at least as high as at any former periods[13].

As already indicated, it is very doubtful that accounting recognition was being effected with the forethought of retaining capital systematically for renewing rolling stock in the future by GJ

---

[13] *Minutes of the Special General Meeting of the Proprietors of the Grand Junction Railway Company etc.*, January 29th 1841, p. 60.

Railway. Rather, if there should be sufficient excess earnings to secure dividend assets, rolling stock asset replacement capital would be voluntarily self-financed and, to the contrary in the event of a deficiency thereof, the practice was voluntarily cancelled with various reasons.

A deficit in assets for dividend appeared in the first half of 1841. Then, GJ Railway posted asset revaluation gain based on the Asset Revaluation Method and secured distributable earnings (Table 7-5). Naturally, they did not carry out self-finance meaning recognition of fixed asset depreciation and placement of a reserve for replacement capital. The "Director's Report" relating to the first half of 1841 of GJ Railway states, regarding the above, that "The Directors, however, do not feel assured of the expediency of acting upon a comparative valuation of Stock on all occasions when it may happen to shew an improvement in value[14]", suggesting discontinuation of the Asset Revaluation Method.

(5) Return to the £5,000 Fixed Amount Method and its new usage

In the latter half of 1841, the operating results of GJ Railway took a turn for the better and there was an abundant amount of excess earnings to open the door again to self-financing for rolling stock replacement (recognition of rolling stock asset depreciation). GJ Railway reapplied the old £5,000 Fixed Amount Method for this purpose.

Mr. Locke, GJ Railway's principal engineer, "objected to the Company's taking credit for some thousand pounds of the supposed improved value of the locomotive power, and showed the impossibility of drawing any correct conclusion from so fallacious a practice, liable as it is to cause great and arbitrary fluctuations in the nominal value of stock according to the persons or the principles of action employed[15]". Therefore, based on this argument, GJ Railway has abandoned the Asset Revaluation Method in favor of the £5,000 Fixed Amount Method". This was explained in the "Director's Report" as follows.

The Directors have therefore resolved to abandon the publi-

---

[14] *Minutes of the Ninth Annual General Meeting of the Proprietors of the Grand Junction Railway Company etc.*, August 6th 1841, p. 66.

[15] *Minutes of the Special General Meeting of the Proprietors of the Grand Junction Railway Company etc.*, February 1st 1842, p. 74.

cation of Comparative valuations, and recommend instead that a certain sum be periodically laid aside, as a fund for the improvement of the Stock, and to meet that insensible but sure decay which is perpetually going on, and which no care or expense can prevent. The Sum they would propose to appropriate to this purpose on the present occasion is £5,000[16].

The above opinion indicates that the directors understood the effectiveness of the £5,000 Fixed Amount Method for self-financing of rolling stock asset purchase capital as opposed to the Asset Revaluation Method. When there are sufficient excess earnings thanks to favorable operating results, self-financing is conducted by recognizing the rolling stock asset depreciation amount as £5,000 and, conversely, when there was no excess earings, this practice was not effected by the directors even for the latter half of 1841 and beyond.

We should note that the £5,000 Fixed Amount Method applied for the latter half of 1841 and beyond has a vastly different meaning in terms of accounting practice as compared with the £5,000 Fixed Amount Method applied in the first and latter half of 1839. In the first and latter half of 1839, the "surplus" (or retained earnings) that fulfilled the function of self-financing was not explicitly indicated in the accounting report meaning that it was a "secret reserve" and, in the first half of 1842 and beyond, the retained "surplus" was indicated as "Depreciation and Renewal of Stock Fund" making that amount open to the stockholders (Historical Document 7-1)[17].

In other words, the £5,000 Fixed Amount Method reapplied for the latter half of 1841 not only deducts £5,000 from operating income, the bottom line of the income account, for the depreciation and renewal of stock, but also newly establishes a corresponding account therefor, the "Depreciation and Renewal of Stock Fund," which is ascribed as "account set aside for the depreciation and renewal of stock" in the Director's Report. Current assets accumulated internally and self-financed are treated as financial assets to earn interest, and the interest acquired from these

---

[16] *Minutes of the Special General Meeting of the Proprietors of the Grand Junction Railway Company etc.*, February 1st 1842, p. 74.

[17] "Depreciation and Renewal of Stock Fund" account is not directly related to the statement of receipts and expenditure, however, it was a part of the accounting report between the first half of 1842 and the latter half of 1844.

166   Fair Value Accounting in Historical Perspective

Historical Document 7-1 Depreciation & Renewal of Stock Fund (First Half of 1842), GJ Railway Co.

Depreciation & Renewal of Stock Fund — viz.	
Set aside December 31-1841	£5,000. –
Interest on — do —	40. 7. 6.
Set aside as above	5,000. —
	£10, 040. 7. 6.

Source: Grand Junction Railway Company, *Minutes of the Tenth Annual General Meeting of the Proprietors*, 1st August 1842, p. 82.

financial assets is not recognized as revenue, but rather credited in the account of "Depreciation and Renewal of Stock Fund[18]".

(6) Relationship between carrying over to the "Depreciation and Renewal of Stock Fund" and paying dividends — Abandonment of the £5,000 Fixed Amount Method

In the latter half of 1841, GJ Railway abandoned Asset Revaluation Method and returned to the £5,000 Fixed Amount Method that systematically enables the self-finance function. What they did next is described below. Table 7-6 shows the transition of the Depreciation and Renewal of Stock Fund from the latter half of 1841 to the latter half of 1844 and its relationship with the excess earnings (Table 7-1) of each fiscal term. From the latter half of 1841 to the latter half of 1842, the company posted £5,000 in rolling stock asset depreciation every fiscal term with ample excess earnings. However, in the first half of 1843, the £5,000 Fixed Amount Method, applied as a means to self-finance capital provisioned for future rolling stock replacement became distorted in its relationship with the dividend policy of the GJ Railway. In other words, in the first half of 1843, £601. 6. 8. was deducted from the Depreciation and Renewal of Stock Fund thus creating

---

[18] The journalizing of this transaction is shown as follows. The interest of £40. 7. 6. was imposed on £5,000 placed in reserve at the accounts settlement of the latter half of 1841. This was essentially the same concept as the sunking fund method.

December 31, 1841   (£. s. d.)
Surplus   5,000. 0. 0. / Depreciation and Renewal of 5,000. 0. 0.
                                    Stock Fund
Financial assets   5,000. 0. 0. / Cash   5,000. 0. 0.
Cash   40. 7. 6. / Depreciation and Renewal of   40. 7. 6.
                                    Stock Fund

Table 7-6 Relationship among Performance, Dividend and Depreciation and Renewal of Stock Fund in GJ Railway Co.

(£ s. d.)

Period	a	b	c	d	e	f	g
1841 ②	145,829 16. 0.	132,198 0. 0.	—	—	5,000 0. 0.	—	5,000 0. 0.
1842 ①	122,487 13. 0.	110,165 0. 0.	5,000 0. 0.	40 7. 6.	5,000 0. 0.	—	10,040 7. 6.
1842 ②	125,082 6. 3.	110,165 0. 0.	10,040 7. 6.	250 18. 9.	5,000 0. 0.	—	15,291 6. 3.
1843 ①	110,781 7. 5.	110,165 0. 0.	15,291 6. 3.	337 10. 0.	—	601 6. 8.	15,027 9. 7.
1843 ②	127,793 1. 1.	110,165 0. 0.	15,027 9. 7.	281 5. 0.	5,000 0. 0.	500 0. 0.	19,808 14. 7.
1844 ①	121,141 5.10.	55,082 10. 0. / 55,082 10. 0.	19,808 14. 7.	425 7. 6.	—	850 0. 0.	19,384 2. 1.
1844 ②	140,442 4. 9.	55,082 10. 0. / 55,082 10. 0.	19,384 2. 1.	944 12. 6.	—	2,500 0. 0.	17,828 14. 7.
1845 ①	44,861 0. 0.	44,066 0. 0. / 1,101 13. 0.	unknown	unknown	unknown	unknown	unknown

Source : Grand Junction Railway Company, *Minutes of Annual and Special General Meeting of the Proprietors*, 1841–1845.

Notes : First half = ①
Latter half = ②
a = Pre-Disposal Earning (= Dividable Income – Depreciation)
b = Determined Dividend
c = Balance of Depreciation and Renewal of Stock Fund Account at the beginning of each Period
d = Interest added to Depreciation and Renewal of Stock Fund Account
e = Amount added to Depreciation and Renewal of Stock Fund Account at the end of each Period
f = Amount deducted from Depreciation and Renewal of Stock Fund Account
g = Balance of Depreciation and Renewal of Stock Fund Account at the end of each Period

rolling stock replacement capital, but there was no addition of £5,000 to this fund account at term-end account settlement. At the ordinary general shareholders' meeting held on August 3, 1843, the directors stated the following with regard to the reasons for suspending the £5,000 Fixed Amount Method.

> The Directors do not recommend the Proprietors to add anything to their Fund for depreciation and renewal of Stock on the present occasion; but at the Summer Half-year is always much the most profitable, they will be enabled at the close of the year to make such allowance, as to the Proprietors may then appear desirable[19].

The reason for not posting the depreciation amount of rolling stock assets was because of the significant decrease in operating revenue compared to the previous fiscal term due to the great fall in GJ Railway passenger ticket sales in the first half of 1843[20]

---

[19] Minutes of the Annual General Meeting of the Proprietors of the Grand Junction Railway Company etc., August 3rd 1843, p. 87.

resulting in a drastic drop in excess earnings. To maintain stable dividends, the policy of carrying over to the Depreciation and Renewal of Stock Fund was discontinued. Earnings prior to disposal for the first half of 1843 were £110,781. 7. 5., but because dividends amounted to £110,165. 0. 0., excess earnings allocatable for self-financing, which is the difference between the two, was only £616. 7. 5. If having added £5,000 to the Depreciation and Renewal of Stock Fund, as was done in the previous fiscal term, there would have been a deficit of surplus of £4,383. 12. 7. (= £110,781. 7. 5. − £5,000. 0. 0. − £110,165. 0. 0.) to pay the determined dividend. GJ Railway's directors, who hated to dip the dividend payout below previous levels due to downturns in operating results, decided to stop the deduction of the rolling stock depreciation amount of £5,000, which was the cause of the drop in dividend resource. The accounting practice of recognizing the depreciation amount of fixed assets was not applied consistently to all fiscal terms, while profit levels and dividend demands were taken into consideration, only in good performance years was depreciation recognized, but not in bad years. This meant that depreciation practice at the time, was contingent[21].

Accounting practices regarding the recognition and measurement of depreciation of fixed assets undertaken by GJ Railway were determined based on the accounting policies of directors concerned with the securement of dividend resource. This means that rather than looking to the qualitative value of acquisition cost or market value as accounting information, directors' prioritized judgment calls either for acquisition cost or market value for the purpose of securing a certain level of distributable earnings. The market value information in the £5,000 Fixed Amount Method and the Asset Revaluation Method was used flexibly by directors to solidify their way of thinking, which made discontinuance of the recognition of the depreciation possible.

---

[20] The total revenue for the first half of 1843 was £185,093. 2. 8., which is about 10.9% lower than that of the previous fiscal term. However, the passenger ticket revenue for that period was £132,976. 6. 9., or about 17.6% lower year on year. *Minutes of the Special General Meeting of the Proprietors of the Grand Junction Railway Company etc.*, January 31st 1843, p. 85. and *Minutes of the Annual General Meeting of the Proprietors of the Grand Junction Railway Company etc.*, August 3rd 1843, p. 88.

[21] The same indication is found in the following contribution. Nakamura [1991], p. 197.

7-3. The Role of Market Value Information in the Accounting Practices of Neuchatel Asphalte Co.

(1) Lawsuit overview

Lee v. Neuchatel Asphalte Co. (1889) is a typical litigation case that greatly impacted the fixed asset valuation procedures of general registered companies. Mr. Lee, a shareholder of Neuchatel Asphalte Co., which was a mining company in 19th Century England, sued the company and the directors thereof claiming in court that in the fiscal year ended December 31, 1885 of Neuchatel Asphalte Co., the depreciation expense (depletion) of intangible fixed assets (mining rights) was not correctly accounted for and the profit was non-existent , and requested a judicial mandate for desisting the payment of dividends by the company out of the amount posted as earnings for that term. The presiding judge in the first instance and the appeal ruled for the defendant (Neuchatel Asphalte Co.) in compliance with the company's articles of association, which prohibits the recognition of depletion with respect to mining rights, stating that there is no need to take depletion into consideration in calculating the profit. Moreover, the basis for the exclusion of mining rights' depletion besides the provisions of the articles of association was the repetitive emphasis at trial by the defendant on the fact that the valuation of the value (market value) of minig rights at the time of the trial (first instance, 1888; appeal, 1889) was significantly higher than the acquisition cost thereof at the time they were purchased when the company was founded. This point is expounded in more detail below.

(2) Market value information that supports the validity of the decision not to deplete assets

Neuchatel Asphalte Co. was established on July 1, 1873 as a result of the merger between six mining companies and incorporated as a limited liability company with nominal capital of 1.15 million pounds (authorized capital) classified into 35,000 shares of preferred stock and 80,000 shares of common stock at 10 pounds per share respectively. In exchange for shares, it acquired the special rights (for mining) of one of its absorbed companies, pavement maker Neuchatel Rock, in other words, exclusive rights to acquire bituminous rock (to make asphalt) from the Val de Travers and all the mines, structures, offices, real estate and current assets of Neuchatel Rock, as well as all the assets of the five other absorbed companies.

The accounting report of Neuchatel Asphalte Co. for the fiscal year ended December 31, 1885 posted surplus of 17,140 pounds leading directors to propose a payout of 9 shillings per share as dividend for preferred shares holders (total 15,369 pounds). Although the general shareholders' meeting approved this proposal, Mr. Lee (plaintiff: holder of 628 shares of common stock and 16 shares of preferred stock of the company) sued the company and its directors in order to restrain them from paying that dividend. The basis of his accounting complaint was that the value of the special rights (mining) had depreciated thus losing a great portion of the company's capital and therefore this company would not have sufficient earnings to apply towards the payment of dividends without compensation for such a loss and depreciation. In other words, Neuchatel Asphalte Co. failed to appropriately account for the depletion costs of the mining rights and treated almost the entire amount of proceeds from asphalt sales as dividable. As a result, Mr. Lee ultimately claimed that the company had returned capital to shareholders in the form of dividends.

At the first instance trial and appeal, the court ruled in favor of the defendant supporting its claim. The basis for the judgment was the provisions of the Neuchatel Asphalte Co. articles of association. Article 100 thereof states as follows.

> 100. The directors may, before recommending any dividend on any of the shares, set aside out of the net profits of the company such sum as they think proper as a reserved fund to meet contingencies or for equalizing dividends, or for repairing and maintaining the works connected with the business of the company, or any part thereof, and the directors may invest the sum so set apart as a reserved fund, or any part thereof, upon such securities as they may select; but they shall not be bound to form a fund, or otherwise reserve moneys, for the renewal or replacing of any lease, or of the company's interest in any property or concession[22].

In other words, it was prohibited to provide for replacement capital by the recognition of depletion of mining rights, which are intangible fixed assets of the company. What has to be noticed here is the de facto recognition of a hike in the value (market value) of mining rights by a judge. This was emphasized as follows in the the judgment.

I do not say that no part of the assets has ever been lost, but on the evidence before us the assets of this company are of greater value than at the time of the formation of the company in 1873. They then had, it is true, a concession, but for a shorter period than the one they have now got, and the royalty was very heavy. Now they have a longer time for the concession to run than they had in 1873, and they have got very much more profitable terms than they had at the first. In my opinion, so far from there being any loss of assets, the company has now in its possession a larger amount of assets than it had at the time it was first formed.....Here all that was taken by this company from the first companies was their assets, and in my opinion those assets has increased in value, ...[23].

It was observed in this case that disregarding depletion of mining rights valuated at acquisition cost was not only required by the articles of association but supported by the rise in their market value, which was understood by the court.

7-4. The Role of Market Value Information in the Accounting Practices of Natal Land and Colonization Co.

(1) Overview of litigation

Bolton v. Natal Land and Colonization Co. [1892] is an example of a case influenced by the judgment delivered at Lee v. Neuchatel Asphalte Co. [1889][24]. Natal Land and Colonization Co. valuated land at market value at the end of December 1882 accounts settlement to write off bad debts in a lump sum using the posted land revaluation gain[25]. Then, in 1885, the company accounted for

---

[22] [1889] 41 Ch.D. p. 3.

[23] [1889] 41 Ch.D. p. 15.

[24] This judgment was called the "Lee Principle" which means that capital expenditures for the acquisition of fixed assets and decreases in their value are irrelevant to the calculation of dividable income and on the other hand, reductions in the value of the floating or circulating assets, or any expenditures for the purchase thereof must be treated as deductions from current term revenues. Chiba [1991], p. 184

[25] In Ammonia Soda Company, Limited v. Chamberlain Ch.D. [1918], land revaluation gains were recorded for to offset past cumulated losses and improve on the issuance requirements of shares. Even in the accounting practices in the US in the 1920s, there are many cases of asset revaluation for the purpose of loss compensation.

profit in its income account and dividends were proposed based thereon. When this occurred, Mr. Bolton, the company's shareholder, filed a complaint stating that the offsetting made in 1882 was erroneous on the grounds that there would have been a significant loss and thus no capital for dividends. Mr. Bolton (the plaintiff) then sued the directors (the defendant) of the company demanding to halt the proposed payment of dividends, because the land valuation was not based on any appropriate advice or opinion of independent specialists and there was large decrease in value for several pieces of land, which was not posted in the debit side of the income and loss account of 1885. The judgment was in favor of the defendant, whose objection to the claim of the plaintiff was as follows: ...the Court will not interfere unless it can be shewn that the company is doing something ultrà vires the articles. The case is entirely covered by the principle of Lee v. Neuchatel Asphalte Company. No company is bound to keep its capital intact and to replace all losses that have been incurred, and not to pay dividends until all those losses have been replaced[26].

The detailed description of the accounting treatment of land market valuation will be shown below.

(2) Land revaluation gain adjusted to the amount for offsetting bad debts

Natal Land and Colonization Co. was founded on December 4, 1860 for the following purpose.

- The purchasing, holding, settling, building upon, or improving, managing, cultivating, planting, clearing, letting, subletting, farming, selling, granting, alienating, exchanging, mortgaging, charging, or otherwise dealing with and making a profit of lands and hereditaments in the Colony of Natal, South Africa, and the British possessions adjacent.
- The lending or advancing money upon real or personal security in the said Colony of Natal, or the British possessions adjacent, or upon produce of the said colony or possessions, or upon goods or merchandise, or bills of lading or goods or merchandise shipped therefrom or thereto[27].

Moreover, Article 113 of the company's articles of association

---

Saito [1984], p. 59.
[26] [1892] 2 Ch.D. p. 130.
[27] [1892] 2 Ch.D. pp. 124-125.

approves the provisioning of capital as deemed necessary by directors prior to surplus distribution as follows.

113. The Directors may, if they shall think fit, before recommending a dividend, set aside, out of the profits of the company, such a sum as they think proper as a reserved fund to meet contingencies, or for equalizing dividends, or for repairing or maintaining the works connected with the business of the company, or any part thereof; ....[28].

Land as a focus of this lawsuit was appraised at market value in the 1882 accounting settlement of Natal Land and Colonization Co., taking the following into consideration, which had been apparent from the explanation of an officer in charge of general administrative affairs[29].

- the prices produced by such portion of the company's lands as were already sold, which had, on the average, realized more than double the amount at which they stood in the company's books
- the upset price fixed by the Natal Government for lands similar to or which could reasonably be compared with the company's lands
- the letters, reports, and other documents (though not being in themselves valuations) from time to time received by the company from their general manager
- the recommendations of the general manager

As is shown in the balance sheet as of the end of December 1882, the land of the company valued at an acquisition cost of £360,766 9s. 8d. was revaluated at a market value (Present estimated value) of £681,053, recording a revaluation value of £430,000. As a result, £69,233 10s. 4d. (£430,000 0s. 0d. − £360,766 9s. 8d.) in increase was posted as revaluation gain to offset bad debts of £72,326 4s. 5d. in the profit and loss account. In this case, the lump-sum writing off of bad debts was not treated as a loss and a charge on profit and loss calculation was avoided, therefore, this land revaluation brought the company distributable earnings without the loss carried over the next term. However, it must be noted that market revaluation gain was calculated intentionally as mentioned above. In other words, the revaluation amount was brought down to £430,000 enough to offset bad

---

[28] [1892] 2 Ch.D. p. 126.
[29] [1892] 2 Ch.D. pp. 128–129.

debts, instead of the actual market value of £681,053. Historical Document 7-2 shows that market value was used to secure distributable earnings intentionally by company directors.

7-5. Conclusion

What was most important to GJ Railway directors was not only the continuous rapid and stable provision of railway transportation services but also the stable payout of dividends to shareholders. To attain the former objective, it was necessary to appropriately replace rolling stock and improve capacity. To achieve this, there was the issue of procuring huge amounts of replacement capital. They chose to self-finance capital through the depreciation of fixed assets. Specifically speaking, they adopted the "£5,000 Fixed Amount Method" and the "Asset Revaluation Method." However, the decision on the provision for actual rolling stock replacement capital was affected by the level of excess earnings minus a certain amount of dividends paid per fiscal term. In order to secure a certain amount of dividends, the calculation of reserves for rolling stock replacement was greatly affected by the amount of surplus remaining after the dividend was deducted from profit. Therefore, from an accounting perspective, the measurement of rolling stock asset depreciation was manipulated and distorted. GJ Railway's

Historical Document 7-2 Natal Land and Colonization Co. 1882 accounting report (partial)

Balance Sheet
31st December, 1882

		Cr.
Assets		
By Land Department: —	£	s. d.
Land-As per Schedule		
447,190 acres — at cost to the		
House and Town Properties, &c. — Company — £360,766 9. 8.		
Present estimated value — 681,053 0. 0.		
But taken only at — 430,000 0. 0.		
Below ommited		

Source: Interleaf in Chiba [1991], pp. 180–181.

accounting practices was characterized as prioritizing corporate finance and the selection of accounting methods was totally random. On this occasion, the method that fit to secure dividend assets was selected and applied.

Natal Land and Colonization Company's accounting practices for fixed assets also featured the flexible selection of acquisition cost or market value in the preparation of accounting information from the point of view of securing a certain level of dividend assets. Thus we see that the relationship between the shareholders who desired a certain level of dividends and the company directors who acted to meet the expectations of shareholders had a great impact on the selection of either acquisition cost or market value in preparing the accounting reports.

[References in English]
[Documents]
Grand Junction Railway Company [1833-1846] *General Meetings*, RAIL220 (7). British Transport Historical Records, Railway Companies. Surrey: Public Record Office (The National Archives)
[Legal cases]
Ammonia Soda Company, Limited v. Chamberlain [1918] 1 Ch. D. 266-299.
Bolton v. Natal Land and Colonization Company [1892] 2 Ch. D. 124-133.
Lee v. Neuchatel Asphalte Company [1886-1889] 41 Ch. D. 1-28.

[References in Japanese]
Chiba, Junichi [1991] *Modern English Accounting System –Inquiry into its Development Process*, Chuokeizai-sha Inc.
Nakamura, Manji [1991] *Historical Study on British and American Railway Accounting*, Dobunkan Shuppan.
Saito, Shizuki [1984] *Historical Study of the Asset Revaluation Movement*, University of Tokyo Press.
Sasaki, Shigeto [2010] *History of British Railway Accounting in the 19th Century*. Kunimoto Shobo.
Urasaki, Naohiro [2002] *Fair Value Accounting*, Moriyama Shoten.

Chapter 8

The Evolution of Audit Thought on Asset Verification during the Period 1880−1940: in the UK and the US practices

Kei Okajima

Takushoku University

Abstract

The traditional British professional audits are often characterized as bookkeeping audits in technical aspects. Late nineteenth and early twentieth century auditors, who were tasked to verify the accuracy of book entries by looking back at the original source of transactions along the process by which the balance sheet was drawn up, attempted to improve the quality of their audits by effectively making use of a procedure called the "vouching". Some verificatory procedures, which embrace the physical inspection of assets appearing in the balance sheet, were already in use even before the 1880s, however, after the mid-1890s, there were several cases concerning auditor's duties in which it was reasonably expected for auditor to perform specific verificatory procedures applied depending on individual circumstances, resulting in their overwhelming acceptance. This development also involved an examination of the values at which assets were shown in the balance sheet. Although the arguments would not have necessarily been based on the uniform grounds, the common understanding that it is the auditor's role to verify the value of assets at the balance sheet date through any means possible would seem to have been established by the 1930s.

Quite contrastingly, the newly emerged audit approach adapting to the US situation, called the "balance sheet audit", did not intend to trace back at the original source of transactions, and thus from the very first American audits did not have to depend on the transaction-based examination unlike the traditional British audits. Therefore, in comparison with the British audits, more proactive asset verification was possible, allowing for the savings of many audit times. The responsibility of the auditor with respect to the values of assets at the balance sheet date could be more aggressively accepted than in Britain. This research demonstrates that in the face of different circumstances, British and American auditors have developed the methods for verifying the existence and the values of assets in a different way, thus the developmental processes in two countries for physical verification took on a different aspect.

Keywords

professional audit, bookkeeping audit, transaction-based examination, verification of assets, verificatory procedures, balance sheet audit, Montgomery, physical tests

8-1. Introduction

The purpose of this Chapter is to clarify from an historical perspective just how professional auditors have treated the "value" aspect of balance sheet items in carrying out their audit program. As a means of verification, auditors have to deal with accounting values and valuations of each assets or liabilities appearing in the balance sheet at various levels or phases. How auditor grapples with these values depends on the circumstances, based on what audit principles and under what constraints, including his relationships with the client company, his works are fulfilled.

In this Chapter, the research is made for the purpose of determining what approach auditors employed in the conduct of audits, especially how they responded as to the value aspect of the items to be examined, by reviewing audit methods and methodologies described in the audit literatures including the major audit textbooks published between 1880 and 1940 in both the UK and the US.

Note that, as with this research, with regard to the research method heavily relying upon audit literatures as an historical source, one may suspect as to whether the descriptions in the audit textbooks reflect current actual practices. Such a methodological issue has been recognized and fully considered in similar previous researches[1]. We assume here that the best practice of that era is well reflected in the writings of the author as a leading practitioner. Moreover, the concern of this research is with underlying principles of auditing rather than with audit technique itself, so the very fact that it is, even if not commonly used as procedure, systematically explained in audit textbooks underscores its value in terms of historical material. Of course, the problem as to whether such explanations truly reflect contemporary practices still remains unsolved. In this Chapter, however, we shall discuss verification methods, accepting the above fundamental limitations while supposing the level of audit conceptualization[2].

8-2. Verification Structure Underlying the British Professional Audit

(1) **Early professional audit** — bookkeeping audit

Historical sources for what the auditors of the days actually did are extremely limited. Up to 1880 when the Institute of Chartered Accountants in England and Wales was formed, *The Accountant*, a periodical published since 1874, contained little material about audit practices or principles[3]. Also until then, there was almost no audit textbook dealing with auditor's work. In 1881, F. W. Pixley, one of prominent professional accountants wrote his textbook *Auditors: Their Duties and Responsibilities* with the intention of enlightening superiority of professional audit over amateur audit,

---

[1] Myers [1985], pp.69-70; Power [1992], p. 39; Chandler *et al.* [1993], p. 444.

[2] In British audit textbooks during that period by the practitioner-writer, such as Pixley, Dicksee, Spicer and Pegler, and de Paula, the descriptions are centered on particular procedures necessary to conduct the audits, related statutory provisions and case law decisions, and considerations in the case of the audit for specific class of business. As already indicated, we need to bear in mind that there appear merely descriptions of technical procedures while *"general* audit principles" are not specified (Power [1992], p.49). Therefore, what was the audit principle underlying technical procedures is a matter of interpretation.

[3] Littleton [1933], pp.315-318; Chatfield [1977], pp. 120-121.

which provided general information on related statutes and case laws and other auditor's duties.

However, Lawrence R. Dicksee's *Auditing: A Practical Manual for Auditors*, the first edition of which was published in 1892, provides a wealth of professional auditing procedures in detail, and is later to go through many editions and become the most influential audit literature in Britain during the period 1890–1930. In Dicksee's *Auditing*, the entire audit process at work is explained as in the summary below. It starts with checking the postings from one account book or ledger to another, with a check of castings and examination of vouchers (vouching), and after these "mechanical[4]" procedures are effected, then the deriving process of the balance sheet drawn up from the trial balance so verified is subjected to auditor's examination. Actually, in his textbook, under "Auditing up to the Trial Balance", checking posting, checking castings, vouching and other procedures are explained, and under "From Trial Balance to Balance Sheet" audit procedures for the drafting balance sheets are explained. From this explanation format we can surmise that the audit evidence process is divided into "Auditing up to the Trial Balance" and " (Auditing) From Trial Balance to Balance Sheet[5]".

The audit function here is generally understood as checking whether the client's bookkeepers are accurately doing their work. This is an explanation of why it is characterized as a "bookkeeping audit[6]". The technical characteristics as detailed checks of bookkeeper's work apparently suited to statutory requirements in that, as Michael Chatfield put it, "its primary goals were the verification of managerial stewardship and the detection of fraud[7]". It was probably found advantageous to examine all transactions occurred

---

[4] Dicksee [1892], pp. 12, 14; Pixley [1897], p. 77.

[5] The chapters of Dicksee's *Auditing* first edition are as follows: Chapter 1: Introductory, Chapter 2: Auditing (up to the Trial Balance), Chapter 3: Methods of Account (suggested in the course of Audit), Chapter 4: Special Considerations in Different Classes of Audits, Chapter 5: From Trial Balance to Balance Sheet, and Chapter 6: The Attitude of the Auditor, with the appendices with additional materials on the related provisions of various statutes and the case law decisions. The content provides auditing tasks in Chapters 2 and 5, wherein Chapter 2 is well enough informative, but it is unclear as to whether Chapter 5 can serve as part of the "audit" process.

[6] Matthews [2006], p. 24.

[7] Chatfield [1977], p. 119.

in terms of ascertaining the legitimacy and honesty in the managerial behaviors as the traces of managerial behaviors *must* be well reflected in the accounting records. It was therefore necessary to monitor the process by which the accounting records are prepared.

Moreover, such a feature as bookkeeping audit tends to be linked with the objective of fraud detection. Roy Chandler *et al.* (1993), discussing the shifting audit objectives from fraud detection to verification of financial statements during the period 1840-1940, seem to implicitly understand that technical characteristics as checks on the bookkeeping staff were reinforced by the demands for effective attainment of the audit objective of fraud detection[8]. From such a perspective, the professional auditors of the day would likely not be making *independent* verifications of financial statements but rather concentrating merely on the effectiveness of finding the irregularities concealed in the financial statements. Nonetheless, is the stance of this research that the history of audit techniques and audit objectives may be discussed separately. In this Chapter, though acknowledging that technicality of audit procedures might have been affected by emphasis on the discovery of frauds and errors, we might usefully examine what assumptions professional audits were being based on in the audit evidence process, in terms of the structure of the verification activities.

(2) **Strong inclination to vouching in the verification structure**

Now we shall discuss the issue as to on what audit principles the auditor's works were conducted in those days. Dicksee observed a wide difference of opinion regarding the extent of the auditor's work such that "some claiming that an Auditor's duty is confined to a comparison of the Balance Sheet with the books, while others assert that it is the Auditor's duty to trace every transaction back to its first source[9]". He went on to say "it cannot be denied that...a minute scrutiny of *every* item would be quite impossible to the Auditor, although it is in the highest degree desirable that every undertaking should possess the means of making such an examination for itself[10]" thus indicating the necessity for test checking. Michael Power (1992) comments on this Dicksee's

---

[8] Chandler *et al.* [1993], pp. 446-447.
[9] Dicksee [1892], p. 7.
[10] Dicksee [1892], p. 7. Italics in original.

statement to the effect that "this issue is partly triggered by the demands for higher quality of verificatory work in which a mechanical approach gives way to one in which transactions are traced to first source[11]". The extension of auditor's work to include looking back to the source of transactions is interpreted as bringing about the situation that "a minute scrutiny of *every* item would be quite impossible[12]". In short, he contends that the heightening of the "depth" of the audits resulted in forcing limits on the "scope" of the audits.

An important method of maintaining the quality of auditor's work under the aforementioned notion was vouching, which was presribed as an examination of the circumstances and documents of the original transactions. From the mid-1890s, as the case laws touching on the auditor's duties were developing, the auditor became more likely to be expected to go behind the client's books of accounts, and consequently this perspective led to the formulation of a concept that makes vouching necessary. This notion was representatively demonstrated by the 1908 prize-winning essay in the Chartered Accountant Students Society of London entitled "Vouching in an Audit", which described the object and importance of vouching as follows: "The process of vouching is the means by which the auditor goes behind the books, ...The value of this process lies in the fact that vouchers generally furnish evidence from sources wholly outside the business under review, and it should be the aim of the auditor to revert to the origin of the transactions. The more original the voucher, the more effective will the audit be[13]".

As shown in the testimony of William Quilter, an early professional accountant at a parliamentary committee in 1849[14], in the formative years of professional audits, vouching had not been considered merely as conventional reference. This in itself suggests that vouching may have been significant in the depth of an audit from the earliest times[15]. Either way, we can infer that early British professional auditors conducted their work primarily with a heavy focus on vouching from the perspective of going

---

[11] Power [1992], p. 48.
[12] Power [1992], p. 48.
[13] Pike [1908], p. 906.
[14] British Parliamentary Papers [1849], Minute 2218.
[15] Matthews [2006], p. 27.

beyond the books. Frederic R. M. de Paula's *Principles of Auditing* (1914) has the following to say about the significance of vouching:

Vouching is the very essence of auditing, and the whole success of an audit depends upon the intelligence and thoroughness with which this part of the work is done. Vouching does not mean merely the inspection of receipts with the Cash Book, but includes the examination of a business together with documentary and other evidence of sufficient validity to satisfy an auditor that such transaction is in order, has been properly authorised, and is correctly recorded in the books. By this means the auditor goes behind the books of account and traces the entries to their source, and it is this way alone that he can ascertain the full meaning and circumstances of the various transactions. ...The entries in the books show only such information as the book-keeper chooses to disclose, and such information may be purposely or unintentionally contrary to the true fact — therefore, only by examining external evidence can an auditor possibly ascertain the real state of affairs[16].

Further, de Paula emphasized the importance of vouching as distinguished from "routine checking", which was prescribed as checking of bookkeeping details such as castings and postings, and as a mechanical work that took up the majority of audit times (actually, articled clerks engaged in this part of the work)[17]. This is reflected in a detailed explanation of vouching. The first edition (1914) of his textbook has 29 pages about vouching, compared to only 7 about routine checking. Even in the eighth edition (1936), it remains almost unchanged, and the same trend is demonstrated to some extent in Spicer and Pegler's and other audit textbooks as well.

8-3. Conception of "Verification of Assets"

(1) Verification of assets

The balance sheet, as is known today, was regarded at these days as more than a detailed statement of ledger accounts which is the culmination of the double-entry system of bookkeeping, and indicating the composition of corporate capital, which is highly important to shareholders as a means to determining the distribu-

---

[16] de Paula [1914], p. 29.
[17] de Paula [1914], p. 8, p. 22.

table profits[18]. When verifying such a balance sheet, merely checking arithmetical details or simply examining the vouchers will not allow an audit to attain its objective thus necessitating some kind of verificatory procedure. Such a concept not only sheds light on how the balance sheet reflects all the recorded facts, but it especially points to whether truthful data is indicated at the balance sheet date[19]. What became necessary were the procedures for verifying physicality of the assets and liabilities.

It is not clear when such kind of procedure began to be employed in verifying the balance sheet. A. C. Littleton, surveying audit procedures in the 1880s based on several addresses delivered before student societies and published in professional periodicals during that decade, concludes that even at that time some verificatory procedures for balance sheet items were already in use, with the reservation that "audit technique was weaker at this point than in the examination of bookkeeping details[20]".

Dicksee's *Auditing* barely refers to the verification of assets in its part of "(Auditing) From Trial Balance to Balance Sheet", which follows "Auditing up to the Trial Balance" in the entire audit process. Dicksee explains there that, when checking bookkeeper's work of drawing up the balance sheet from the trial balance, the auditor's attention should be devoted to the basis of asset valuation. After giving general consideration on the subject of asset valuation, he enumerates under the heading "Verifying Existence of Assets" evidential materials available for verifying existence of particular assets[21]. The significance of recommending the substantiation of the existence of assets by obtaining the enumerated materials when verifying assets was articulated in a little over one

---

[18] Littleton [1933], p. 309.
[19] Littleton [1933], p. 309.
[20] Littleton [1933], p. 312.
[21] The text of his explanation reads in part: "The evidence necessary in each class of assets would be as follows: LAND AND BUILDINGS: The Title-Deeds of the property. STOCK-IN-TRADE: The original Stock Sheets, signed by the stock-taker, calculator, checker, and manager. Most accountants would, in addition, consider it essential that the extensions and additions be re-checked by one of their own staff. ..." (Dicksee [1892], p.122). The enumerated asset items are, in addition to above two items, "Investments in Stocks and Shares", "Book Debts", "Plant, Machinery, Fixtures, etc.", "Bank Balance", "Bills Receivable", "Cash in Hand", and "Work in Progress". This explanation format stays the same in later editions and continues untouched all the way to the fifteenth edition published in 1933.

page in length in the textbook's first edition (1892) (however, depreciation of fixed assets and provision for bad debts are discussed elsewhere in his textbook). Thus, we can see that Dicksee was rather pessimistic with regard to auditor's verification of assets in his first edition.

However, from the mid-1890s onward, an auditor's views on asset verification became changing gradually as the case laws concerning the extent of auditor's certification were developing. These cases focused on the need for auditor to perform proper verificatory procedures under particular circumstances[22]. More generally, in the *London Oil Storage Company, Limited* case (1904), in which discussed regarding the counting of petty cash, it was held that it was the duty of auditor to take proper steps to verify the existence of assets stated in the balance sheet.

In such circumstance, E. E. Spicer and E. C. Pegler's *Practical Auditing* in 1911 gives one independent chapter for the verification of assets (Chapter 5), which starts with as follows:

The most important duty of the Auditor...is verification of the assets appearing in the Balance Sheet. If the transactions have been correctly recorded in the books, evidence will appear therein of all the assets that have been acquired in the course of business; but it is not sufficient for the Auditor to verify the correctness of the Balance Sheet as shown by the books — he must go further, and verify, by actual inspection or otherwise, the existence of the assets. The fact that there is an entry in the books recording the asset does not prove that the asset itself exists, *even though the Auditor may have vouched the accuracy of the entry. ...*[23].

In this explanation, it is emphasized that even if a transaction is accurately recorded, the related assets will not necessarily exist at the balance sheet date. Even if vouching has been appropriately conducted, it is not sufficient enough for auditor to satisfy himself as to the existence of assets, and therefore a different kind of procedure from routine checking and vouching is needed just for

---

[22] Chandler *et al.* [1993], p. 454. The verificatory procedures which the courts considered as reasonable for auditors to perform included the examination of the bank pass book (1897), the examination of outstanding invoices (1900), the counting of petty cash (1904), the examination of bad debts provision (1920), the examination of investment securities (1924) and the examination of stock records (1932).

[23] Spicer and Pegler [1911], p.159. Italics added.

asset verification. Actually, Spicer and Pegler dwelt on specific audit procedures for 12 asset items from "Land and Buildings" to "Copyrights" in 23 pages[24].

de Paula's *Principles of Auditing* (1914) also systematically discusses the subject of asset valuation and verification in one chapter (Chapter 5)[25]. He, on the same basis as Spicer and Pegler, stresses that auditor should satisfy himself that assets are actually in the possession of the company at the date of the balance sheet[26]. Further, in another textbook authored by young A. E. Cutforth, although no mention being made of such verification concept, audit procedures with regard to balance sheet items are described in an integrated format, and some of physical checks of assets included here from the first edition (1908)[27]. Meanwhile, Dicksee's *Auditing* explains the verification of existence of assets in just over one page in its first edition (1892), but 11 pages in the ninth edition (1912) and up to 15 pages in the fifteenth edition (1933)[28].

(2) Auditor's responsibilities with regard to asset values

As to how auditors responded to asset values in balance sheets, Pixley's audit textbook offers fragmentary details[29]. The examination of the value or amount of assets seems to have been recognized as included in the scope of the auditor's work, but it is not clear whether these procedures were demanded in terms of asset verification under the foregoing concept.

Dicksee's *Auditing* states in connection with the matter of secret reserves: "... it is very undesirable that valuable assets should be omitted from the Balance Sheet *in toto*, because in such a case the Auditor is very liable to omit to verify their existence[30]". The involvement of the auditor here is not completely negated.

---

[24] Spicer and Pegler [1911], pp. 162–184. As a matter of convenience, their explanation for verification of "Cash in Hand and at Bank" is included in a deferent chapter.

[25] de Paula [1914], pp. 75–103.

[26] de Paula [1914], pp. 75–76.

[27] Cutforth [1908], pp. 9–20.

[28] Dicksee's audit textbook differs from those of Spicer and Pegler's and de Paula's in that it does not contain a specific chapter that lays forth a system for asset verification. One reason is that, as indicated by Chandler *et al.*, even if there were multiple editions, the formulations from the first edition of his audit textbook could not be easily changed (Chandler *et al.* [1993], p. 453).

[29] Pixley [1881], p. 126, p. 141.

However in its first edition, there were no specific details on the involvement of auditor with respect to asset values, in the context of asset verification. Subsequently, from the fifth edition (1902), which reflected legal decisions concerning the responsibilities of auditors such as the *London and General Bank* case (1895) and the *Kingston Cotton Mill* case (1896), just before the aforementioned section of "Verifying Existence of Assets", was inserted a section entitled "Responsibility for Values", which summarizes:

> a much-debated point is the extent of responsibility incurred by the Auditor in relation to the values set upon the assets of a company in the published accounts of the directors. The opinion arrived at in the Court of Appeal in the London and General Bank case upon this most important point appears to be that the Auditor incurs no responsibility whatever so long as, after exercising reasonable care and diligence, he has honestly arrived at the opinion that the accounts are correct[31].

He stresses here that while it has already been required in case law for auditor to employ certain procedures for verifying the existence of asset, auditor's responsibilities with respect to accounting values in this case are severely limited. It is interesting to note that after Dicksee's death, his successor, S.W. Rowland, completely deleted this section in the fifteenth edition (1933).

Quite contrastingly, Spicer and Pegler's *Practical Auditing* (1911) recommend more proactive involvement of auditors with respect to asset values, on the grounds that the improper inflation of assets values is, as well as the fictitious book entry of non-existent assets, assumed as a form of fraud, which the verification of assets serves to guard against, thus asserting that "The verification of assets...should include not only the verification of the existence of the asset, but also of the value at which it appears in the books, as far as it is possible for the Auditor to satisfy himself of this[32]".

However, the items to which Spicer and Pegler actually referred as subject to verification of values were only "Investments" and "Stock-in-trade". In addition to presenting investment accounts at the acquisition cost or under, they explained: "brokers' bought notes will be sufficient evidence of the price paid. The necessity or advisability of providing for depreciation can only be considered in

---

[30] Dicksee [1892], p. 137.
[31] Dicksee [1902], p. 184.
[32] Spicer and Pegler [1911], p. 161.

relation to the present value of the Investments...[33]". Regarding stock-in-trade, as they put it, "[the Auditor] is not a valuer, and the technical knowledge of the trade concerned, which he may or may not possess, will not as a rule be sufficient to enable him to for an opinion as to the correct valuation of the stock. He is usually unable, therefore, to verify the existence of this asset, either by reference to the financial books or by actual inspection, and he cannot assure himself of *the accuracy of its value* by the methods which are available in the case of other assets, such as Investments[34]". Whereas the authors contended that the verification of values must be included in the scope of an audit when discussing for all assets generally, they acknowledged that the verification of inventory values is forced to be limited exceptionally.

Meanwhile, de Paula discussed this issue without necessarily associating it with asset verification itself. Regarding the stance of auditors with respect to valuation of assets in general, he stated that "the actual valuations are made by the proprietors or officials of the concern, who have a special knowledge of such assets, and that an auditor's duty is confined to testing the valuations as far as he can...[35]" stressing that an auditor is not a valuer but a reviewer of values determined by the client company. Accordingly, the main duties of auditors in the verification of inventory values are to verify merely whether "the valuations appear to be fair and reasonable", i.e. whether the valuation principles actually employed are rational, and whether the elements applied under these principles, namely cost, market price, etc., are appropriate.

Between Spicer and Pegler and de Paula, there are great discrepancies in the way in which auditors are to deal with asset values, but there are little variances in the procedures necessary for actual inventory verification as they both agree as to the inherent difficulty of verifying the value aspect of stock-in-trade, based on the assumption that an auditor is not tasked with determining inventory values. While Spicer and Pegler, considering all assets, see the setting of some limitations on the verification of inventory assets as an exception, de Paula sees the existence of such restrictions as applicable generally to all asset verification. However, despite these discrepancies in opinion on some

---

[33] Spicer and Pegler [1911], p. 168.
[34] Spicer and Pegler [1911], pp. 169–170. Italics added.
[35] de Paula [1914], p. 75.

fundamentals, they do supposedly concur in the need for auditors to verify both the existence of assets and their value.

More broadly, we can see that the newly developed verification concept, which embraces not only verification of the existence of assets but also their value, became accepted by the 1930s. The following is stated in Taylor and Perry's (1932) textbook, which was a well-known guide to accounting students during the 1930s:

...the substantiation of an entry under the date on which it is made does not prove the existence of the related asset or liability at the date of the Balance Sheet, nor is the value or amount of such asset or liability necessarily the same as on the date of the original entry. The Auditor has the further duty of substantiating the *existence and value of such items as at the date of the Balance Sheet*, and this work is known as "verification." ...This work must be distinguished from vouching...[36]

In the context of audit methodology, the issue here is, on the whole, whether to prioritize continuous accounting records reflecting the transactions occurred during the period or physical existence of the assets and liabilities at the end of the period. We can conclude properly that the British auditors came to put far more emphasis on the verification of assets and liabilities than before. Yet on the other hand, we also acknowledge that during the same period the British auditors were still rather reluctant to assume the responsibility for asset values, especially of stock-in-trade.

Derek Matthews draws his conclusion that no enough audit resource was devoted for asset verification at that time, from the space for description of Dicksee's work in its 1904 edition with its 205 pages of examination of bookkeeping details and 55 pages of verification of assets such as stock or plant and machinery, etc. (in the 1969 edition, the ratio was still 128 pages vs. 33 pages, respectively)[37]. He also emphasizes that many, but not all, British auditors drew up the client's accounts prior to conducting the audit at that time[38]. Indeed, one leading accountant, the then President of the Institute of Chartered Accountants in England and Wales, regarding his experiences around the First World War period, recalled: "an audit consisted of 80 per cent. checking everything possible, and 20 per

---

[36] Taylor and Perry [1932] p. 77. Italics added.
[37] Matthews [2006], p. 26.
[38] Matthews [2006], pp. 11–22.

cent. preparing the final accounts. ...Balanced books were the exception rather than rules. Thus the audit started with the knowledge that the books were more than likely to be out of balance[39]". This is one reason why the circumstances at that time still necessitated the application of audit time to checking of the book of accounts. Further, Matthews argues that, as late as the 1930s (even in the 1960s!), this trend still lingered[40]. If this is so, then we can suppose that in Britain at that time it would have been somewhat difficult to spare any audit time for asset verification so that more effective techniques for that purpose cannot readily be developed.

8-4. American Balance Sheet Audit and Verification of Assets therein

(1) The emergence of the "balance sheet audit"

The development of the American auditing in its early years was largely contributed by British chartered accountants who settled there on behalf of British clients in the late 1880s and the 1890s. Therefore, the first American audits were modeled after British general audits[41]. However, in the first decade after the turn of the century, the American auditing progressed immensely fitting with peculiar American environments. American accountants began to emphasize the verification of assets and liabilities in the balance sheet accordingly. This is amply illustrated by Arthur Lowes Dickinson, an English accountant practicing in the US market for many years, who stated in a speech in 1902 before American audience that:

> the most important feature of the independent audit of the accounts of a corporation, large or small, is the verification of the assets and liabilities in the Balance Sheet, the determination of proper and adequate rates of depreciation, and of proper reserves for bad and doubtful debts. ...the auditor is able...by a comparison of prices in the inventory with current market quotations, ...in many case by actual test of quantities remaining on hand as compared with quantities purchased and sold, to satisfy

---

[39] Mosley-Roberts [1937], p. 416.
[40] Matthews [2006], pp. 21-22.
[41] Moyer [1951], p. 3.

himself whether the valuations both of book debts and of inventories are fair and reasonable[42].

In a similar vein, Walter A. Staub noted in a prize-winning essay at the First International Congress of Accountants held in St. Louis in 1904:

A balance sheet is a statement of assets and liabilities as of a given date, hence an audit of it will embrace, (a) the verification of the existence of the assets, ascertaining whether any have been omitted, and, as far as it lies within the province of the auditor, judging their values, or at least determining the bona fides and the methods of derivation of those items whose statements of value are open to question; (b) the verification of existence and amount of the liabilities ...[43]

Probably the determinant factor for attracting more attention to verification of assets and liabilities was urgent need from the bankers, which had very close interests in the auditor's certificates regarding the balance sheet for credit purpose.

Further, *The American Business Manual* published in 1911, in its chapter entitled "Auditing," mentions that there were two alternative approaches to be adopted in proving the balance sheet: "an audit directed principally to transactions prior to and leading up to a balance-sheet[44]" and "an audit which very largely takes for granted the integrity of the current operations and in which the chief interest devolves upon the assets and liabilities[45]". The latter was called the "balance-sheet audit". The distinct feature of the balance sheet audit is that it is not an audit approach that tracks the entries of books and ledgers back to the original transactions but rather an audit approach that devotes audit resources mainly to the verification of assets and liabilities in the balance sheet, without focusing on the accuracy of bookkeeping details to be ascertained through comparison between the figures in the books or ledgers.

The writer of this part, Robert H. Montgomery further elaborated on the principles of balance sheet audits and provided the audit program thereupon, in his own textbook entitled *Auditing: Theory and Practice* (the first edition of which was published in 1912).

---

[42] Dickinson [1902], p. 747.
[43] Staub [1904], p. 233.
[44] Montgomery [1911], p. 353.
[45] Montgomery [1911], p. 353.

According to his explanations, the balance sheet audit is to be made alternatively to the "detailed audit", another approach mentioned above[46]. Specifically, when conducting a balance sheet audit, he explained, "if the auditor has satisfied himself that the system of internal check *is* adequate, he will not attempt to duplicate work which has been properly performed by some one else. His duty will then be to verify the assets and liabilities, and to make such an analysis of the Profit and Loss Account as will enable him to certify that it has been properly stated[47]".

Before Montgomery's *Auditing* was published, American accounting literatures on this subject merely had introduced the British traditional audit methods[48]. However, after its publication, the other author's textbooks as well as Montgomery's endorsed not the traditional British structure of transaction-based examination, but rather prioritized such procedures as focusing attention on the balance sheet[49]. So both the term and concept of the "balance sheet audit" would have become gradually accepted in the other author's audit textbooks, while whether the description of Montgomery's truly reflected or was ahead of current practices is still unknown.

Naturally, the audit methods explained in American audit literatures stress even more the need for verificatory procedures of balance sheet items, especially of assets items. As mentioned above, British audit textbooks, as late as the 1930s and beyond, still had many pages dedicated to the explanations of the archaic procedures of routine checking and vouching, which were diminishing in American counterparts. In the sixth edition (1933) of de Paula's work, there remain 36 pages on routine checking and vouching, and 36 on verificatory procedures of balance sheet items.

---

[46] Montgomery [1912], p. 80.

[47] Montgomery [1912], p. 82. Italics in original.

[48] Audit literatures published in the 1900s prior to Montgomery's *Auditing* include, in addition to American editions of Dicksee's *Auditing* (1905, 1909), which Montgomery himself edited, *The Science and Practice of Auditing* (edited by E. H. Beach and W. W. Thorne; 1903), *Renn's Practical Auditing: A Working Manual for Auditors* (authored by George B. Renn; 1905, 1907, 1909) and so on. For details on American audit literatures of the 1880s and 1890s, see Moyer [1951].

[49] For example, Eric L. Kohler and Paul W. Pettengill's *Principles of Auditing* (1924), William H. Bell's *Auditing* (1924), and William B. Castenholz's *Auditing Procedure* (1925) prioritize the verification of balance sheet items in the composition of their textbooks.

Spicer and Pegler's seventh edition (1936) also has the same procedures explained over 78 pages and 28 pages, respectively. In contrast, the American Kohler and Pettengill's textbook (1924) has routine checking and vouching described along with other basic auditing methods in 12 pages, with 64 pages devoted to verificatory procedures. Similarly, Bell's *Auditing* (1924) has 48 on the former and 75 on the latter. It may not be reasonable to understand the degree of importance placed on those items solely within those pages of explanation, but we can assume that more man-hours would have been devoted to asset verification in the audit program for the items subjected to more detailed procedures. So we shall argue, in the American-style balance sheet audits, there would have been more audit work done with respect to verificatory procedures than in the traditional British audits.

(2) Verification of assets in the balance sheet audit

In the balance sheet audit, unlike the traditional British audits, much more emphasis was placed on the verification of assets and liabilities. Montgomery, prior to discussing in detail specific procedures for each asset item, noted first of all that "an entry on the books which purports to record an asset is *nothing more* than a *book* record, and there can be no good excuse for accepting such entry as final. The data supporting the entry may be in order, but it is the auditor's duty to *verify independently*, as far as possible, the fact that the asset still exists, or did exist at the date of the balance sheet[50]". In as such, he stressed an *independent* verification of the existence of assets in general[51].

The problem here is how the verification of asset values at the date of balance sheet is demanded in Montgomery's textbook. In Montgomery' *Auditing* there is no description generally dealing with the auditor's involvement of with respect to asset values but only indicating how auditors should respond to asset values within

---

[50] Montgomery [1912], p. 88. Italics in original.

[51] Montgomery prescribed as one of the principles of balance sheet audits: "(1) The auditor must ascertain that all of the assets shown by the books to have been on hand at a certain date were actually on hand" (Montgomery [1912], p. 87), an important point in auditing as to whether assets actually exist. Meanwhile, regarding the verification of liabilities, he stated that "in a balance-sheet audit nothing is more important than to ascertain whether or not all the liabilities of any nature whatsoever appear and are properly stated" (Montgomery [1912], p. 148), stressing the verification of the *completeness* of liabilities.

the explanations of audit procedures for each asset. Thus purposefully choosing inventory item among all asset items, we examine what sort of verification was required for auditors with regard to the value of inventory in Montgomery's textbook from his explanations of audit procedures for that item.

According to Montgomery, the basis of inventory valuation should be "cost *or* market, whichever is the lower", the safest rule that would never result in the deceit of "the banker, creditor, and stockholder, who have a right to believe that the values stated are real values as of the date of the balance sheet[52]". Here, he suggested that auditors were to verify values accepting as a basis of valuation the lower of cost or market rule[53].

More significantly Montgomery asserted to distance himself from traditional British auditors, "those who maintain that an auditor, *not* being a valuer, has no right to attempt to pass upon physical valuations, including stock-in-trade and plant[54]", thus stressing that an auditor's duty is not properly performed unless he does all that his experience and skill enable him to do. In addition, he pointed out that "the physical condition and salability of the stock must also be considered[55]" and specifically that "if there is deterioration or if part of the stock is out of date, or otherwise unsalable, the asset loses its most important aspect, availability. ... [the auditor] must depend upon his own intuition and inquiries to determine whether or not the stock is in good condition or merchantable ...[56, 57]". The explicit requirement for the verification of the quality and current status of physical inventories

---

[52] Montgomery [1912], p. 104.

[53] Regarding this point, there is almost no discrepancy with other authors of his time. For example, Kohler and Pettengill's *Principles of Auditing* also explains that, assuming that the generally accepted inventory valuation standard is lower of cost or market, "purchase invoices furnish data as to cost while market quotations can be obtained from trade journals. Market price is generally accepted as the average bid price current at the date of the inventory. ...In referring to market prices consideration should be given to the question of quantity discounts if allowed; ...The question of what cost to use when checking the prices of materials which have been purchased over the past years is usually decided by taking the cost shown by the most recent invoice, ..." (Kohler and Pettengill [1924], p. 79).

[54] Montgomery [1912], p. 106.

[55] Montgomery [1912], p. 104.

[56] Montgomery [1912], pp. 104-105.

[57] Specific audit procedures provided by Montgomery in his rules for the verification

was departure from the traditional British practices. These features such as quality and current status are incidental to physicality of assets, thus for auditors to pay attention to such features has had a significant meaning to the verification itself.

The greater concerns directed to the valuation of inventories relates to the economic conditions existing in the United States at that time. The market turmoil of 1920 brought commodity prices crashing down, and thereby led to widely broadened discussions as to the basis of inventory valuation. In the preface to the third edition (1921), responding to such a crisis, Montgomery asserted: "when values fluctuate widely, ...balance sheets do not reflect the "full and true financial position" which is the goal of the auditor. ...If auditors in their discretion fail to write values up in an advancing market, why does not sound judgment dictate that in a period of steady declining prices, value shall be *written down below* apparent market at date of balance sheet?[58]" He apparently recommeded more positive auditor's involvement regarding the values.

Some accounting firms would have changed their inventory auditing procedures when faced with tumbling commodity prices of 1920. For example, one commissioned work on the history of Price, Waterhouse & Co. tells that "With the fall of commodity prices in 1920 the firm [i.e. Price, Waterhouse & Co.] considered it prudent to enlarge the contents of letters to be obtained from clients relative to inventories to include more specific statements regarding market and realizable values of merchandise, commitments and possible rebates to be allowed on goods held by customers[59]". This suggests that the fall in commodity prices would have had a significant impact on the way in which inventory values were verified.

---

of inventories include the following item relating to the quality and status of inventory as stock: "12. ...apply the knowledge so acquired to answering the following questions: (a) Is any of the stock damaged, depreciated in quality, or have the styles or shapes changed? (b) Is any of the stock obsolete, out of date, of a size or quality no longer used?" (Montgomery [1912], p. 109).

[58] Montgomery [1921], pp. iv-v. Italics added.

[59] DeMond [1951], p.267. "Prior to 1910", this author also writes, "the usual procedures of the firm was to obtain a letter signed by responsible officials in which general statements were embodied that the inventories had been taken by physical count, weight or measurement, that there was no obsolete or unsalable stock included therein" (*Ibid.*).

While this was a time of fervent debate as to the proper basis for the valuation of inventories, it cannot be ignored that the concept of tasking auditors with respect to asset values at a certain date has been established during this period. This tendency was evident in the definition of the balance sheet audit by one contemporary contributor of *The Journal of Accountancy* (1922), who prescribed that "the object of balance-sheet audit is to verify by satisfactory evidence the existence, possession and ownership of all assets and the values at which they are shown in balance-sheet and to ensure the disclosure thereon of all liabilities — all as at a particular moment of time[60]". In William H. Bell's *Auditing* (1924), he claimed that "there can be no doubt that the verification of inventory valuations is generally regarded as comprehended in the scope of an audit, and it is an indispensable part of an audit; neither is there any doubt that the professional auditor should be eminently qualified to pass upon such valuations[61]". This is the same concept as Montgomery's whereby professional auditor is able to make judgments on physical valuations of inventories even though not being a valuer, and therefore this further underscores the notion that, the auditor should do all that his training and experience qualifies him to do in satisfying himself that inventory is fairly valued. More specifically, Bell continued that "the verification of valuations seldom requires that all prices be investigated, but tests should usually be made covering at least one-quarter to one-third of the total amount of the inventory[62]" thus instructing the auditors to allocate adequate audit time for this task.

(3) Verification of quantities

Another important feature of the American audit literatures, which became apparent from the 1920s, is that these commonly used a unique category for discussion entitled "verification of inventory quantities". As Bell put it in the context of the extended auditor's responsibility:

the verification of the quantitative feature of inventories is not generally regarded as comprehended in the scope of an audit. The basis for this common understanding appears to be the

---

[60] Buist [1922], p. 182.
[61] Bell [1924], p. 157.
[62] Bell [1924], p. 157.

notion that professional auditors are not qualified or equipped to do that kind of work. In many, if not most, cases this belief is utterly fallacious. It is admitted that...an auditor...is seldom qualified to take an inventory independently of the persons familiar with the stocks; but there is a distinct difference between such independent action and *the procedure necessary to enable the auditor to satisfy himself regarding the quantities so that he may certify to the inventories without reservation*[63]. Regarding the latter procedure above, he insisted that "in order to be in a position to certify to the quantitative feature of an inventory it is necessary only that the auditor supervise the counting, weighing, or measuring of a considerable part of the stock as represented in the values[64]", thus explaining the particular procedures regarding inventory quantities. However, at the very least, most of the procedures mentioned were merely the methods which made use of the quantities presented on the inventory sheet or the perpetual inventory record prepared within the client company.

In Kohler and Pettengill's *Principles of Auditing*, there is also an explanation on inventories stating "a simple expedient on the part of the executives of a company who desire to make paper profits is to twist either the quantities or pricing of the inventories to suit their needs[65]" dividing inventory verification into quantities, pricing, clerical accuracy. In addition, as with Bell, it describes verification procedures for inventory quantities stating "sometimes it is possible and advisable for the auditor to make a test-check of quantities by having a count made under his supervision at the time of the audit. This count can be compared with the stock records, if any, ...[66]".

Such categorization was succeeded even by the audit guidance for the practices before federal agencies such as the Federal Reserve Board and the Federal Trade Commission. The first version of such bulletins, *Uniform Accounting* in 1916 did not explicitly employ that category, but in the Federal Reserve Bulletin of *Verification of Financial Statements* published in 1929 by the American Institute of Accountants, auditor responsibilities regarding inventories are stipulated in three areas, namely "Clerical

---

[63] Bell [1924], pp. 152–153. Italics added.
[64] Bell [1924], p. 153.
[65] Kohler and Pettengill [1924], p. 75.
[66] Kohler and Pettengill [1924], p. 77.

accuracy of computations, footings, and recapitulations", "Basis of pricing" and "Quantities, quality, and condition[67]". The above distinguishes, with respect to inventories, the verification of values in the form of looking at the prices used for the inventory purpose or the balance sheet purpose by the client company and, separately, the verification of quantities. This may be understood only as dividing inventory values presented in the balance sheet into quantities and prices, and making them subject to separate verification, however, such style of reasoning can also be interpreted as reflecting the peculiar audit concepts abound in American auditing.

Now turning back to Montgomery, we examine how his *Auditing* dealt with the methods of verifying inventories in later editions. After the recession from 1920 to 1921, America benefited from an economic boom from 1922 to 1929. The third edition (1921) was written in a time of economic recession, and thus Montgomery must have considered the problem arising from violent inventory fluctuations as getting ignorable during that period[68]. Even then, however, the subject of verification of inventory quantities was still controversial within the profession. For example, in the fourth edition (1927), he argued that:

> it is urged by some accountants that the verification of quantities is not generally regarded as included in the scope of an audit, that the public should assume that at present, even though there is no qualification, it is implied that the verification has covered values only. The author [i. e. Montgomery] does not agree with this view. Unless there is a distinct qualification, the public has a right to assume that the auditor has satisfied himself with regard to values and that whatever method he may have adopted to assure himself of the correctness of the quantities, he has found nothing which leads him to question them[69].

In his opinion, professional auditor *should* verify not only the values of inventories but also their quantities, as far as possible.

---

[67] AIA [1929], pp. 7–11. Incidentally, regarding "Basis of pricing", it is stipulated that "He [the auditor] must undertake sufficient investigation of the inventories to satisfy himself...that the goods are valued in accordance with the usual commercial practice — that is, at cost or market price, whichever is lower" (AIA [1929], pp. 7–8).

[68] This resulted in the deletion in the fourth edition of a large portion of the text detailing inventory valuation basis added in the third edition.

[69] Montgomery [1927], p. 143.

Based on this understanding, Montgomery listed specific audit procedures to verify quantities of inventory at the end of period. Inventory verification procedures in the third and fourth editions are revised and expanded, but most notable is the subtle and incremental inclusion of audit procedures particularly based on the important standpoint of "physical tests" that would bring auditors into physical contact with inventories. The emphasis on inventory quantity verification resulted in more explicit requirement for auditors to get into physical contact with inventory stock.

Furthermore, in the fifth edition (1934), the verification of values is explained as "the determination of the amount at which the inventory shall be stated on a balance sheet involves not only a verification of the prices used in its determination, but also consideration of whether such prices are suitable for use in a given balance sheet[70]" whereby the verification of values only through a superficial comparison between price used in inventory valuation and market value became stressed as insufficient. It is interesting to note that verification in this light had a complementary role so as to allow for a more thorough verification of values.

8-5. Conclusion

The purpose of this research was to provide an overview of the development of audit methods and methodologies for verifying the value or amount of assets. The research intended to examine whether there occurred any methodological changes in the structure of the verification activities in the course of this development and, if any, to identify them. In conclusion, this historical review of verification methods shows that the transaction-based examination as represented by routine checking and vouching, which developed in the late nineteenth and early twentieth century was less worthy in terms of verifying physical existence and value, and cannot function as an effectual means of substantiating the assets in existence at a definite date. However, it is also evident that the verification of the values of assets cannot attain its intrinsic aim, unless the fundamental viewpoint of the verification activities is placed on such an aspect of the assets as a sort of physical things.

---

[70] Montgomery [1934], p. 202.

The UK and the US differed circumstantially in terms of basic audit environments, and therefore British and American auditors have adopted the verification methods for asset values in a different way. The greatest deterrent to such developments would have been the auditor's passive mentality based on the traditional notion that an auditor is not entitled or equipped to pass upon physical valuations of assets such as inventories due to lack of necessary qualifications. However, it is a fact that, in either country, at a certain level, it was gradually recognized the verification of asset should include not only verification of the existence of assets, that is, whether related assets actually did exist *at the balance sheet date*, but also the values of assets, that is, whether the amount actually reflected *the values thereof at the balance sheet date*. At whatever level this verification was effected, in theory, any auditor will not be able to make professional judgment on asset values without properly conducting physical examination of the assets. From this perspective, especially in the case of audits of inventory, the process by which physical tests became generally accepted and ordinarily used by auditors was very crucial in the course of the historical development of professional auditing not only in terms of audit techniques but also in conceptual terms.

[References in English]

American Institute of Accountants [1929], *Verification of Financial Statements*, Washington.

Bell, William H. [1924], *Auditing*, New York.

British Parliamentary Papers [1849], *House of Lords Select Committee on the Audit of Railway Accounts*, First and Second Reports and Minutes of Evidence, x, 1. Third Report and Minutes of Evidence, x, 469.

Buist, George B. [1922], "Purposes and Limitations of Balance-sheet Audits", *The Journal of Accountancy*, Vol. 34, No. 3, September 1922.

Chandler, Roy A. [1997], "Judicial Views on Auditing from the Nineteenth Century", *Accounting History (NS)*, Vol. 2, No. 1.

Chandler, Roy A., John Richard Edwards and Malcolm Anderson [1993], "Changing Perceptions of the Role of the Company Auditor, 1840-1940", *Accounting and Business Research*, Vol. 23, No. 92.

Chatfield, Michael [1977], *A History of Accounting Thought*, revised edition, New York.

Cutforth, Arthur E. [1908], *Audits*, London.

DeMond, C. W. [1951], *Price, Waterhouse & Co. in America: a history of a Public Accounting Firm*, New York.

de Paula, Frederic R. M. [1914], *The Principles of Auditing: A Practical Manual for Students and Practitioners*, London.

Dickinson, Arthur L. [1902], "The Duties and Responsibilities of the Public Accountant", *The Accountant*, 26 July 1902.
Dicksee, Lawrence R. [1892], *Auditing: A Practical Manual for Auditors*, London.
────── [1902], *Auditing: A Practical Manual for Auditors*, 5th edition, London.
Kohler, E. L. and P. W. Pettengill [1924], *Principles of Auditing*, Chicago & New York.
Littleton, A. C. [1933], *Accounting Evolution to 1900*, New York.
Matthews, Derek [2006], *A History of Auditing: The Changing Audit Process in Britain From the Nineteenth Century to the Present Day*, London & New York.
Montgomery, Robert H. [1911], "Auditing", in Edward M. Carney *et al.*, *The American Business Manual Vol. III: Administration*, New York.
────── [1912], *Auditing: Theory and Practice*, New York.
────── [1921], *Auditing: Theory and Practice*, 3rd edition, New York.
────── [1927], *Auditing: Theory and Practice*, 4th edition, New York.
────── [1934], *Auditing: Theory and Practice*, 5th edition, New York.
Mosley-Roberts, A. E. [1937], "Mechanisation and the Auditor", *The Accountant*, 20 March 1937.
Moyer, C. A. [1951], "Early Developments in American Auditing", *The Accounting Review*, Vol. 26, No.1.
Myers, J. H. [1985], "Spiraling Upwards: Auditing Methods as Described by Montgomery and His Successors", *Accounting Historians Journal*, Vol. 12, No. 1.
Power, Michael K. [1992], "From Common Sense to Expertise: Reflections on the Prehistory of Audit Sampling", *Accounting, Organizations and Society*, Vol. 17, No. 1.
Pike, Basil G. [1908], "Vouching in an Audit", *The Accountant*, 20 June 1908.
Pixley, Francis W. [1881], *Auditors: Their Duties and Responsibilities*, London.
────── [1897], *The Profession of a Chartered Accountant*, London.
Spicer, E. E. and E. C. Pegler [1911], *Practical Auditing*, London.
Taylor, E. Miles and Charles E. Perry [1932], *Principles of Auditing with one hundred questions and answers*, 5th edition, London.
Staub, Walter A. [1904], "Mode of Conducting an Audit", paper presented at the First International Congress of Accountants in St. Louis, reproduced in *The Accounting Review*, Vol. 18, No. 2.

Chapter 9

Classical Inflation Accounting and Fair Value Measurement

Hideki Kubota
Konan University

Abstract

In this Chapter the accounting for changing prices for which experiments for systematization were conducted from the 1970s to the 1980s after being developed up to the 1960s in the US is referred to as "classical inflation accounting". Up to the 1960s, the history of classical inflation accounting theories was so important that it could be referred to as the history of American accounting theories in themselves. In the 1970s, classical inflation accounting developed by precedence of idea gave way to systematization of classical inflation accounting by the FASB. However, subsequently when in the 1980s inflation drew to an end, this experiment was ceased.

For inflation adjustments in classical inflation accounting, whether adjustment by general price index or adjustment by index specific to the assets, both centrally involved the adjustments of historical data. Contrastingly, for the fair value measurement of financial instruments, it is not by the adjustment of historical data but by the methods for valuation that appropriately reflect the pricing on market. Consequentially, the fair value measurement of financial instruments is very different from the adjustment of historical data in classical inflation accounting which was developed by precedence of idea.

First, this Chapter provides summary of the history of classical inflation accounting and the experiments for systematization of classical inflation accounting, and new financial instruments project in the US. Next, it provides an overview of the accounting modernization process in Japan after WWII focused on valuation of assets and it considers how the valuation at current price and fair value measurement have been accepted in accounting based on the Securities Exchange Law. Lastly, it shows that in *"the Exposure Draft of Accounting Standard for Fair Value Measurement and its Disclosure"* published by the Accounting Standards Board of Japan (ASBJ) in July 2010 it was not sufficiently recognized the difference between current price and fair value. For entity specific assumptions as the basis of valuation at current price is decidedly different from market participant assumptions as the basis of fair value measurement.

Keywords
Accounting for financial instruments, entity specific assumptions, fair value, Fair Value View, inflation accounting, market participant assumptions, Stewardship View

9-1. Introduction

In this Chapter the accounting for changing prices for which experiments for systematization were conducted from the 1970s to the 1980s after being developed up to the 1960s in the US is referred to as "classical inflation accounting". In *"A Statement on Accounting Theory and Theory Acceptance"* (AAA [1977]) by American Accounting Association (AAA), Paton [1922], Canning [1929], Sweeney [1936], MacNeal [1939], Edwards / Bell [1961], Moonitz [1961], Sprouse / Moonitz [1962] and others are classified as "true income" theory. "They drew on the teachings of neoclassical economic theory and on their observations of economic behavior to propose that accounting, which had been preoccupied with historical data and conservative measurement, should be restructured to reflect current costs or values" (AAA [1977], p. 6). In other words, their theories defended classical inflation accounting. Up to the 1960s, the history of classical inflation accounting was so important that it could be referred to as the history of American accounting theories in themselves. That means that classical inflation accounting had the characteristic of precedence of idea.

The fair value measurement of financial instruments and other products that became main accounting issues from the 1980s onward differs from classical inflation accounting that was developed to remove the impact of inflation on the distribution of resources. For the shift to the floating rate system and the start of the deregulation of finance followed by an increase in volatility due to the globalization of economies made fair value measurement of financial instruments accounting issues to be dealt with directly.

This Chapter provides summary of the historical background of classical inflation accounting and the experiments for their systematization in the US and shed light on the features of fair value measurement which is different from valuation at current price. In light of the above, this Chapter provides the outline of accounting modernization in Japan centered on the valuation of assets after WW II and the history of acceptance of valuation at current price and fair value measurement in accounting based on the Securities Exchange Law in Japan. Then, it shows that in *"the Exposure Draft of Accounting Standard for Fair Value Measurement and its Disclosure"* published by the Accounting Standards Board of Japan (ASBJ) in July 2010 it was not sufficiently recognized that fair value measurement based on market participant assumptions is decidedly different from valuation at current price based on entity specific assumptions.

9-2. Experiments for Systematization of Classical Inflation Accounting and the New Financial Instruments Project in the US

(1) History of classical inflation accounting in the US

In the US, the need for classical inflation accounting became apparent when the doctrine of Sweeney (Sweeney [1936]) emerged though there were not any actual problem with inflation in the US in the 1920s. For example, Sweeney referred to valuation issues relating to inflation in the 1920s using German case as example. Inflation was not a problem in the US also thereafter either so any attention was not paid to the theory of Sweeney.

As inflation emerged during World War II and in the following years, classical inflation accounting saw a renaissance of interest. However, the Committee on Accounting Procedure (CAP) concluded in Accounting Research Bulletin No. 33 *"Depreciation and High Costs"* (AIA [1947]) that there was no need to change the accounting to reflect the effect of decrease of purchasing power of the money. Subsequently, ARB No.43 *"Restatement and Revision of Accounting Research Bulletins Nos. 1-42"* (AIA [1953]) which was published in 1953 also concluded that no such change would be necessary for accounting.

Prices of commodities in the US increased afterwards and the Accounting Principles Board (APB), the successor of the CAP, concluded at a special meeting held in 1961 that ignoring the fluctuations of the purchasing power of the money was not realistic. In response to this, a special committee on inflation issues led by Moonitz was formed. Then, the need to focus on inflation accounting was emphasized in ARS No. 3 *"A Tentative Set of Broad Accounting Principles for Business Enterprises"* (Sprouse / Moonitz [1962]). In 1963, the recognition of the impact of the change of purchasing power of the money was reemphasized in ARS No. 6 *"Reporting the Effects of Price Level Changes"* (AICPA [1963]). According to this, an adjustment by price index in the financial statements would have made financial statements more accurate and useful for users.

Then the classical inflation accounting is characterized by precedence of idea went on systematization. After oil crisis in 1973, the inflation rate in the US rose to 10.89% (calculated based on the consumer price index in the economic indicators of the OECD). This continuous and rapid advance of inflation led to a sudden burst of interest in accounting for changing prices. Systematization of classical inflation accounting was advocated by the Financial Accounting Standards Board (FASB), which succeeded the role of setting accounting standards from the APB.

The FASB published in February 1974 an essay that dealt with the problems on inflation entitled Discussion Memorandum *"Reporting the Effects of General Price Level Changes in Financial Statements"* (FASB [1974a]). Based on the discussion memorandum and the reactions thereto, the Exposure Draft *"Financial Reporting in Units of General Purchasing Power"* (FASB [1974b]) was published in December of that year. The main conclusion of this exposure draft was that all corporate financial statements must include comprehensive supplemental data based on the unit of general purchasing power of the money. However, this exposure draft did not result in the statement of financial accounting standard.

(2) Experiments for systematization of classical inflation accounting in the US

In March 1976, the Securities and Exchange Commission (SEC) published Accounting Series Release No. 190 *"Notice of Adoption of Amendments to Regulation S-X Requiring Disclosure of Certain Replacement Cost Data"* (SEC [1976]). In the release the SEC required certain publicly held corporations to submit supplemental data based on replacement cost.

The publication of ARS No. 190 by the SEC made the FASB partially postpone its efforts for systematization of inflation accounting. But it followed up in December 1978 with the publication of Exposure Draft *"Financial Reporting and Changing Prices"* (FASB [1978b]), and then Exposure Draft *"Constant Dollar Accounting"* (FASB [1979a]) in March 1979. These exposure drafts proposed the reporting of information about change of general price level, recommended by both of announcements in 1974. Their main discrepancy with the ones published in 1974 is the shift from full correction to partial correction of data and the switch from the GNP deflator to the consumer price index of the all urban consumer (CPI (U)). The work of the FASB resulted in the publication of the Statement of Financial Standards (SFAS) No. 33 *"Financial Reporting and Changing Prices"* (FASB [1979b]) in September 1979. This required certain large corporations to disclose both information adjusted by general price index and information adjusted by specific price index.

In November 1984, five years later from the publication of SFAS No. 33, SFAS No. 82 *"Financial Reporting and Changing Prices: Elimination of Certain Disclosures"* (FASB [1984a]) was published. This did not require companies which disclosed information adjusted by specific price index to disclose information about general purchasing power of the money. In December 1984, Exposure Draft *"Financial Reporting and Changing Prices: Current Cost Information"* (FASB [1984b]) was published. It arranged and integrated all statements of financial accounting standards regarding the heretofore published financial reporting and changing prices with the intention of finalizing the disclosure of information adjusted by price index. However, because the general response was not favorable, this did not lead to the statement of financial accounting standard.

Subsequently, although a new project began with the goal of disclosing the more effective and useful information adjusted by price index, the inflation rate that reached as high as 13.48% in 1980 decreased to 6.15% in 1982 and then again down to 1.9% by 1986 (calculated based on the consumer price index in the main economic indicators of the OECD). Meanwhile, in September 1986 a proposal was made to remove the requirement of disclosing information adjusted by price index in a newly published Exposure Draft *"Financial Reporting and Changing Prices"* (FASB [1986a]), which became later SFAS No. 89 *Financial Reporting and Changing Prices* (FASB [1986b]) which made the disclosure of information adjusted by price index voluntary. As inflation was drawing to an end in the first half of the 1980s, the FASB's experiment on systematization of inflation accounting was in essence halted.

(3) The new financial instruments project and fair value measurement

In the late 1970s when the shift to assets and liabilities view occurred, the problems brought upon by new financial instruments did not directly cause this shift because this was prior to the rapid growth of new financial instruments which occurred in the 1980s. Because in the 1970s accounting of financial assets and liabilities was not the prevalent accounting issues, it was outside the scope of this shift.

The new financial instruments project started in 1986. In 1990, SFAS No. 105 *"Disclosures of Information about Financial Instruments with Off-Balance-Sheet Risk and Financial Instruments with Concentrations of Credit Risk"* (FASB [1990]), and then in 1991, SFAS No. 107 *"Disclosures about Fair Value of Financial Instruments"* (FASB [1991]) were published.

SFAS No.107 states that movements in fair values, and thus in market returns, during the period that a financial asset is held or a financial liability owed provide a benchmark with which to assess the results of manager's decisions and success in maximizing the profitable use of an entity's economic resources and in minimizing financing costs (FASB [1991], para. 44).

In 1993, SFAS No. 115 *"Accounting for Certain Investment in Debt and Equity Securities"* (FASB [1993]) was published, which requires the fair value measurement for all securities held by enterprises other than securities held for ownership until maturity. For securities held for the trading purpose fair value measurement is required, on the other hand for securities held for ownership until maturity valuation at historical costs (including amortized cost method) is required. These mixed cost-fair value approaches established in SFAS No.115 have become the mainstream of accounting rules in developed countries afterwards.

In 1989, the International Accounting Standard Committee (IASC) and the Canadian Institute of Chartered Accountants (CICA) started a joint project to formulate comprehensive standards on the recognition, measurement and disclosure of financial instruments. Then, the IASC published in September 1991 Exposure Draft 40 *"Financial Instruments"* (E40) (IASC [1991]). In response to wide-ranging criticism against it, the IASC published in 1994 Exposure Draft 48 *"Financial Instruments"* (E48) (IASC [1994]). Because this was also met with a strong critical reaction, the management committees of both the IASC and the CICA decided to divide the project into two phases, starting with the publication of IAS No.32 *"Financial Instruments Disclosure and Presentation"* (IASC [1997]) in 1997.

Recognition and measurement of financial instruments was the theme of *"Discussion Paper: Accounting for Financial Assets and Financial Liabilities"* (IASC/CICA [1997]) published by the IASC and the CICA in March 1997. That proposal called for the measurement by enterprises of financial assets and financial liabilities at fair value after initial recognition. Further, in 2001, the Joint Working Group of Standard Setters (JWG) comprising of standards setters and professional bodies from Australia, Canada, France, Germany, Japan, New Zealand, the five Northern European countries, the UK, the US and the IASC published Draft Standard *"Financial Instruments and Similar Items"* (JWG [2001]). The Draft Standard called for the measurement of almost all financial assets and liabilities at fair value.

Then, in September 2006 the FASB published SFAS No. 157 *"Fair Value Measurement"* (FASB [2006]) and, based thereon, the IASB published the Exposure Draft *"Fair Value Measurement"* in May 2009. In addition, IASB and FASB published on May 12, 2011 new guidelines on fair value measurement and disclosure requirements in IFRS and US GAAP. These guidelines appear in IFRS No. 13 *"Fair Value Measurement"* (IASB [2011]) and in the Amendments of FASB's Accounting Standards Codification, Topic 820 (formerly

SFAS No. 157).

9-3. "Entity Specific Assumptions" versus "Market Participant Assumptions"

Discounting of future cash flows in itself is not particular to financial innovation. American economist Fisher's concept of income depended on the discount calculation of future cash flows (Fisher [1906]). He also subsequently attempted to introduce his concept of income directly into accounting. This led to the development of J. B. Canning's work (Canning [1929]) and "economic concept of income" in West Germany. The economic concept of income is defined as ideal income which is concept of income under certainty. The economic income model values capital on the base of discounted future net cash receipt, based on the fundamental compound discounting principle. Because of the necessary prediction of future benefit for discounting purposes and the choice of an appropriate discount rate, much of the economic approach to income and capital is founded on subjective judgment and estimation. Because the accountant is traditionally an advocate of objective and verifiable measurements, he find hard to accept as feasible and valued for financial reporting purpose (Lee [1974], p. 11).

Most real firms do not operate in a certain world. In most cases, the prediction of future cash flow is a matter of conjecture and is usually considered to be unacceptable as a base for calculating income for the firm (Jaedicke/Sprouse [1965], p. 25).

Whether inflation adjustment in classical inflation accounting is adjustment by general price index or adjustment by index specific to the assets, both are centered on adjustment of historical data. On the other hand fair value measurement of financial instruments is effected not by adjustment of historical data but by methods for valuation that suitably reflected the pricing on market. The important points of financial innovation are the setting of financial dealings as future cash flows and the recognition of them as present value by discounting the flows with an adequate discount rate.

Even with no observable market price of financial instruments, the fair value can be estimated by a technique using factors in information on capital market pricing principles and current market conditions. This technique is sometimes applied in the market price determination process enabling many types of measurements at a rational cost, using widely available software. Therefore, the fair value measurement of financial instruments is different from adjustment of historical data in classical inflation accounting characterized by precedence of idea.

The IASB and the FASB, as the result of the joint project for developing conceptual framework, published some announcements on the conceptual framework for financial reporting (FASB [2006], [2008a], [2008b], [2010a], [2010b]). They reflect "Fair Value View" that focuses on usefulness for economic decisions (Whittington [2008], p. 157). And "Fair Value View" assumes that markets are relatively perfect and complete and that, in such a setting, financial reports should meet the needs of passive investors and creditors by reporting fair values derived from current market prices" (Whittington [2008], p. 139).

Whittington gives the following as the main features of "Fair Value View".

"Market prices should give an informed, *non entity specific* estimate of cash flow potential, and *markets* are generally sufficiently complete and efficient to provide evidence for representationally faithful measurement on this basis" (Whittington [2008], p. 157).

"Fair Value View" is supposed to be the descendant of the following" assets and liabilities view:"

"Earning normalization is a responsibility of the user of financial statements as a part of his assessment of an enterprise's earning power, not a responsibility of the preparer of those financial statements" (FASB [1976], p. 20).

According to Whittington the basis for the view of the world "Fair Value View "is the thought that financial reporting should be independent of stewardship (Whittington [2008]). Because the word "stewardship" reminds a preference for historical cost measurement, Whittington calls his view of the world "Alternative View" (Whittington [2008], p. 157). But in this Chapter, it is called the "Stewardship View". "Stewardship View" assumes that markets relatively imperfect and incomplete and that, in such a setting, financial reports should meet the monitoring requirements of current shareholders (stewardship) by reporting past transactions and events using entity-specific measurements that reflect the opportunities actually available to the reporting entity" (Whittington [2008], p. 139).

Whittington gives the following as the main features of "Stewardship View".

"The economic environment is one of imperfect and incomplete markets in which market opportunities will be entity-specific." (Whittington [2008], p. 159) And he gives the following as the implications of "Stewardship View". "The financial statements should reflect the financial performance and position of a specific entity, and entity specific assumptions should be made when these reflect the real opportunities available to the entity" (Whittington [2008], p. 159).

"Stewardship View" is supposed to be descendant of the following "revenues and expenses view:" "the preparer of financial statements is in a better position to do the normalizing than the user" (FASB [1976], p. 20).

Basically, classical inflation accounting was developed to remove the impact of inflation on the distribution of resources. On the other hand, in international accounting standards "price" based on the definition of fair value is "exit price" which shows the current expectations for future cash inflows relating to assets and future cash outflows relating to liabilities from the <u>perspective of the market participant</u>.

The opposition between "Fair Value View" and "Stewardship View" is not merely at the level of accounting procedure but the view of the world, "market participant assumptions" versus "entity specific assumptions". The contention of theses accounting basic assumptions could be traced back to the difference between "assets and liabilities view" and "revenues and expenses view".

9-4. History of Acceptance of Valuation at Current Price and Fair Value Measurement in Japan after World War II

In Japan, accounting based on the Commercial Code (or the Companies Act) and capital market-oriented accounting based on the Securities and Exchange Law (SEL) (or the Financial Instruments and Exchange Act) exist in parallel. For business accounting and accounting research in the postwar age in Japan, it was important to reconcile these two accountings.

However, looking back again at the history of the modernization of business accounting in Japan, in the field of accounting based on the Securities Exchange Law which is separate from accounting based on the Commercial Code, experiments such as the introduction of interim financial statements and cash flow statements, and the disclosure of the market value information of securities were performed. Even on the side of accounting based on the Commercial Code, by applying a system already tested in the field of accounting based on the Securities Exchange Law, it was possible smoothly to introduce, for example, audit by certified public accountants and consolidated financial statements into its own field. The interaction and compartmentalization of both these accountings after the World War II played a significant role in the modernization of business accounting in Japan.

In Japanese history of modernization of business accounting, in a field outside the Commercial Code, the project of establishing accounting standards to supplement accounting based on the Commercial Code started with *"the Working Rules of Financial Statements by the Ministry of Commerce and Industry"* (hereafter referred to as *"the Working Rules"*) in 1930s. In 1940s the project was subsequently continued with *"the Exposure Drafts of Working Rules of Financial Statements for Manufacturing Industry by the Planning Bureau"* (hereafter referred to as *"the Exposure Drafts"*). And in 1950s the project was performed by *"the Tentative Business Accounting Principles"* by the Investigation Committee on the Business Accounting System (See Kubota [2013]). In *"the Exposure Drafts"* large companies on a basis of amount of stated capital, and in *"the Accounting Principle"*, listed companies were the target of "experiments" that pushed forward the modernization of accounting in Japan. The following is an overview of the history of acceptance of valuation at current price and fair value measurement in Japan after World War II.

(1) Rule for valuation of marketable securities in "the Tentative Business Accounting Principles" (1949)

"The Regulations concerning Terms, Formats and Preparation Methods of the Financial Statements" (the Regulation No.18 of the Securities and Exchange Commission) was enacted based on part of *"the Tentative Business Accounting Principles"* and *"the Working Rules for the Preparation of Financial Statements"* in 1950. Standardization of format of financial statements was tried by *"the Working Rules"* and *"the Exposure Drafts"* before the end of World War II, but it was not performed. *"The Regulation No. 18"* mandated the

format of financial statements in Japan for the first time.

In *"the Tentative Business Accounting Principles"* (version of 1949), valuation of marketable securities was defined as follows: "Marketable securities held temporarily should be measured on the market price" (Principles of Balance Sheet, 5 B) (underlined by this chapter's author).

This provision was taken almost verbatim on the revise in 1954, but on the revise in 1963 it was defined in step with the Commercial Code amended in 1962 as mentioned below.

"Marketable securities held temporarily should be measured on the acquisition cost. However, when the market price is considered to have fallen significantly and as unrecoverable, the marketable securities should be stated at the market price in the balance sheet" (underlined by this chapter's author).

In May 1950, "the Investigation Committee on the Business Accounting System" was renewed to "the Business Accounting Standard Deliberation Council". This council published *"the Auditing Standards"* and *"the Working Rules of Field Work"* in July 1950. In 1951, *"the Regulations concerning Audit Certificate"* (the Regulation No. 4 of the Securities and Exchange Commission) which was the basis for partially legislating the *"the Auditing Standards"* was enacted. Finally, as the Japanese accounting system, a full set of modernized accounting regulations was realized by *"the Tentative Business Accounting Principles"*, *"the Regulation No. 18"* and *"the Auditing Standards"*. After government reform as the result of the independence in 1952, the Economic Stabilization Board was reorganized into the Economic Deliberative Agency, and the council was also reorganized into an advisory body of the Ministry of Finance named "the Business Accounting Deliberation Council".

"Kaikei Seido Kansa" (this means a sort of "accounting system review") based on *"the Tentative Business Accounting Principles"*, *"the Regulation No.18"* and *"the Auditing Standards"* in accordance with the Securities Exchange Law were carried out between 1951 and 1956. The initial and second audits were carried out during the postwar occupation, and after the independence the third, fourth and fifth audit were carried out. And since a period beginning on January 1, 1957, regular financial statements audit has been conducted.

(2) "The Opinion on Disclosure of Information about Changes of Price Level in Corporate Disclosure System" (1980)

Under worldwide inflation after the 1973 oil crisis, *"the Opinion on Disclosure of Information about Changes of Price Level in Corporate Disclosure System"* (hereafter referred to as *"the Opinion (1980)"*) analyzing the effects of changes of price level on business accounting and importance of the disclosure of information on the effects of those fluctuations was published in May 1980. It discussed trends in the US, the UK and West Germany and suggested a direction for the disclosure of information on changes of price level in Japan. *"the Opinion (1980)"* listed the following four problems that changes of price level would bring to business accounting.

1) For non-monetary assets valuation, there is only insufficient information which reflects economic realities;
2) holding gains and operating margin for inventories and depreciable assets are not presented separately;
3) there is only insufficient information on whether enough fund necessary for depreciable assets replacement is placed in reserve; and
4) no information is provided on the effects on business accounting of changes of purchasing power of the money brought upon by changes of price level.

As shown by the problems listed above, *"the Opinion (1980)"* proposed ways to overcome problems in historical cost accounting from the perspective of classical inflation accounting. However, any concrete proposals as to what indication of changes of purchasing power of the money should be selected, and in the case where current cost in itself is objectively difficult to find were not shown. It reguired only a discussion regarding the content and method of disclosing financial information on changes of price level as a first step for the social consensus and there was no progression to any actual systematization. After "the Opinion (1980)" was published, inflation was coming to a halt and no systematization took place in Japan.

(3) "The Opinion on Accounting Standard for Financial Insruments" (1999)

The switch to the floating rate system in 1971 caused the problem that foreign exchange rates and interest rates began to fluctuate violently as the monetary policy target went from interest rates to money supply. To counter this development, new computer technologies brought about global money market which led to new financial instruments created to hedge against risks by new risk valuation methods. The valuation of these financial instruments became a new issue for business accounting.

As a accounting standard for financial instruments, "the Business Accounting Deliberation Council" first published in May 1990 *"the Opinion on Accounting Standard for Future and Option"* to provide a disclosure standard for current prices of future, option and marketable securities. Afterwards, the disclosure of current prices was expanded into forward exchange transaction and all other derivatives.

Subsequently "the Business Accounting Deliberation Council" published *"the Exposure Draft of the Opinion on Accounting Standard for Financial Instruments"* in June 1998 and *"the Opinion on Accounting Standard for Financial Instruments"* (hereafter referred to as *"the Opinion (1999)"*) in January 1999. In "the "positioning of this opinion" "of *"the Opinion (1999)"* it is stated that though the rule for valuation of assets is provided in "the *Tentative Business Accounting Principles*", for the valuation of financial instruments, in principle, the rule in *"the Opinion" (1999)* shall control.

In *"the Opinion (1999)"*, "current price" is defined as follows.

"Current price signifies fair value, which represents amounts that are based on price, quotes, and indices formed in the marketplace (hereafter, "market price"). If market prices are not available, fair value should be the amount that is reasonably calculated" (III Scope of Financial Assets and Financial Liabilities, etc. 2 Current Price).

As shown by the above definition, the current price in *"the Opinion (1999)"* is different from that is defined in classical inflation accounting, and more like "fair value" in western world. However, the term "current price" has been used subsequently in *"the Opinion on Accounting Standard for Impairment of Fixed Assets"* (2002), *"the Opinion on Accounting Standard for Business Combination"* (2003) and *"the Opinion on Accounting Standard for Real Estate for Rent"* (2008).

In the amendment of the Commercial Code in 2002, the provisions of the rules for assts valuation, deferred charge, allowance and increase in amount of net assets by revaluation of assets etc. that were included in the Commercial Code at the time of the amendment of the Commercial Code in 1962 were transferred into *"the Ordinance for Enforcement of the Commercial Code"*. An officer in charge at the Legal Affairs Ministry at the time explained that this transference into the Ordinance of Ministry attempted to remove obsolete by the Commercial Code in changing accounting based on the SEL (Kanda et al. [2003], p. 8). In other words, *"the Accounting Standards"*, which make up the substance rule of accounting based on the SEL, could be formulated in response to the globalization of the financial sector without any hindrance by the Commercial Code. This substantially changed the relationship between *"the Accounting Standards"* as global standards and the Commercial Code as domestic law.

Then in the Companies Act and the Ordinance on Company Accounting enacted in 2006 the substance rule of accounting based on the Companies Act has been entrusted to *"the Accounting Standards"*.

9-5. Conclusion

The Accounting Standards Board of Japan (ASBJ) published in August 2009, based on the measures made by the IASB and the FASB in response to the financial crisis, *"the Preliminary Views on Fair Value Measurement and Its Disclosure"* , and after further examination, published in July 2010 *"the Exposure Draft of Accounting Standard on Fair Value Measurement and its Disclosure"* (hereafter referred to as *"the Exposure Draft (2010)"*). *"The Exposure Draft (2010)"* cited the release of SFAS No. 157 *"Fair Value Measurement"* shown above and the Exposure Draft of *"Fair Value Measurement"* by IASB as the background of its release.

In *"the Exposure Draft (2010)"*, as shown below, it is said that there is no significant discrepancy in the accounting conceptual reasoning between "current price" in Japanese standards and "fair value" in the international accounting standards.

"These accounting standards are applied for accounting and disclosure based on fair value. In using "current price" under other accounting standards, it is to be replaced with "fair value" (para. 3).

But, the discrepancy between "current price" and "fair value" is not made clear and, in its "Background of Conclusion" the following opinion is shown; In international accounting standards, price based on the definition of fair value is "exit price". This indicates the current expectations with regard to future cash inflows for assets and future cash outflows for liabilities from <u>perspective of market participant</u> (para. 30, underlined by this chapter's author). On the other hand, <u>such a perspective is not presented</u> in the Japanese concept of "current price", there may be some cases that <u>the use of entry value is more appropriate</u> rather than using exit value (para.31, underlined by this chapter's author).

Further in measuring fair value based on market participant assumptions, if there are no observable transactions, the enormous influence of corporate capability and intention cannot be avoided in measuring fair value from perspective of "market participant assumptions". As the result, there may be <u>some cases that in essence fair value is similar to value from perspective of "entity specific assumptions"</u> such as "value-in-use" in accounting for impairment of fixed assets (para. 36, underlined by this chapter's author).

Ultimately, it states <u>there is a crucial difference in concept because fair value measurement should be made separate from measurement from perspective of "entity specific assumptions"</u>. Even if observable transactions are nonexistent, they conclude that the use of <u>"market participant assumptions" is necessary</u> (para. 36, underlined by this chapter's author).

However, it is not sufficiently understood that "market participant assumptions" which is the basis for fair value measurement are determinately different from "entity specific assumptions" which is the basis for conventional valuations. For the difference between "market participant assumptions" and "entity specific assumptions", the explanation provided by T. S. Kuhn (historian of science) as follows based on the concept of "paradigms" regarding the transformations which occurred in the history of physics might be true.

"We have already seen several reasons why the proponents of competing paradigms must fail to make complete contact with each other's viewpoints. Collectively these reasons have been described as the incommensurability of the pre- and postrevolutionary normal-science traditions, and we need only recapitulate them briefly here. In the first place, <u>the proponents of competing paradigms will often disagree about the list of problems that any candidate for paradigm must resolve. Their standards or their definitions of science are not the same</u>" (Kuhn [1962], p. 148; underlined by this chapter's author).

In the case of measuring fair value of debt for changes in credit worthiness, the net gain or loss results from changes in the credit risk of an enterprise's interest-bearing liabilities. Though it is necessary to recognize such gain or loss from perspective of "market participant assumptions", it is strange from perspective of "entity specific assumptions". As the premise on the debate regarding fair value measurement, there is discrepancy at the level of the view of the world between the conventional current price on the base of "entity specific assumptions" and fair value measurement on the base on "market participant assumptions". The purpose of fair value measurement is supposed to be the removal of arbitrary measurements that may be exercised under "entity specific assumptions". Consequently, the replacement of "current price" with "fair value" might bring about relativization of these *heterogeneous concepts*.

[Refereces in English]
American Accounting Association (AAA) [1977] *"A Statement on Accounting Theory and Theory Acceptance"*.
American Institute of Accountants (AIA), Committee on Accounting Procedure [1947] Accounting Research Bulletin No. 33, *"Depreciation and High Costs"*.
────── [1953] ARB No. 43, *"Restatement and Revision of Accounting Research Bulletins Nos. 1-42"*.
American Institute of Certified Public Accountants (AICPA), Accounting Research Division [1963] ARS No. 6, *" Reporting the Effects of Price Level Changes"*.
Anthony, Robert N. [1984] *Future Directions for Financial Accounting*.
Canning, J. B. [1929] *The Economics of Accountancy*, New York.
Chiba, Junichi [1998] "The Designing of Corporate Accounting Law in Japan after the Second World War", Tokyo Metropolitan University Journal, Keizaitokeizaigaku (*Economic and Economics*), No. 85.
Edwards, Edgar O. /Bell Philip W. [1961] *The Theory and Measurement of Business Income*, University of California Press.
Financial Accounting Standards Board (FASB) [1974a] Discussion Memorandum *"Reporting the Effects of General Price Level Changes in Financial Statements"*.
────── [1974b] Exposure Draft *" Financial Reporting in Units of General Purchasing Power"*.
────── [1976] *"Scope and Implications of the Conceptual Framework Project"*.
────── [1978] Exposure Draft *"Financial Reporting and Changing Prices"*.
────── [1979a] Exposure Draft *"Constant Dollar Accounting"*.
────── [1979b] SFAS No.33 *"Financial Reporting and Changing Prices"*.
────── [1984a] SFAS No.82 *"Financial Reporting and Changing Prices: Elimination of Certain Disclosures"*.
────── [1984b] Exposure Draft *"Financial Reporting and Changing Prices : Current Cost Information"*.

―――― [1986a] Exposure Draft *"Financial Reporting and Changing Prices"*.
―――― [1986b] SFAS No. 89 " *Financial Reporting and Changing Prices"*.
―――― [1990] SFAS No. 105" *Disclosures of Information about Financial Instruments with Off-Balance-Sheet Risk and Financial Instruments with Concentrations of Credit Risk"*.
―――― [1991] SFAS No. 107 " *Disclosures about Fair Value of Financial Instruments"*.
―――― [1993] SFAS No. 115 " *Accounting for Certain Investment in Debt and Equity Securities"*.
―――― [2006] SFAS No. 157 " *Fair Value Measurement"*.
―――― [2006] Discussion Paper *"Preliminary Views on an improved Conceptual Framework for Financial Reporting: The Objective of Financial Reporting and Qualitative Characteristics of Decision-Useful Financial Reporting Information"*
―――― [2008a] Exposure Draft *"Conceptual Framework for Financial Reporting: The Objective of Financial Reporting and Qualitative Characteristics of Decision-Useful Financial Reporting Information"*
―――― [2008b] Discussion Paper *"Preliminary Views on an improved Conceptual Framework for Financial Reporting: The Reporting Entity"*
―――― [2010a] Exposure Draft *"Conceptual Framework for Financial Reporting: The Reporting Entity"*
―――― [2010b] Conceptual Framework for Financial Reporting: *"Chapter 1, The Objective of Financial Reporting, and Chapter 3, Qualitative Characteristics of Useful Financial Information"*.
Fisher, Irving [1906] *Income and Capital"*, in: Parker, R. H./Harcourt, G.C./Whittington, G. [1986] *Readings in The Concept and Measurement of Income"*, 2nd ed., Oxford.
IASC [1990] International Accounting Standard No. 32 *"Financial Instruments Disclosure and Presentation"*.
―――― [1991] Exposure Draft 40 *"Financial Instruments"*.
―――― [1994] Exposure Draft 48 *"Financial Instruments"*.
IASC/CICA [1997] Discussion Paper *"Accounting for Financial Assets and Financial Liabilities"*.
IASB [2011] IFRS No. 13 *"Fair Value Measurement"*.
Jaedicke, Robert K. / Sprouse, Robert T. [1965] *Accounting Flows : Income, Funds, and Cash*, Prentice-Hall.
Joint Working Group of Standard Setters [2000] Draft Standard *"Financial Instruments and Similar Items"*, International Accounting Standards Committee.
Kubota, Hideki [2013] "The 'Japanese Type' Modernization of Accounting Regulations in the First Half of Showa Period", *Konankeieikenkyu (Konan Business Review)*, Vol. 54, No. 2.
Kuhn, Thomas S. [1962] *The Structure of Scientific Revolutions* ,University of Chicago Press.
Lee, T. A. [1974] *Income and Value Measurement : Theory and Practice*, A. Wheaton & Company.
Lennard, Andrew [2007] "Stewardship and the Objective of Financial Statements: Preliminary Views on an Improved Conceptual Framework for

Financial Reporting: The Objective of Financial Reporting and Qualitative Characteristics of Decision-Useful Financial Reporting Information", *European Accounting Review*, Vol. 4, 2007.

MacNeal, Kenneth [1939] *Truth in Accounting*, University of Pennsylvania Press.

Moonitz, Maurice [1961] Accounting Research Study No. 1 "*The Basic Postulates of Accounting*".

Paton, W. A. [1922] *Accounting Theory*, New York.

Securities and Exchange Commission [1976] Accounting Series Release No. 190 "*Notice of Adoption of Amendments to Regulation S-X Requiring Disclosure of Certain Replacement Cost Data*".

Sprouse, Robert T. / Moonitz, M. [1962] AICPA ARS No. 3 "*A Tentative Set of Broad Accounting Principles for Business Enterprises*".

Sweeney, Henry W. [1936] *Stabilized Accounting*, New York.

Whittington, Geoffrey [1983] *Inflation Accounting : an introduction to the debate*, Cambridge University Press.

―――― [2008] "Fair Value and the IASB/FASB Conceptual Framework Project : An Alternative View", *ABACUS*, Vol. 44, No. 2.

[References in Japanese]

Arai, Kiyomitsu *et al.* [1978] "Round-table conference; A Basis of Business Accounting Systems", *Kigyokaikei (Accounting)*, Vol. 30, No. 12.

Japanese Institute of Certified Public Accountants (the compilation committee of 25 years history of JICPA) [1975] *The History of Certified Public Accountants in Japan*, Doubunkan Shuppan.

Kanda, Hideki *et al.* [2003] "Round-table conference; The Amendment of Commercial Code in 2002 and Rules on Accounting", *Shojihomu (Commercial Law)*, No. 1672.

Kubota, Hideki [2001] *The Materialization of 'Japanese-type' of Accounting*, Zeimukeiri-Kyo-Kai.

―――― [2008] *The Transition of Accounting Regulations in Japan,* Chuokeizai-sha.

Kurosawa, Kiyoshi [1954] "On Revise of the Tentative Business Accounting Principles and its Commentary", *Kigyokaikei (Accounting)*, Vol. 6, No. 8.

Prime Minister's Office [1948], *"Resolution"*, National Diet Library, [Call Number] Honkan-4E, 036-00, Number of Reels 001400.

Chapter 10

Various Aspects of Divergence from Fair Value Accounting in History

— Actual Requirements for Application of Market Value Accounting —

Takemi Ono
Tokyo Keizai University

Abstract

This report asserts that the status of both market and internal corporate liquidity determines the suitability of applying market value accounting. In other words, application of market value accounting comes with assumptions and under certain conditions. For example, if the market liquidity is high, then the probability of executing contracts at market value for assets being currently traded on that market would also be high. Conversely, if market liquidity is low, then the probability would also be expected to be low. In other words, the level of market liquidity determines the applicability of market value accounting.

However, the application of market value accounting is not automatic, even under permissible circumstances. For example, if shares of a subsidiary are traded actively on the market, then the application of market value accounting would be rendered possible. However, whether it is adequate to do so would require separate consideration. In this report, I shed light on the actual requirements for the application of market value accounting by providing historical debates and precedents from the perspective of market and internal corporate liquidity.

The Bagehot debate examined in this thesis and the precedents set by the insurance industry and zaibatsu (financial combines) before World War II can be used to determine how accounting is to be applied, particularly how treatments under market valuation are to be effected, when the market loses liquidity and when faced with matters involving affiliate shares as business assets. These are case examples about handling valuation when market liquidity (the precondition for market valuation) is lost and advanced embodiments regarding the adequacy of application under circumstances that permit market value accounting.

Keywords
financial crisis, market liquidity, market value separation theory, W. Bagehot, Showa Depression, financial combine, market value accounting application avoidance, fair price (iustum pretium)

10-1. Introduction: Basic Stance Regarding Market Value Accounting Application

This report states that the suitability of applying market value accounting is determined by the status of market and internal corporate liquidity. In other words, application of market value accounting does not come without assumptions. For example, if the market liquidity is high, then the probability of executing contracts at market value for assets being currently traded on that market would also be high. Conversely, if market liquidity is low, then that probability would also be expected to be low. In other words, the level of market liquidity decides the applicability of market value accounting.

However, whether or not the application of market value accounting is automatic (even under permissible circumstances that would allow it) is an issue that should be examined separately. For example, if assets held to maturity (e.g., investment securities and subsidiary shares) are traded actively on the market, then (if market liquidity is sufficiently secure) the application of market value accounting with respect to those assets would be possible. However, whether it is adequate to do so should be considered separately. In other words, depending on the level of importance of the liquidity of those assets (or liabilities) within the company (i. e., whether to hold or dispose thereof based on some chronology), managers may sometimes face the question of whether application of market value accounting is appropriate (see Table 10-1).

Consequently, whether or not to apply market value accounting becomes a question of feasibility and appropriateness that depends on the status of market and corporate liquidity. In this thesis, I will attempt to analyze past debates and facts regarding market value accounting from the perspective of market and corporate liquidity and find actual requirements for the application (or non-application) of market value accounting.

[Table 10-1]

Market Liquidity	Long-term financial instruments	Short-term financial instruments
	Long-term business assets	Short-term loans

Internal Liquidity in Corporations

Note: Items appearing in the Table above are examples.

10-2. An Interpretation of the Financial Crisis and Easing the Application of Market Value Accounting Application

The global financial crisis spawned by the US subprime loan fiasco in 2007 unintentionally exposed the limitations of the systemization of modern market value accounting. As Vinals [2008] reported, "When financial markets are active, the prices traded on them conceivably reflect consensus between buyers and sellers about the future cash flows of financial instruments, and on the degree of uncertainty surrounding them[1]". In addition, Allen and Carletti [2008 (b)] found that, "However, in crisis times when there is a shortage of liquidity, mark-to-market values do not reflect future earning power and cannot be used to assess the solvency of financial institutions[2]". Therefore, these studies exposed the fact that one cannot always purely state that the market value of financial instruments is fair.

---

[1] Viñals [2008], pp. 123-124.
[2] Allen and Carletti [2008b], p. 5.

As Fujii [2009] put it, "Market value is the first step towards knowing the facts[3]", and "accounting standards mirror the actual conditions of an enterprise and serve as the basis for the drafting of financial statements which constitute information that supports the decision-making of investors, therefore, the freezing of market valuation of financial instruments when financial markets are in a period of turmoil cannot possibly be acceptable". This extremely straightforward argument is provided in the "Chairman's Statement[4]" published by The Japan Institute of Chartered Accountants. However, one should not forget that this "argument" was made during normal markets. Market value accounting, which has fulfilled the function of providing valuable information during normal markets, has also exposed a fundamental defect in the form of collapse of market value from a lack of liquidity in the market when it is acting abnormally, such as during a financial crisis (particularly, the appearance of market values that do not reflect the fundamentalism of the clearance sale price and losses from the inability to attain a sale or purchase contract, among other aberrations). Consequently, it is said that "the current turmoil in the international financial system has highlighted some of these limitations of fair value (accounting)[5]".

Furthermore, when market value accounting is suspended, it is necessary to "continue to find the best way to calculate market value when the markets are in turmoil with no active market and few indicators to interpret the signs that would help in that task", thus presenting anxiety toward "emergency market value" as opposed to "normal market value[6]". In other words, the suspension of market value accounting during financial crises should not be interpreted only in terms of government meddling in accounting regulations but rather as a fundamentally contradictory exposure of the loss of any accurate market value brought upon by a lack of liquidity latent in market value accounting.

---

[3] Fujii [2009], p. 66.
[4] Masuda [2008]. However, regarding the series of steps taken during the financial crisis, he states that "handlings relating to measurements, etc. of bonds, etc. with very low liquidity are effected within the framework of current standards," meaning that treatments are to be done at all costs within the framework of market value accounting.
[5] Viñals [2008], p. 125.
[6] Sakamoto [2009], pp. 138–139.

10-3. Function of Liquidity in Market Value Accounting[7]

Liquidity is defined as either "being able to transact with ease whenever wanting to transact" or "being provided ample opportunities to transact whenever wanting to[8]"; the reason liquidity is important in market value accounting is its effect on price volatility. Generally, "prices fluctuate either when new information is known that fundamentally changes the value of an item, or there is no new information but some large order or other occurrence impacts the market[9]." However, the abrupt price increases in times of low liquidity, as in the latter case, is predictable. Thus, according to Allen and Carletti [2008a], "When liquidity is scarce, asset prices are determined by the available liquidity or in other words by the cash in the market[10]". Therefore, slight change in supply or demand may cause the prices to fluctuate significantly. In addition, modern financial systems allow such price fluctuations to be conveyed instantly between financial institutions or other major stock market players. However, the contagion of such price fluctuations is related to the use of mark-to-market accounting[11]". Consequently, if the valuation of the balance sheet is based on *book value* instead of *market value*, there would be no negative chain spread from the initially infected financial institution to others. Therefore, we must not ignore the fact that there should be an endogenous expansion of shocks to the (financial) system for the *market valuation* effected under balance sheet safety regulations to generate synchronicity amongst financial institutions using price signals[12].

If there is sufficient liquidity on the market, and price fluctuations reflect changes in the fundamentals, then the application of market value accounting would be useful to information users' decision-making. However, it must be noted that "when markets do not work perfectly and prices do not always reflect the value of fundamentals as in the case where there is cash-in-the-market

---

[7] See Obinata [2012] for a comprehensive description of the relation between fair value accounting and market liquidity/holding purpose.
[8] Ota, Uno, Takehara [2011], p. 4.
[9] Ota, Uno, Takehara [2011], p. 14.
[10] Allen and Carletti [2008a], p. 12.
[11] Allen and Carletti [2008a], p. 14.
[12] Takemori [2008], p. 208.

pricing, mark-to-market accounting exposes the value of the balance sheets of financial institutions to short-term and excessive fluctuations, and it can ultimately generate contagion[13]". In other words, when market liquidity is lost, there is the extreme possibility that generated prices deviate from the intrinsic value of items traded on the market. In this case, market value does not reflect fundamentals but rather liquidity at a point in time[14] and market prices (value) cease to be an indicator of fair value. The reliability of price signals was a core concept for economists; therefore, market value accounting was proposed on the basis of this trust[15]. However, the lack of market liquidity has caused the loss of intrinsic reliability of market prices.

10-4. Market Value Deviation Theory and Abandonment of Market Value When Liquidity is Lost

A lack of liquidity on the market has been seen several times in history during stock market panics, leading to various debates over the years about how to handle sharply plummeting securities prices. I will now provide a few examples to bolster my examination of market valuation when market liquidity is lacking.

(1) Market value deviation theory during panics

The crash of securities prices during stock market panics is an inevitable, concomitant phenomenon. Walter Bagehot suggested a rather aggressive remedy to this situation. Allen and Garletti [2008b] describe Bagehot's concept thus: "Bagehot (1873), for example, suggested that in response to crises, central banks should value bank collateral weighting panic and pre-panic prices as market prices are not accurate measure of values in those circumstances[16]".

The debate proposed by Bagehot is widely known as the "Bagehot Principle" or the "Bagehot Rule." He states that, "during a panic, the Bank of England should provide as much credit as the public

---

[13] Allen and Carletti [2008a], p. 14.
[14] Takemori [2008], p. 252.
[15] Takemori [2008], p. 252.
[16] Allen and Carlettip. [2008b], p. 1.

demands even at a high rate of interest and make every effort to maintain ample reserves to that end[17]". The reason for this is that "the lack of any new infusion of capital during a panic rendering impossible the sale of securities held and there, and large amounts of cash that would enable such immediate purchases are nowhere to be found in the country in such a situation[18]". Therefore, the Bank of England must provide cash as a Lender of Last Resort (LLR): "The lender of last resort stands to halt a run out of real and illiquid financial assets into money by making more money available[19]". What is seen here is fundamentally the problem of capital supply by a central bank in times of scarce liquidity; however, this presents a deeply interesting concept as to how collateral is evaluated as a precondition to capital supply. In other words, he states the following: "As we have seen, principle requires that such advances, if made at all for the purpose of curing panic, should be made in the manner most likely to cure that panic. And for this purpose, they should be made on everything which in common times is good 'banking security'. The evil is, that owing to terror, what is commonly good security has ceased to be so[20]". This means that during a panic, liquidity dries up along with any accurate evaluation of security. Therefore, "all banking security that is of excellent quality in normal times" should be used to lend out capital. Indeed, the valuation of security in such times is meaningless as a clearance price, and there are no market prices available when financial crises erupt; thus, valuation would be under market prices as set in normal times[21]. In other words, the debate on security valuation in Bagehot's LLR theory may be interpreted as the virtual market-value deviation theory regarding security valuation during panics.

Although the valuation of security assets at market prices in normal times is opposed to the recent trend of market valuation, Bagehot's Principle assumes that the loans of a central bank LLR should be restricted to solvent entities with a temporary lack of liquidity. The value of security assets with respect to financial institutions as solvent, going concerns is obviously different from that

---

[17] Kanei [1989], p. 129.
[18] Kanei [1989], p. 136.
[19] Kindleberger [2002], p. 146.
[20] Bagehot [1873], pp. 204–205.
[21] Oguri [2001], p. 143.

of insolvent entities[22].

(2) Market value avoidance in life insurance industry during the Showa Panic

The problem of securities valuation in the life insurance industry becomes more acute during a time of economic crisis. For example, during the interwar period, Japan faced a reactionary crisis in 1920, a financial crisis in 1922, the Showa Panic of 1927, and a slight repetition of the latter in 1930 and 1931, all of which had a devastating effect on corporate operations at that time. Although there were structural reforms featuring a combination of banks in the aftermath of the Showa Panic, I will instead focus on life insurance companies, which are a kind of financial institution on par with banks. I will look for suggestions regarding market value accounting from the independent methods employed to solve the accounting problems that appeared at that time.

The financial crises and the Showa Panic caused "securities values to plummet, interest rates to fall and loans to become irrecoverable having disastrous financial ramifications that pushed life insurance companies in dire straits[23]" while their "total assets featured excessive holdings of securities[24]". The ratio of securities in total assets was over 50%, with approximately 20% in stocks (see Table 10-2).

Furthermore, the plummet of securities prices was not only limited to stocks but also affected bonds. "The set interest-bearing object of government bonds, regional bonds, and corporate bonds, among others, did not significantly lose value (seemingly). This is justifiably a superficial problem much like the bonds of a certain combine whose market value became unavoidably stuck at a certain level due to the lack of any trading so that in actuality the value ought to be much lower[25]". Table 10-3 shows the actual valuation losses posted by life insurance companies.

Although it can be observed that during the Showa Panic, the life insurance industry's asset valuation losses, particularly its securities valuation losses, increased exponentially, the Big Four insurers (namely Nippon Life, Daiichi Life, Chiyoda Life, and Teikoku

---

[22] Oguri [2001], p. 143.
[23] The Life Insurance Association of Japan [1970], p. 5.
[24] The Life Insurance Association of Japan [1970], p. 42.
[25] The Life Insurance Association of Japan [1970], pp. 55–56.

[Table 10-2] Assets Held by the Life Insurance Industry

	Total Assets (Thousand yen)	Securities (Thousand yen)	Stocks (Thousand yen)
T13	765,334	329,042 (43)	96,979 (13)
T14	893,717	416,316 (47)	117,969 (13)
S1	1,036,473	508,551 (49)	150,806 (15)
S2	1,166,430	582,125 (49)	186,087 (16)
S3	1,315,212	689,572 (52)	249,589 (20)
S4	1,454,881	768,002 (53)	269,890 (20)

Note 1: T = Taisho, S = Showa
Note 2: Percentage of securities in total assets.
Source: The Life Insurance Association of Japan [1970], pp. 42–43.

[Table 10-3] Asset Valuation Loss or Gain of Life Insurers

	Valuation gain (thousand yen)	Valuation loss (thousand yen)	Difference (thousand yen)
T13	5,090	6,204	1,114 (loss)
T14	6,777	6,269	508 (gain)
S1	5,368	8,209	2,941 (gain)
S2	6,432	12,444	6,012 (loss)
S3	6,432	12,941	6,509 (loss)
S4	4,949	39,133	34,184 (loss)

Note 1: T = Taisho, S = Showa
Note 1: Although valuation gains and losses include items related to real estate, debt, etc., 90% or so relates to securities.
Source: The Life Insurance Association of Japan [1970], p. 48.

Life) saw a great deterioration in earnings because of their accounting of large disposal and valuation losses during the Showa Panic[26]. However, such large valuation loss postings relate to the way in which life insurance is managed. In other words, securities whose book values were decreased by accounting for valuation losses in advance were sold after the fact at market value, with the unrealized gains therefrom added to earnings[27]. As such, the

---

[26] Takeda [2009], p. 70.

reason for the posting of valuation losses was not only a reflection of the fall in the market price of securities but also a result of managing securities. The life insurance industry could not avoid the enormous burden of these losses.

Under these circumstances, the life insurance industry petitioned the Ministry of Commerce and Industry, its regulator, for the implementation of accounts settlement easing methods regarding the market valuation of securities, demanding that "for investments in securities by life insurers, regarding valuations with no discussion of long-term investment in consideration of the nature of the business and without any objective of profiting from price fluctuations, while we should consider yields, etc. from long-term investments free of instability due to price falls, the Commercial Code calls for measurement based on market value which can result in many companies becoming insolvent when prices of securities held fall thus bringing down accounts settlement results which creates anxiety amongst general policy holders and can lead to a bleak future for the insurance business[28]". However, it also stated that "ultimately, with the issue price of government bonds taken from Item 16 of the June 30, 1932 Act and the adoption of the Depreciation Act upon the revision of the 1939 Insurance Business Act, the Average Share Price Act was never passed[29]". In other words, despite consideration for bonds with regard to market valuation, no thought whatsoever was given to stocks.

(2)-1 Establishment of Life Insurance Securities and Deviation from Market Value

Under these circumstances, the life insurance industry formulated additional measures on the basis of the "new concept of not only having a pool of one type of securities but also establishing an investment trust in the form of a stock holding company that would work to prevent and avoid falls in prices of held securities[30]". This concept led to the establishment of the Life Insurance Securities Company (hereinafter, "the Company"), with capital infusion from 32 life insurers in October 1931[31]. "The shares of the Company were underwritten only by life insurance companies with some excep-

---

[27] Takeda [2009], p. 73.
[28] The Life Insurance Association of Japan [1970], p. 6.
[29] The Life Insurance Association of Japan [1970], p. 6.
[30] Ogawa [1994], p. 151.
[31] The Japan Life Insurance Association [1970], p. 93.

tions where underwriting was not allowed...in other words, this is a deviation from the market valuation of individual, directly held listed stocks, meaning that the greatest consideration was made to allow the conversion to lump-sum valuation of unlisted stocks of the stock holding company through direct holding thereof[32]". The main intention of the establishment of the Company was "to purchase and hold safe stocks through the building of a joint entity with the infusion of the stock investment assets of insurance companies with a considerably large volume of assets under management...of course, there were no unsound motivations for the start of this body...[33]". However, this move has been criticized since its first implementation. For example, the Toyo Keizai Shimpo (September 13, 1930) published an editorial titled "Against the Establishment of the Life Insurance Securities Company", which harshly criticized the move, stating that the Company "constitutes a swindling public deception and temporary loss concealment apparatus that will lead to none other than the suicide of the life insurance companies that comprise it[34]".

The industry's government regulator, the Ministry of Commerce's Insurance Section, stated that "from the perspective of government insurance policy, in the event that illegal measures to increase stock prices are committed only to prevent losses from a decrease in the value of a life insurance company on the part of the Life Insurance Securities Company, meaning that speculative trading was effected on the market, two or three warnings are necessary prior to establishment[35]". However, ultimately, circumstances at the time indicate that "according to the media, Deputy Minister Tajima, acting on behalf of Minister Tawara, invoked state powers and ordered the indecisive Insurance Section Manager Inuzuka to approve the Life Insurance Securities Company[36]".

(2)-2 Effects of life insurance securities company and its accounting significance

The Company was launched during an extremely tough business environment, and the degree to which it affected the industry is questionable. In fact, the number of shares owned by the Company

---

[32] Ogawa [1994], p. 153.
[33] The Japan Life Insurance Association [1970], p. 81.
[34] The Japan Life Insurance Association [1970], p. 89.
[35] The Japan Life Insurance Association [1970], p. 80.
[36] Ogawa [1994], p. 155.

was about a few percent of the number of shares owned by the life insurance companies that infused capital therein[37]. On the basis of this alone, it can be said that the effect was not that pronounced; however, some of these companies are of the opinion that its effect was substantial. For example, it is stated that "when reducing the number of shares held, Aikoku, Yasuda, Chiyoda, Meiji, Teikoku and other life insurers with relatively high amounts of capital invested in the Company vis-à-vis their total shares could be exempted from the market valuation of directly held listed shares and convert them to the unlisted shares of the Company, a very highly effective move[38]". In particular, investments in the Company represented 15.6% of the total shares of Yasuda Life in FY 1930, 11.2% of those of Chiyoda Life, and 8.14% of those of Teikoku Life during the same period, constituting the reason for waiving market valuation[39]. In addition, the stock price index at that time fell to approximately 27% (compared to 41% for the stock price index of public corporations), demonstrating that for these companies, the effect of exempting from market valuation was not insignificant.

The Company's incorporation by the life insurance industry and its purchase of the shares of member life insurance companies was not the shifting of individual listed shares held by life insurers to the Company but rather avoiding market value fluctuations of listed shares by holding unlisted shares of the Company. This can be interpreted as an attempt by the Company at distancing themselves from listed stock market value fluctuations using actual measures to insulate their accounting from market value.

10-5. Debating the Appropriateness of Market Value Accounting Application and its Avoidance

(1) Appropriateness of market value accounting application

On the basis of the existing debate, it is evident that a liquid market is an essential precondition for market value accounting application. However, should market value accounting be applied

---

[37] Ogawa [1995], p. 12.
[38] Ogawa [1995], p. 17.
[39] Ogawa [1995], p. 17.

Chapter 10: Various Aspects of Divergence from Fair Value Accounting in History

constantly when the market is liquid? That it, when the application of market value accounting is possible, would it be appropriate to do so at any time? What is important here are asset realities that could become the object of market value accounting, more than their outer form. Thus, the appropriateness of market value accounting is decided by asset realities. However, it should be noted that "decisions are made depending on the actual nature of the investment, whether financial or operational[40]". Therefore, "for financial investments, cash flows calculated with the held asset and liabilities position as is are results that were expected prior to such investment and directly linked to the market value of such held assets and liabilities[41]". In comparison, business investments are made to obtain "not proceeds from converting facilities and raw materials into money, but rather the fruit of business activities such as selling items given a higher value[42]". Such results "vary depending on the know-how and sales efforts of the entity undertaking the business; therefore, the value of those assets is not the same as if someone held them because the market price of simple assets, or the market value, does not demonstrate the inherent value of the entity[43]".

To elaborate on this concept, being external financial assets, some of these are not subject to market valuation. They are shares of stock of subsidiaries and affiliates held not as a financial investment but rather as a business investment. "This constitutes a business investment controlling the operations of another entity whereby the gains generated therefrom are measured the same way as gains of their own company on a consolidated basis by the equity method under which the market value of the shares is ignored[44]". Thus, not conducting market valuation becomes an appropriate move even if market valuation is possible with respect to the financial assets. Consequently, under the current accounting system, generally, shares of subsidiaries and affiliates appearing in a parent company's financial statements are maintained at historical cost valuation unless it becomes necessary to valuate downward by force. However, we cannot forget that accounting

---

[40] Saito [2009], p. 40.
[41] Saito [2009], p. 40.
[42] Saito [2009], p. 39.
[43] Saito [2009], p. 57.
[44] Saito [2009], p. 159.

policies prioritizing the cost method for affiliate shares were applied since before such accounting regulations existed. This can be demonstrated using the example of the zaibatsu that existed prior to the Second World War in Japan.

(2) Market value accounting application avoidance by pre-war Zaibatsu

Here, the head offices of Mitsubishi and Sumitomo will be used as examples, along with their valuation method of subsidiaries. The function of a holding company within a combine is to own the stock of the operating companies thereunder. There were cases where such holding companies controlled and managed those group companies on the basis of such stock ownership. However, their results are affected by the valuation of the stocks held and absorption of their dividends. Therefore, the manner in which stock is valued constitutes an extremely important managerial policy.

First, let us take a look at Mitsubishi. From 1925 to 1932, over 90% of the stocks it owned were of its affiliated companies (i. e., operating companies under its direct control). Beyond this period, this figure was maintained at over 80%[45]. In addition, the investment income rate of affiliates' stocks is much higher and more stable than that of non-affiliates and the latter's frequently incurred large capital losses[46]. In particular, between 1925 and 1936 "losses from the disposal and valuation of securities was continually being posted, a large portion thereof generated by valuation losses of the company stock of Toyo Weaving, Toa Industries, Chunichi Industries and other non-Mitsubishi companies[47]". Such stock valuation continued thereafter, and the posting of valuation, losses including capital reduction losses with respect to non-affiliates, continued to occur between 1937 and 1944 (see Table 10-4).

Next, we will look at Sumitomo. In 1921, it reorganized into Sumitomo Ltd. and "its securities balance increased to the point of doubling in 1930 from the approx. 80 million yen balance in 1921 and gradually increasing thereafter[48]". A look at the proportion of securities in total assets shows that between 1929 and 1931, it

---

[45] Okazaki [2000], Table 1 on pp. 166–167.
[46] Okasaki [2000], p. 190.
[47] Okazaki [2000], p. 191.
[48] Asajima [1983], p. 440.

Chapter 10: Various Aspects of Divergence from Fair Value Accounting in History 237

[Table 10-4] Valuation Losses Accounted for by Mitsubishi (Unit: Yen)

Year	Loss	Issue that resulted in a valuation loss
1925	411,769	Koa Industries: 250,000; Chunichi Industries: 96,600; Tokyo Kaikan: 37,500; Meiji Fisheries: 27,669
1926	341,889	Kita-Sakhalin Mining: 249,144; Daigen Mining: 92,745
1927	21,116	Electrochemical Industries: 11,116; Manchoho bonds: 10,000
1928	1,240,449	Toyo Weaving: 1,080,478; Kanjo Bank: 6,250
1929	1,651,912	
1935	228,131	Toyo Weaving: 210,631; Nichiro Industries: 15,000; Argentine Farms: 2,500
1937	26,460	Miyako Hotel investment loss: 22,500; Japan Refractories and Antiseptics capital reduction loss: 3,960
1938	41,750	Tsurumi Harbor Railroad: 30,000; International Telephone merger loss: 11,750
1939	381,396	Shanghai Mitsubishi Warehousing recapitalization loss: 379,549; Izumo Railway capital reduction loss: 1,848
1940	173,550	Fuji Textiles merger loss: 173,550
1941	175,000	Kyowa Mining merger loss: 175,000
1942	189,594	South Sea Pearls: 189,594
1943	179,160	Taiwan Colonization: 95400; South Sea Colonization: 83,760

Note: A breakdown of 1929 valuation losses is not available.
Source: Okazaki [2000], Tables No. 19 and 43, taken from Mitsubishi Ltd. "Accounts Ledger" and "Mitsubishi Magazine".

went to about 80%[49], with a breakdown of securities owned by Sumitomo Ltd. being "6–7% general stocks and about 90% Sumitomo affiliate stocks[50]". The decrease in stocks held was caused in part by a decrease in capital and valuation decrease with little finance related causes[51]" (see Table 10-5).

In Sumitomo's case, we sometimes come across the posting of valuation losses or gains by operating companies under its umbrella whereby "increases in stock valuation were mainly by

---

[49] Asajima [1983], p. 439, Table 166.
[50] Asajima [1983], p. 486.
[51] Asajima [1983], p. 494.

[Table 10-5] Valuation Losses (Gains) Accounted for by Sumitomo Ltd.

(Unit: Thousand yen)

Year	Sumitomo issues	Other issues
1925		Bank of Japan, Tokyo Marine: 328
1926	Osaka North Port: 264	Toa Industries, Chunichi Industries: 347
1927	Osaka North Port (depreciation): 439	Taiwan Bank (capital decrease): 58, Toa Industries, etc. (depreciation): 405
1929		Hanshin Electric Railway: 169
1930		Bank of Japan, Hanshin Electric Railway: 2280
1931		Japan Electric Power: 1917
1932	Sumitomo Bank: 86	
1940	Sumitomo Metals (valuation gain): 8966, Sumitomo Mining, etc.: 3801	North China Gold: 5165
1941	Sumitomo Metals, etc. (valuation gain): 2115, Sumitomo Mining, etc.: 297	Japan Gold: 1818

Source: Asajima [1983], Table 195 and 202, taken from Sumitomo Ltd. "Status Report" and Sumitomo Collection Archives.

Sumitomo Metals, which grew with the times, and decreases mainly caused by a halving of net profits and lowered dividends by Sumitomo Mining[52]". The balance of securities held was an extremely low proportion. Other stocks held "were mostly listed.... On the surface, Sumitomo affiliate stocks had a high depreciation rate caused by valuation losses, but this is a reflection of market conditions and low corporate results, which contrasts with Sumitomo affiliate stocks that the company continued to hold at historical cost[53]".

These prewar zaibatsu would often apply the cost method for affiliate stock valuation with the intention of holding long term in contrast with general stocks issued by non-affiliates; however, this can be interpreted as "insolation from market value" from the

---

[52] Asajima [1983], p. 505.
[53] Asajima [1983], p. 499.

perspective of adequacy of market value accounting application.

10-6. Conclusion: Requirement of Market Value Accounting Application

When the market liquidity is scarce, it is highly possible that the market prices will be decided on the basis of benchmarks that do not reflect fundamentals. "Valuation losses or gains of fair value that reflect financial bubble prices (speculative prices) are illusionary gains or losses of no substance that may mislead short-term investors[54]". In other words, the application of market value accounting in a financial crisis is not fair value accounting. For market value accounting to constitute *fair value accounting* a very liquid market is required. The application of market value accounting lacking this precondition was almost never considered problematic.

The debate on *fair price* is rooted in the Middle Ages in Europe. This debate on *iustum pretium* (fair price) waged by the scholastics can be exemplified as follows:

· "Price determinations must be in conjunction with collaborative civil entities. With no exception, they must match price levels during normal markets[55]".

· "Even is a price is agreed upon by the buyer and seller on the market, it is unfair if such price is forced upon as a result of one of the parties' ignorance or need[56]".

· "Collaborative determination of market prices is not merely a legal or formal undertaking, but rather based on natural law, whose righteousness sheds light on any unfair consents forced on the other party due to ignorance or need[57]".

As Noonan, Jr., [1957] states, "The scholastics... condemn attempts to manipulate the market price artificially by monopolistic restriction of the supply or by purely speculative purchases[58]". This view of *fair price* clearly presupposes a normal market undergoing liquid trading. The expression *forced by need* means that the price

---

[54] Koga [2009], p. 7.
[55] Oguro [2006], p. 72.
[56] Oguro [2006], p. 74.
[57] Oguro [2006], p. 74.
[58] Noonan, Jr., [1957], p. 88.

is not fair even if both the seller and the buyer agree that it is very suggestive, even in a modern day setting.

Meanwhile, even if market value accounting can be applied, there are cases where the adequacy of its application is doubtful, such as when the object asset is considered as a business investment. Even if (where the object is affiliate company stocks acquired as a business investment while also constituting financial assets) market value accounting for listed stocks is applied, the adequacy of such application is unverified. It is noteworthy that these prewar combine holding companies did this on their own without using any accounting system.

Many prewar combine affiliates were not publically issuing their stock, and it was not until the 1930s that more operating companies began gradually placing their shares on the market. Although these affiliated operating companies with publically issued shares were not the target of constant market valuation by holding companies, other non-affiliate shares held were market valuated, and aggressive measures were taken whenever valuation losses were accounted. They drew a line separating what would be targeted for market value accounting application and what would not, suggesting that they debated the adequacy of such application.

The debates and examples shown in this thesis to answer the question of how to treat affiliate stock issues acquired as business investments under an illiquid market, and particularly whether to apply market valuation, are perhaps best understood as vestiges of the struggles of our ancestors. This report presents some empirical cases of what to do when markets lose their liquidity, a precondition of market valuation, and practical examples regarding the adequate application of these methods under permissible conditions.

[References in English]
Allen, F., and E. Carletti [2008a]. "The Role of Liquidity in Financial Crises", prepared for the 2008 Jackson Hole Symposium.
―――― [2008b], "Should Financial Institutions Mark-to-Market," Financial Stability Review (Banque de France), No. 12.
Bagehot,W. [1873], *Lombard Street, a Description of Money Market*, Henry S. King & Co.
Kindleberger, C. P. [2002], *Manias,Panics and Crashes:A History of Financial Crises*, 4th ed. Palgrave .
Noonan, Jr., J. T. [1957], *The Scholastic Analysis of Usury*,Harvard University

Press.

Vinals, J. [2008], "Improving Fair Value Accouting", Flinancial Stability Review (Banque de France), No. 12.

[References in Japanese]

Asajima, Shoichi [1983], *The history of Sumitomo financial combine management in interwar period*, University of Tokyo Press.

Fujii, Mariko [2009], *Financial innovation and Market crisis*, Nikkei publishing Inc.

Kanai, Yuichi [1989], *Formation of the Bank of England monetary policy*, The University of Nagoya Press.

Koga, Chitoshi [2009],"Financial crisis and the future of fair value accounting — Toward a construction of financial reporting — ", *Kigyo Kaikei (Accounting)*, Vol. 61 No. 3.

Masuda, Kouichi [2008] (the chairperson of JICPA), "Comment on the current value accounting and so on".

Obinata,Takashi. [2012], *Financial crisis and accounting regulation : fallacy of the fair value accounting mesurement*, Chuokeizai-sha. Inc.

Ogawa, Isao [1994], "The Showa panic and life insurance management (I) — the establishment of Life Insurance Securities Corp.", *Bunken Ronshu*, No. 109, Life Insurance Culture Research Institute.

——— [1995], "The Showa panic and life insurance management (II) — the establishment of Life Insurance Securities Corp.", *Bunken Ronshu*, No. 110, Life Insurance Culture Research Institute.

Oguri,Seiji [2001], "Reconsideration on W. Bagehot — the 'last resort' function of the Central Bank", *Hikone Ronshu* , No. 332.

Oguro, Shunji [2006], *Lie and Greed: the view on commerce, merchants in the West Middle Ages*, The University of Nagoya Press.

Okazaki, Tetsuji [2000], "Financial structure of the Mitsubishi financial combine head office — an analysis of 1925-1944 year financial statements"), *Mitsubishi Shiryoukan Ronshu*, Vol.1.

Ota, Wataru, Jun Uno and Hitoshi Takehara [2011], *Stock market liquidity and Investors behaviour*, Chuokeizai-sha. Inc.

Saito, Shizuki [2009], *Study on Accounting Standards,* Chuokeizai-sha. Inc.

Sakamoto, M. [2009], "The interview : Did financial crisis change the current value accounting ? the argument over the current value and institutional correspondence of each countries", *Kigyo Kaikei (Accounting)*, Vol. 61 No. 2.

Seimeihoken Kyokai (Life Insurance Association of Japan) [1970], *Showa-seimeihoken shiryo*, Dai 1 kan (*Life insurance documents*", Vol. 1)

Takeda, Haruhito [2009], "Investment behavior of life insurance companies in Japanese capital market before the World War II", *Kinyu Kenkyu (Journal of Financial Research* published by Institute for Monetary and Economic Studies in Bank of Japan), Vol. 28 No. 2.

Takemori, Shunpei [2008], *Do you dislike Capitalism?*, Nikkei publishing Inc.

Chapter 11

A Warning Bell from History on giving too much Emphasis to the Usefulness Approach[1]

Izumi Watanabe
Osaka University of Economics

Abstract
Double-entry bookkeeping, which first came about in the northern city-states of early thirteenth century Italy as a memorandum of receivables and debts, developed over the next hundred years into a means of verifying earnings from physical inventories. Once the cornerstone of structural calculation in accounting, it took on the role of progenitor of verification methods based on transaction facts. In other words, the most important aspects of accounting and double-entry bookkeeping are that the earnings measured therewith are the results of commerce based on fact and that they must possess reliability that is verifiable by anyone.

However, the usefulness approach for decision making in the modern age, in which usefulness and relevance are excessively emphasised, has become more important than reliable information whose accuracy and verifiability are guaranteed based on fact, which is the root of accounting, even if there are, for example, uncertain components included in that information but still

---

[1] The Author expresses much gratitude to J. Roger Mace, who is a former senior lecturer in Accounting and Finance at the University of Lancaster, for his perceptive and helpful comments and modifications of my English.

considered as useful. Information should be considered as useful because its content is reliable and for no other reason.

Comprehensive income information sought under the Asset and Liability View, which regards only today's results as important, is contaminated with uncertain forecasts based on future cash flows that significantly add noise to accounting rooted in reliability. The purpose of this thesis is to affirm the original role of accounting or double-entry bookkeeping and sound a warning bell from the perspective of history with respect to the qualitative revolution of the profit information provided by the usefulness approach, which is overemphasised today.

Keywords
Reliability, usefulness, verifiability, market valuation, fair value, market value, verification method

11-1. Introduction

It is not an exaggeration to say that the accounting perspective that was created by the FASB-developed "Asset and Liability View" invaded modern accounting and caused a Copernican revolution in historical cost-based accounting founded on the accrual basis method passed down for eight centuries.

The most fundamental role of modern accounting is information provision. However, in recent years, because the aspect of information useful for decision-making has been overly emphasised, I cannot help getting the impression that financial accounting has exceeded its original boundaries of structural computation and bitten into the forbidden fruit of forecasting and anticipation, thus deviating from its role as presenter of results based on fact. That's because even if information useful for investors and speculators represented in all manner of funds neither constitutes reliable information on past transaction results nor is based on fact, it is strikingly appealing to those living in the world of expectations and pink figures. As a result, illusions are created as to the usefulness of forward-looking statements estimable on the market over and above simple historical facts.

The FASB publicised SFAS No. 130 in 1997 requiring the disclosure of comprehensive income. However, "the component of SFAS130 'other comprehensive income' merely adds noise to comprehensive income[2]" indicated by empirical research released at the same time to be meaningful. Therefore, we can say that including results generated by forecast-comprising management accounting into the historical fact-based financial accounting[3] severely warps the reliability of information backed by financial accounting fact-based verifiability.

The reason why double-entry bookkeeping, the backbone of structural computation of accounting, has been passed down continuously for 800 years from the early 1200's to the present day is because it is a reliable profit calculation system that is accurate and verifiable by anyone based on fact. Under the theme of "usefulness and relevance," is it at all possible for accounting to supply truly useful information to investors and creditors using the Asset and Liability View, which, I would go as far as saying, is not based on a continuous record? What and how well-grounded were the arguments supporting fair value accounting, that were sufficient to drive the Revenue and Expence View into a corner?

The purpose of this Chapter is reconsider what role double-entry bookkeeping had throughout history as it buttressed accounting and its profit and loss computation structure and then to compare it with the role of modern accounting, which places the information provision role as the primary concern, and finally to use the findings to reexamine the true nature of accounting. I want to view the dangers lying in the path being taken by modern accounting, whose centre of gravity has shifted from reliability to usefulness, or from verifiability to relevance, through the lens of history and to sound the warning bell for all to hear.

11-2. True Nature of Accounting: Historical Cost as Guarantor of Evidentiality

AAA defines accounting as "the process of identifying, measuring, and communicating economic information to permit informed judgment and decisions by users of the information[4]". It goes without saying that accounting is the act of conveying the

---

[2] Dahlia, Dan, Subramanyam and Trezevant [1999], p. 47.
[3] Matsumoto [2008], p. 57.
[4] AAA [1969], p. 2.

results of a company's business activities over the course of a year to stakeholders. Therefore, the role of accounting is generally two-fold: information provision and interest adjustment; so the primary function of financial accounting is to provide external stakeholders, investors and creditors with period income information acquired by a company during a fiscal year from start to end. This is the reason why financial accounting is called as external report accounting and past accounting. The primary role of financial accounting is to calculate the realised income for one year and to report it to stakeholders. The positioning of distributable realised earnings based on the accrual principle as being useful information for decision-making is the traditional standpoint of accounting.

However, if emphasising the point of providing information useful for decision making, the world is moving away from past imtormation of profit and being lured towards future information assuming the acquisition of some profit going forward. A multitude of investment funds and analysts that strive to meet every desire of general shareholders universally forecast future corporate income and estimate future cash in-flow to determine the value of a company and their forecast results can potentially become useful information in investment decision making. In other words, for these fund investors and analysts, and by extension the investors and speculators that refer to their forecasts, the substance of useful information has shifted from actual, distributable earnings acquired over the past year to the more appealing corporate value information obtained from comprehensive income and market cap data that includes unrealised earnings estimates based on fair value.

The new accounting perspective spawned in the wake of the "Big Bang" accounting reforms is a paradigm shift in the content of the information provided by accounting to interested parties from net income to comprehensive income, or simply to corporate value constituting a move from historical cost to fair value and the measurement standards thereof. If the purpose of accounting is to provide corporate value, then eight centuries of double-entry bookkeeping that supported accounting's structural computation framework would be rendered useless because corporate value measurements are not necessarily based on continuous records. Corporate value measurement is the concern of financial researchers on a plane well beyond that of mere accounting.

It is obvious that information useful to decision-makers provided by traditional accounting, constitutes current term net income measured on the accrual basis backed up by historical cost, or simply allocatable realised earnings. Since the 1960s, we saw the emergence of a concept that valued not simple historical information but future information as useful for investment decision making even if it contained uncertainties including forecasts.

Here lies the large trap of false representation and window-dressing into which modern accounting is likely to step. The reason is that when discrepancies arise between forecasts and reality, people have the tendency to change those forecasts to match reality in an effort to justify their own forecasts. This is falsification in the form of window-dressing or reverse window-dressing. Forecast information, which exists in the world of make-believe, is drafted to give the beholder a false sense of objectivity, accuracy and reliability through plausible explanations and figures, the latter of which are mysterious numbers in the form of future cash flows and discounted present values. Even if one claims to have disclosed these figures, they do not ensure the transparency of genuine accounting.

In recent years, the hobbling of reliability to expedite usefulness has caused reliability and verifiability to retreat from being the fundamental characteristics of financial reporting useful to decision making and has ushered in the new concept of faithful representation in an effort to justify reliability's demise.

11-3. Fundamental Role of Double-Entry Bookkeeping as a Pillar of Accounting's Structural Computation

In its earliest stage, double-entry bookkeeping served not to compute income but had the dual purpose of providing a memorandum on receivables and debts and, in times of trouble, providing evidentiary documentation and notarised certificate. Human memory is limited. Thus double-entry bookkeeping is the act of writing down of figures so as to avoid troubles in the future. If a dispute arose, ledgers were used as evidence in court. Double-entry bookkeeping is a technique by which evidence of daily transactions is written down in a manner verifiable by anyone. In order to enhance its evidentiality and consequently give it the same validity as a notarized certificate, up to the late 1500s, a bookkeeper would draw up a crucifix with the inscription "Al Nome di Dio, Amen" (In the Name of God, Amen) on the heading.

Amounts recorded as evidence had to be, without a doubt, accurate and reliable figures that anyone at any time could immediately authenticate. For all people to trust those numbers, they were required to be, first and foremost, accurate and objective and based on fact without any predictions and, second, represent amounts actually transacted that anyone could verify at any time. In other words, those amounts are presumed to be transparent and verifiable. It is precisely the reason why they are trustworthy figures that they constitute potentially useful information to decision making.

Since its creation, the backbone of accounting's structural earnings computation, double-entry bookkeeping, has always served as a calculation method that met all its demands and the basis for the value of things as they are actually transacted, or the transaction value (which is transformed to historical cost with the passage of time). The greatest advantage of calculations based on transaction value is that the resulting price becomes a historical fact whose objectivity, or facts supporting it, can be verified at any time. This is the justification for double-entry bookkeeping's existence and is the most significant factor that assures accounting's reliability. It has passed over eight hundred years since the oldest ledger appeared on the historical stage of accounting. Accounting and double-entry bookkeeping have stood the test of time passed down from the Middle Ages to the present day because it always guaranteed accuracy and transparency, the hallmarks of reliability backed by materiality and verifiability[5].

When double-entry bookkeeping first appeared in the early 1200s, there were still no profit and loss accounts, therefore, an enterprise's comprehensive income could not be calculated by continuous recording[6]. Even so, under such circumstances, Florence's "term partnership" structure did not allow for asso-

---

[5] The origin of reliability in accounting is the use of continuous recording as a means to prove on-hand calculations based on physical inventory count at the time when double-entry bookkeeping was developed in Italy in the Middle Ages to support structural computation in accounting.

[6] Watanabe [2005], pp. 47–48.

ciations by blood relations (*Consulteria*). Unlike aristocratic Venice's "family partnership" structure (*Societas*), a term partnership structure not made up of blood relations (*Magna Societas*) formed[7]. Therefore, faced with the actual need for profit sharing among association members but as yet non-recurring as per need, total income calculations by period were made. Prior to the full development of double-entry bookkeeping, because profit sharing could not be effected under continuous recording, merchants in that era proposed a substitute method: income computation based on *Bilanzio* — earnings appropriation from combined property inventory — centred on physical inventory, which was a pioneering form of periodic income computation practiced prior to the full development of double-entry bookkeeping (early 1300s)[8].

However, with calculation based on the results of a physical inventory count only of items on hand, joint investors doubted the reliability of earnings figures arrived therefrom. They would exclaim, "Is that all the profits the company made?" Accountants were then pressed to find some other means to prove that earnings figures calculated under *Bilanzio* were free of errors and unfairness. The resulting reliable verification method was continuous recording, or income computation under double-entry bookkeeping. In this way, double-entry bookkeeping, which first appeared in the early 1200s, developed into a comprehensive income computation system as late as a century later to prove the correctness of earnings figures calculated by *Bilanzio*. It is this reliability backed by factuality (accuracy) and verifiability (transparency) that directly gave birth to double-entry bookkeeping. This in itself constitutes the foundation upon which double-entry bookkeeping and accounting exists.

As one piece of evidence that double-entry bookkeeping was a tool to verify specific on-hand calculation from the results side based on abstract income calculation generated from the causal side, we can cite *Vierde Stvck Der Wisconstighe Ghedachtnissen* by Simon Stevin (1548 – 1620) in 1605 in Leiden, Holland. Earnings measured by calculating cost and revenue differentials based on continuous recording was used as a means to verify earnings

---

[7] Saito, H. [2002], pp. 301 – 336.

[8] Regarding pioneering term income calculation, refer to Watanabe [2005], pp. 17 – 18, and Watanabe [2008a], pp. 45 – 46, p. 80 and p. 109.

figures measured by calculating increase and decrease comparisons of assets, liabilities and capital as the results of on-hand computation.

Stevin, when closing the main ledger accounts, would calculate term-end equity by drawing up *Staet* (a position statement) as a list of assets, liabilities and capital. The term-end capital is then compared with the beginning-of-term figure to calculate the year's earnings. To prove term earnings calculated from the stock side, he describes a method whereby *Winst en Verlies* (an income statement) is drafted whose accounts are calculated from the flow side as *Staet Proef* (an evidentiary statement) and the earnings figure resulting therefrom proves the earnings figure calculated in the position statement[9]. Therefore, because the earnings appearing in the income statement calculated based on continuous recording is used for evidentiary purposes, its transparency must be verifiable by anyone and its reliability must be absolutely assured. It goes without saying that this reliability is guaranteed by records based on fact, meaning values determined at the time that transactions were effected, which means historical cost.

11-4. Historical Cost and Current Value: Nothing more than Different Points in Time

Historical cost is the current value at the time of transaction (transaction value = market value). The current value at the time the transaction actually occurred is merely transformed into historical cost indicating the past value at the time of accounts settlement conducted in the future. In essence, there is no difference between them. Put differently, the current value at the time of transaction is the same as the historical cost at the time of accounts settlement. Therefore, current value is merely perceived differently as a result of its movement on the time axis and market value can essentially be synonymous with historical cost[10].

Generally, "fair value" takes the name of "current value" and specifically indicates present market value and future cash flow of discounted present value. However, does the time in the "present"

---

[9] Stevin [1605], pp. 34-36.
[10] Watanabe [2010], pp. 2-3.

purported when speaking of "present value" really exist? When representing time chronologically in terms of past, present and future, "present" is the "just now" and lasts only an instant, therefore, the "now" is not a portion of time but only a point of dividing the past and the future. Time called "now" has "neither length nor breadth[11]. Consequently, time is the relation between the present and the past, and the future does not exist in any sense of the word and is absorbed into the present and the past[12].

Therefore, how should we verify the actuality of future cash flow amounts measured at a point in the future, which is a time that does not exist? Accounting and the basis of its structural computation, double-entry bookkeeping, has earned its reliability by providing income information backed by accuracy and verifiability. Even if market value as measured by actual present value is taken out of the equation, in accounting measurements where reliability is paramount, what aspects of these mysterious future cash flows and their discounted present values measured at a non-existing point in the future should we trust?

In the same way, even fair value is essentially on a different plane than market value and discounted present value. Looking at time chronologically, the time called the "present" varies depending on whether it is attributed a certain breadth on the timeline or an instant. Either way, the "instantaneous present" gets immediately absorbed into the past. Therefore, evaluations based on market value assessed in the "instantaneous present" slip into the past an instant later becoming historical cost. Put another way, as long as market value is looked upon as occurring in the present and merely the link between past and future, then there is essentially no difference between market value and historical cost. Considering this, if the past is "the former present[13]", then historical cost is "the former market value." Therefore, for fair value measurements, market value-based valuations (present value) may be transformed into historical cost (past value) by the mere passage of time and categorised within the framework of historical cost accounting. Market value measurement accounting can be regarded as revised historical cost accounting. In other words,

---

[11] Irifuji [2008], p. 21.

[12] Nakajima [2007], p. 194.

[13] This concept is the fruit of trial and error on the movement of time or "flow of time" (Omori [1996], pp. 89-90).

double-entry bookkeeping has been the coexistence of two types of accounting (mixed attribute accounting), current value accounting and historical cost accounting, right from its onset.

The fact is that in ledgers drafted in eighteenth and nineteenth century England, the aforementioned was prevalent, however, impossible for discounted present value (future value) because the future cannot exist in the present in the same form.

This has already been mentioned sufficiently, but take any marketable security, for example, and people will believe that its market value generally possesses objectivity. This is true for small quantities such as 10,000 or 20,000 shares, however, for huge quantities like several million shares, cashing those in all at once at market value would be unrealisable, you would not get the amount imagined. The more one sells, the lower the stock price becomes, and there is a certain quantity of shares that can never be sold completely at the initial price. Where can find a realisable and reliable basis for such market value?

It goes without saying that accounting records reflect economic phenomena. Because of this, it is extremely important that they should be expressed by means that allow for a reconstitution from the transaction's recognised phenomena (journalizing) to original form (transaction). Where in the world can we find reliable value in information that makes corporate earnings dizzyingly fluctuate at the current value's every whim? Modern accounting's future cash inflow is nothing more than a camouflaged forbidden fruit seen through rose tinted glasses.

11-5. Historical Cost and Market Value in Transaction Value Accounting

As everyone knows, fair value is defined in SFAS No. 15, Paragraph 5 as "the monetary amount received from the sale of an asset or payment or transfer of a liability in an orderly transaction between market participants on the measurement date". In Japan, this generally refers to current value (exit value). In other words, according to SFAC, SFAS and IFRS, current value is a fair measuring stick by which to determine an asset's value. Not a single person objects to its measurement based on a fair value. But who in the world was it that defined fair value as current value?

Without digging into this central issue, you may well think that the assumption of current value being a fair value would create a huge pitfall in today's asset measurement. What is important is where to find specific measurement attribute for fair value. In the field of economics, it would be acceptable to measure assets at fair value, however, in accounting, without clarifying specific measurement attribute of fair value, amounts to appear on the balance sheet cannot be determined.

One would rightfully think that people are spreading some kind of myth that values measured based on a market are complete and fair and more objective than any yardstick. However, not all assets and liabilities exist on a market. Those without a market have their prices measured based on an estimate of future cash flow or other forecast. This is also referred to as fair value. Evaluations based on fair value cannot be verified: neither can they be contradicted by anyone. The expression has the added magic of having the word "fair" in it. We must recognise the large gap in sense and weight of the word "fair" as understood by us Japanese as opposed to Western societies.

Originally, the concept of "fairness" customarily employed in the field of accounting refers to the fairness of expression and includes the neutrality of preparation (lack of bias) and expression in financial reporting. In other words, fairness is a word that primarily refers to neutrality without bias toward any other concept. Simultaneously, it covers the fairness and righteousness of all items that result from it. Therefore, the depth of the expert knowledge and cautions expressed and sworn in financial statements guarantees the fairness of corporate financial activities. The word "fairness" plays an extremely important role in accounting and "the conventional nature of the concept of fairness is fairness in presentation, a guarantee that diligence and care in the presentation and attestation of financial statements are to ensure the adequate presentation of the financial affairs of the firm. Because the central meaning of fairness is fairness in presentation, the concept understood in the United States as the fairness doctrine and in Europe as the 'True and Fair' doctrine, pinpointing some of the consequences of its application[14]".

Consequently, a negation of fairness immediately connotes "unfairness". An "unfair" person indicates a biased individualin

---

[14] Monti-Belkaoui and Riahi-Belkaoui [1996], p. 1.

whom all good characteristics are outweighed. Using this sorcery, American and international accounting standards are attempting to force the replacement of transaction value-based measurement, used for eight centuries since the birth of bookkeeping and that partially includes current value-induced correction, with fair value-based measurement without any explanation as to why fair value is considered current value.

Don't you perceive here a clever tactic by standards formulators or some global conspiracy? However, calling this fair value by the name "current value," "market value" or "discounted present value" from the outset, then we can see how the myth that current value is a fair value spread widely controlling the minds of masses. This is terribly suspicious. What is important is how to determine the specific measurement attribution of fair value. In the field of economics, there may be no problem whatsoever in measuring fair value based on the value of things traded on a market. However, in the field of accounting, without clarifying a specific measurement attribute for fair value, the value of balance sheet account items cannot be determined and therefore earnings cannot be determined.

As everyone knows, the Enron and Worldcom bankruptcies of December 2001 and July 2002, the subprime loan crisis at the end of 2006 and the fall of Lehman Brothers in September 2008 blew away the market myth like a house of cards. Only 4 years have passed since the storm. The dangers of overdependence on the market were prophetically heralded in the mid-1980s by Michael Bromwich as follows: "In the practical world, not all resources and investment opportunities can be traded on perfect markets. Examples of the absence of complete markets are provided by the inability to market 'human' assets and to sell enterprise 'goodwill' other than jointly with other assets. The lack of a complete set of forward markets and complete insurance opportunities provides further examples of incomplete markets[15]".

Moreover, Sadao Takatera wrote, while quoting Mary Barth and Guillaume Plantin: There is no need to reiterate that in a market with lots to offer and easy liquidation, market values are reliable standard bearers, therefore, the predominance of historical value measurement in market value measurement cannot be negated. Unfortunately, when markets are incomplete, market values are

---

[15] Bromwich [1985], p. 57.

oftentimes not the true and fair values of assets. Therefore, compared with historical value measurement, the predominance of market value measurement is questionable[16].

Nevertheless, from the beginnings of double-entry bookkeeping, transactions have been made based on market value at the time thereof. This market value (present value) is transformed into historical cost (past value) with the passage of time. From the creation of double-entry bookkeeping, when merchants were faced with discrepancies between present value and past value, they developed means to correct them using present value. The oldest surviving account records consist of two sheets of paper on which are four pages of continuous accounts journalised vertically at a fair in Bologna, Italy in 1211 by a Florentine banker. Because of the limited data, we cannot confirm whether any bad debt account was included in the account items.

However, we can easily surmise from the ledger wording that they fully comprehended the risk of loan becoming bad debts by bankruptcy. It is written that "1211, Orlandino Galigaio from Santa Trinita must give us 26 pounds for mid-May, for buolongnini which we gave him in Bolongna for the San Brocoli market; if they stay longer [the interest] is 4 denari per pound each month. Should he fail to pay, Angiolino Bolongnini Galogaio promised to pay us[17]". We can see that borrowers took on guarantors to prepare against any likely incapacity to reimburse a debt. Certainly this ledger suggests that loan claims were evaluated based on current value. If the borrower failed to reimburse by the deadline, a 20% penalty fee was imposed in addition to 40% of agreed interest rate. The interest on the debt, which matched the interest on the loan, was seen as the loss on expected earnings and considered an average rate of interest in the financial business of those days[18].

Bad debt accounts actually first appeared in ledgers such as those prepared by the Datini Company's Barcelona Branch in the last 1300s[19]. They reevaluated accounts receivable using current value and posted bad debt loss as "irrecoverable accounts". The Datini Company's Florence Branch in 1404 accounted for the

---

[16] Takatera [2008], pp. 236-237.
[17] Alvaro [1974], p. 329.
[18] Alvaro [1974], p. 322.
[19] de Roover [1974], p. 149.

irrecoverable portion of sales proceeds as "cattivo debitore" (bad debt)[20]. Another example can be found in Chapter 3, Paragraph 14 "Inventory Model" of Pacioli's *Summa*, which states "In total I have so many ducats to collect, you will say, of good money, if the money is due from good people, otherwise you will say of bad money[21]".

At that time, for income accounts, all private accounts other than those transferred to asset, liability and capital accounts were transferred and a "miscellaneous" summary account (hotchpotch account) was created simply to close the main ledger[22]. Because of this, the concept of calculating an enterprise's total income using profit and loss account items was rare until as late as the first half of the 1300s. The same can be said concerning the balance account. For the balance account in the February 28, 1483 ledger of Nicolo and Alvise Barbarigo, not only items relating to assets and liabilities but also to cost and revenue were transferred[23].

In this manner, measurement based on current value (market value) appeared at the same time with the birth of double-entry bookkeeping. Therefore, current value at the time of transaction and historical cost at the time of accounts settlement are nothing more than representations at different points in time, and market value can essentially play the same role as historical cost. Although we are entirely uncertain at the present time how the market will act in the future, even if the market is incomplete, we can use transaction prices based on market values at the time of their occurrence as objective facts that cannot be easily refuted. Real income generated as a result of actual trading is essentially different from illusory earnings generated from by the mere possession. The greatest advantage of transaction price, or measurement based on historical cost, is the constant objectivity and transparency the measured monetary amounts as historical facts, or verification based on transaction facts, enabled thereby. Verifiability based on fact is the foundation of double-entry bookkeeping, developed as a means to prove profit using physical inventory, and the greatest factor substantiating the reliability of

---

[20] Penndorf [1933], S. 37–38.

[21] Geijsbeek [1914], p. 37.

[22] This concept of handling profit and loss accounts as "miscellaneous accounts" can be seen in Pacioli's *Summa* (Yamey [1978], p. 109).

[23] Watanabe [1993], pp. 31–32.

accounting.

11-6. Discounted Present Value and Feasibility Concept

A complete definition of fair value was provided in APB Opinion No. 29 "Accounting for Nonmonetary Transactions" in 1973 based on discounted present value, positioned as the foundation of future cash flow in the 1950s[24]. However, even though it is also called fair value, market value, which also generally goes by the name "current value", is essentially very different from the fair value upon which discounted present value is based as the foundation for future cash flow appearing in the 1950s.

The method of revising prices set at the time of transaction using current value came about at the same time as double-entry bookkeeping. The current value evaluation of loan claims, or the accounting practice of bad debt losses and losses on the evaluation of equipment and inventory goods, found here and there in the ledgers of Italian merchants in the thirteenth to fifteenth centuries beginning with the oldest preserved account records has already been mentioned in the previous section. Both measurement based on historical cost and measurement based on current value (market value) coexisted with double-entry bookkeeping from its very beginnings. Double-entry bookkeeping at its creation was a hybrid of current value accounting and historical cost accounting (mixed attribute accounting).

At the moment of a transaction, the market value (present value) is generated and the price that is set is nothing more than its transformation into historical cost (past value) at the time of accounts settlement after time has elapsed.

Described another way, market value accounting is within the wider realm of historical cost accounting (accounting where both past accounting and present account coexist = mixed attribute accounting), or transaction price accounting, and essentially different from discounted present value accounting, which is forward accounting in the same category as fair value accounting. That's because whether records are posted using actual transaction prices based on fact, or using imaginary transaction prices based on estimates,

---
[24] Bromwich [2007], p. 49.

their timelines are fundamentally different. What separates transaction price accounting from fair value accounting is the realisation concept (see the next page diagram).

The biggest problem facing fair value accounting today is how to articulate its realisation concept. The measurement of the value of things is the role of economics, and what is important to business operators is not the current value of goods in their possession but how much they can actually sell them for. However, accounting is a map of actual economic circumstances and never does it reflect estimated or anticipated global economic events. The calculation of earnings based on actual fact has been fulfilled constantly by accounting since its creation even through all the ebbs and flows of time. It is the reason why accounting has been trusted for eight hundred years. We can never eat nothing but pie in the sky. In the same way we cannot expect to be able to measure realised gains by setting aside actual yardsticks and using a type of accounting that is based on holding gains or evaluation profits.

However, today's fair value accounting may not even have a realisation concept or any other meaning. The profits concept that existed at the onset of double-entry bookkeeping is the designation of actual realised gains as real earnings and unrealised earnings and other fictitious figures are pipe dreams that the merchants at that time ignored as meaningless. The essence of earnings calculated by accounting is distributable realised profits and not comprehensive income.

The following Diagram shows the relation between historical cost, market value and discounted present value.

Things that don't have a market cannot be measured based on market value. Because of this, the measurer must decide whether to analogise leveraging the market value of a similar asset (Level 2) or deem a current value amount resulting from estimating that asset and its future cash flow and computing future interest from the present value (Level 3). Level 3 is the estimate squared. An estimate may very well not hit the mark, so how are we supposed to find accounting-based facts and transaction objectivity in discounted present value obtained from multiplying one estimate by another estimate.

I believe that the enigmatic means of evaluation that is discounted present value is unsuitable for the real-life world of accounting centred on reliability[25]. The starting point of

[Diagram] Relation between transaction price accounting and fair value accounting

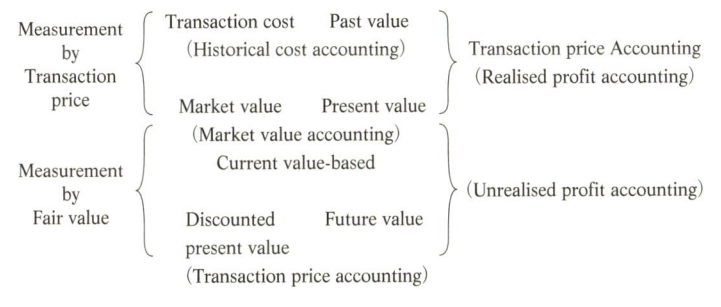

```
                    ┌ Transaction cost    Past value      ┐
Measurement         │ (Historical cost accounting)        │  Transaction price Accounting
   by               │                                     │  (Realised profit accounting)
Transaction         │                                     │
   price            └ Market value       Present value    ┘
                    ┌ (Market value accounting)           ┐
                    │   Current value-based               │
Measurement         │                                     │  (Unrealised profit accounting)
   by               │                                     │
Fair value          │ Discounted          Future value    │
                    │ present value                       │
                    └ (Transaction price accounting)      ┘
```

measurement is transaction price (historical cost). Historical cost's greatest feature is that it is an objective, actually transacted price which is verifiable by actually transacted vouchers. This reliability backed by actuality (objectivity) and verifiability is the root of double-entry bookkeeping, which has supported accounting and its structural computation. It is because it is reliable that accounting and double-entry bookkeeping has been passed down in an unbroken chain for 800 years. Ignoring entirely the world of finance, accounting is definitely not what is being seen today: a triumphantly swaggering, overused decision-making usefulness approach where relevance and usefulness are the main focus affecting the dealings of the corporation.

11-7. Retreat of Reliability and Verifiability and Faithful Expressions

FASB described in SFAC No. 2 "Qualitative Characteristics of Accounting Information" published in May 1980 the essential features necessary to render accounting information useful. It states that "financial reporting should provide information that is

---

[25] Many of the various reserves appeared after the dynamic theory and some believe they most likely computed based on discounted present value. However, taking the allowance for doubtful accounts as an example, is merely based on past experience value, or amounts that actually occurred in the past, and should not be interpreted as a figure resulting from the discounted present value of future cash out flows.

useful to present and potential investors and creditors and other users in making rational investment, credit, and similar decisions[26]", and to guarantee this usefulness, it positions relevance on equal ground with reliability[27]. At this stage of history, experts were still clearly aware that if information is not reliable then it is not useful. However, any intensification of demands and pressure with respect to a company by a few speculators with abundant capital who expect speculative returns, and not general shareholders who expect fixed dividends, will naturally result in action on the part of the company's managers in response to their every demand.

In other words, they have to provide not net income information for the fiscal term under review calculated based on continuous records but on corporate value information that fluctuates every waking instant. Speculators are not interested in the fruits of normal business operations but rather in the amount of speculative returns they can acquire from the sale of the shares they hold in that business. They want information on the liquidation value of a company as a precursor to an M&A. However, what is most important to business operators is how to avoid the risk of bankruptcy and maintain their enterprise as a going concern. They should never be aiming to measure its corporate value with the assumption of dissolution. Although no one is very much interested these days, I would like you to remember that there is a basic presumption to accomplish sound accounting, which is the accounting postulate of the going concern. Accounting is only achieved when the survival of the company is presumed and not when the purpose of liquidation. Such bankruptcy-focused corporate value calculations do not belong in the field of accounting. Accounting is an area of study that cannot exist if its all-important "going concern" assumption is discarded.

Speculators, typically hedge funds, have little interest in net income or other items calculated based on double-entry bookkeeping presuming the going concern but rather focus their energies on finding out what that enterprise is worth now and every subsequent moment thereafter. What is important to them for decision making is not past and present information on actual results posted over the year under review but rather future

---

[26] FASB [1980], No. 2, p. 9.
[27] FASB [1980], No. 2, p. 15, p. 20.

information predicting the amount of future cash inflows that can be generated. As a result, companies, following the orders of large shareholding speculators, prioritise the disclosure of comprehensive income information and corporate value information measured based on fair value over and above net income information from a historical cost-centric accrual basis. Therefore, in the world of financial instruments, all eyes are on the balance sheet and the role of the income statement is greatly diminished. An extreme arguer would label the income statement as an unnecessary document for enterprise value measurement purposes.

As stated in section 3 herein, double-entry bookkeeping on which accounting's structural computation is founded proves the earnings measured from the physical inventory-based *Bilanzio* using the earnings item in the profit and loss summary account based on continuous recording. Put another way, double-entry bookkeeping came to be as an evidentiary tool to enable the on-hand calculation of physical inventory. It is the reliability of earnings figures computed based on fact, and consequently the guarantee of verifiability that allows the confirmation of accuracy and factuality of calculated numbers by anyone, that is the true essence of accounting.

However, as the usefulness of accounting becomes overemphasised, the first sign of reliability's demise is the provision of useful information by SFAS and IFRS, which advocate that it is the very usefulness thereof that makes it reliable. This caused the recent removal of reliability and verifiability from "fundamental qualitative characteristics" established by accounting standards pushing them down to "enhancing qualitative characteristics[28]". This is an about-face that can only be explained as madness.

Regarding the reliability of measurements, IFRS stated in 2010 that "The second criterion for the recognition of an item is that it possesses a cost or value that can be measured with reliability as discussed in paragraph 31 to 38 of this Framework. In many cases, cost or value must be estimated; the case of reasonable estimates is an essential part of the preparation of financial statements and does not undermine their reliability[29]". This removed "reliability" from the new conceptual framework and in its stead introduced the expression "faithful representation."

---

[28] Iwasaki [2011], pp. 31–34. Fujii [2011], p. 32. Tsumori [2012], pp. 21–22.
[29] IASB [2010], Chapter 4, F4–41.

According to IFRS, one of the reasons for this is the often-witnessed criticism of fair value evaluation brought upon by the vagueness of "reliability". That's putting the cart in front of the horse. For any information, the most important factor is reliability. What in the world would a legitimate company do with unreliable information?

It was the raising of "usefulness" on the flag pole by IFRS and SFAS and the consequent removal of all information that deviates from relevance that caused the removal of "reliability" as a basic and essential feature of IFRS accounting standards and its new role as secondary feature, as well as the downgrading of verifiability that relegates reliability to the rank of secondary feature. You would think that, when establishing accounting standards, it wouldn't be reliability that gets the axe but rather information generated based on uncertain estimates under the moniker of "usefulness".

Regarding this point, IFRS states, "Financial reports represent economic phenomena in words and numbers. To be useful, financial information must not only represent relevant phenomena, but it must also faithfully represent the phenomena that it purports to represent. To be a perfectly faithful representation, a depiction would have three characteristics. It would be *complete*, *neutral* and *free from error*[30]". At a glance, the expression "faithful representation" gives the reader the impression that economic phenomenon are being faithfully expressed, however, these are not factual economic phenomena but merely relevant events expressed faithfully. In other words, according to IFRS 2011, if information does not conform to a certain purpose, even if the economic phenomenon being purported to is true, then it cannot be a faithful expression in terms required by investment decision makers and creditors.

11-8. Conclusion: Original Role of Accounting

Double-entry bookkeeping, which originated in the 1200s as a memorandum of receivables and debts developed into a fully-fledged corporate total income calculation system by the first half of the fourteenth century. The primary factor in the development

---

[30] IASB [2010], Chapter 3, QC12.

of double-entry bookkeeping is to confirm the total income of enterprises arrived at by the *Bilanzio* based on physical inventory through continuous recording. In other words, the origin of accounting is as a tool to confirm earnings calculated using physical inventory unrelated to the verifiability-backed, high-reliability continuous recording (double-entry bookkeeping). It is reliability in itself supported by accuracy and verifiability that buttresses accounting's income calculation structure, and is at the same exact time its destination. What has guaranteed accounting's reliability is income calculations based on historical cost (market value) centred on accrued (realised) basis. It is because the earnings figures calculated based on it constituted reliable information that double-entry bookkeeping managed to survive 800 years and continues to be the backbone of accounting's structural earnings computation.

However, as time went on, between the latter half of the 1600s and the early half of the 1700s, as discrepancies emerged between current prices of assets held and those at the time of their acquisition, various contradictions came to light in the earnings computation function, the original role of accounting. There was uncertainty as to whether historical cost-based measurements made for accurate earnings computations. To resolve this problem came the new method or view of accounting that reevaluates these assets at present market values and attach greater importance to comprehensive income than to net profit.

In addition, from the latter 1700s to the turn of the nineteenth century, associations and stock companies heretofore established by licensing were replaced by the gradual emergence of huge, modern corporations transforming the role of accounting. A substantial change in the purpose of accounting occurred from what was the calculation of actual, distributable earnings in a way that was accurate, verifiable and reliable to the provision of useful information for the purpose of investment decision making for the benefit of general investors from whom capital is procured. This was an overturning of accounting's purpose.

The impetus for this movement is the switch to fair value acounting, in which future cash flows are embedded, from distributable realised earnings calculation based on historical cost centred on the accrual basis.

In December 1976, the FASB released a memorandum that advocated an accounting concept based on the Asset and Liability

View and the Revenue and Expense View. Subsequently, new financial instruments spawned and, with the publication of SFAS No.105 in 1990 and SFAS No.107 in 1991, fair value-based accounting spread widely. As you know, 1993's SFAS No. 115 is the spark that placed the "mixed model" historical cost and fair value combination on centre stage. In September 2006, SFAS No. 157 was published on which the exposure draft "Fair Value Measurement" was established by the IASB in May 2009, which led to new guidance from IFRS in May 2011.

As the world became strikingly devoted to fair value accounting, the FASB procrastinated for six months between June and December 2011 on deciding on the evaluation criteria that would determine whether or not to commit to a roadmap for international standards. Under such circumstances, what is Japan to do? Align with the Americans or the international standards? I fear that we here will continue to dangle in the air on this issue. In our quest for stability, we accounting scholars will not encourage swimming with the tide, but rather a return to our roots and a dedication to down-to-earth research on the role of reliability as the essence of accounting, its true role and purpose and not the short-sighted usefulness doctrine.

[References in English and other Languages]
AAA [1957], "Accounting and Reporting Standards for Corporate Financial Statements 1957 Revision", *The Accounting Review*, Vol. 32, No. 4.

AAA [1966], *A Statement of Basic Accounting Theory*, Illinois.

Alvaro, Martinelli [1974], *The Origination and Evolution of Double Entry Bookkeeping to 1440, Part1 and Part 2*, Denton.

Barth, Mary [2006], "Including Estimates of the Future in Today's Financial Statements", BIS Working Paper, No. 208, August.

Bromwich, Michael [1985], *The Economics of Accounting Standard Setting*, Prentice Hall.

────── [2007], "Fair Values: Imaginary Prices and Mystical Markets. A Clarificatory Review", Walton, Peter ed., *The Routledge Companion to Fair Value and Financial Reporting*, New York.

de Roover, Reymond [1974], *Business, Banking, and Economic Though*, Chicago & London.

Dhaliwal, Dan, K.R. Subramanyam and Robert Trezevant [1999], "Is Comprehensive Income Superior to Net Income as a Measure of Firm Performance", *Journal of Accounting and Economics*, Vol. 26, Nos.1−3.

FASB [1976], *An Analysis of Issues Related to Conceptual Framework for Financial Accounting and Reporting: Elements of Financial Statements and Their Measurement*, FASB Discussion Memorandum.

―――― [1980], *Statement of Financial Accounting Concepts*, No. 2 "Qualitative Characteristics of Accounting Information".
―――― [2000], *Statement of Financial Accounting Consepts*, No. 7 "Using Cash Flow Information and Present Value in Accounting Measurements".
Geijsbeek, John B. [1914], *Ancient Double-Entry Bookkeeping*, Denber.
IASB [2010], *Conceptual Framework for Financial Reporting 2010*.
Mace, J.Roger [1977], "Criteria for the Selection of Reporting Method", *OMEGA*, Vol. 5, No. 5.
Monti-Belkaoui, Janice and Ahmend Riahi-Belkaoui [1996], *Fairness in Accounting*, London.
Penndorf, Balduin [1933], *Luca Pacioli Abhandlung über die Buchhaltung 1494*, Stuttgart.
Plantin, Guillaume, Haresh Sapra and Hyun Song Shin [2004], *Fair Value Reporting Standards and Market Volatility*, Working Paper, Carnegie Mellon University, University of Chicago and LSE, October, 2.
Porter, Roy [1982], *English Society in the Eighteenth Century*, (Revised edition 1990), London.
Stevin, Simon [1605], *Vierde Stvck Der Wisconstighe Ghedachtnissen Vande Weeghconst*, Leyden.
Yamey, Basil S. [1978], *Essays on the History of Accounting*, New York.

[References in Japanese]

Ando, Hideyoshi [2012], "A Gap between Financial Accoutring and Financial Reporting", *Kigyou Kaikei (Accounting)*, Vol. 64, No. 4.
Fujii, Hideki [2011], "FASB/IASB Improved Conceptual Framework for Financial Reporting and Its Related Asset-Liability View of Accounting", *The Kokumin-Keizai Zasshi (Journal of Economics & Business Administration)*, No. 204, No. 1.
Izutani, Katsumi [1980], *Original History of Double-entry Bookkeeping*, Moriyama Shoten.
Irihuji, Motoyoshi [2008], *Does The Time Exist Really?*, Kodansha Gendai-Shinsho.
Iwasaki, Isamu [2011], "On the Concept Frameworks of IFRS", *Kaikei (Accounting)*, Vol. 180, No. 6.
Kataoka, Yoshio [1967], *A Study in Pacioli's Summma*, Revised and Enlarged 2nd edition, Moriyama Shoten.
Kimura, Bin [1982], *Time and Oneself*, Chuko-Sinsho.
Kishi, Etsuzo [1975], *Generative History of Accounting-A Study of Accounting Regulations of Ordonnance du Commerce*, Dobunkan Shuppan.
Matsumoto, Toshifumi [2008], "The Intersection of Financial Accounting and Management Accounting-An Analysis of Features of Jsox, Asset Impairment Accounting and Comprehensive Income Concept-", *Kaikei (Accounting)*, Vol. 173 No. 5.
Nakajima, Michiyoshi [2007], *Philosophise "The Time": Where Has Gone The Past*, Kodansha Gendai-Shinsho.
Omori, Shozo [1996], *Time Does Not Passe*, Seidosha.
Saito, Hiromi [2002], *Commerce and Cities in The Latter Medieval in Italy*, Chisen Shokan.

Saito, Shizuki [2012], "Accounting Standards and Standards Research: Consistency, Usefulness and Social Norms", Obinata, Takashi, *The Starting Point of Studies in Accounting Standards*, Chuokeizai-sha, Inc.

―――― ed. [2002], *Conceptual Foundations of Accounting Standards*, Chuokeizai-sha, Inc.

Takatera, Sadao [1988], *Possibility Accounting*, Sanrei Shobo.

―――― [2008], "Market Imperfections and the Limited Application of Market Value Accounting", *Osaka Keidai Ronshu (Jouranal of Osaka University of Economics)*, Vol. 5, No. 2.

Tokuga, Yoshihiro [2011], "Review on Mixed Accounting Models for the Future Accounting Standards", *IMES Discussion Paper No. 2011-J-19*, Nihon-Ginko Kinyu Kenkyusho.

Tsumori, Tsunehiro [2012], "A Study of my 'Meta Theory' in Contemporary Accounting", *Kigyokaikei (Accounting)*, Vol. 64, No. 8.

Watanabe, Izumi [1983], *History of Profit and Loss Accounting*, Moriyama Shoten.

―――― [1993], *History of Closing Procedure*, Moriyama Shoten.

―――― [2005], *The Evolution of Profit and Loss Caluculation*, Moriyama Shoten.

―――― [2008a], *Accounting learned by History,* Moriyama Shoten.

―――― [2008b], "A Pitfall of Modern Accounting", *Kaikeishigakkai Nenpo (Year Book of Accountig History Association)*, No. 27.

―――― [2009], "Paradox of Accounting Purpose-Between Reliability and Usefulness-", *Kaikei (Accounting)*, Vol. 175, No. 5.

―――― [2010], "Historical Cost Accounting and Fair Value" *Kaikei (Accounting)*, Vol. 178, No. 3.

―――― [2011], "The Standpoint of Fair Value from the Viewpoint of History-Historical Cost and Market Value as the Transaction-price-based Accounting-" *Kaikei (Accounting)*, Vol. 180, No. 5.

―――― [2012], *A Warning Bell from History on The Excessive Usefulness Approach of Decision Making,* Working Paper of Osaka University of Economics, No. 2012-1, April.

INDEX

A

Accounting complaint, 170
Accounting mind, 101–103
Accrual basis, 247, 263
Accrual principle, 99
Acquisition cost, 168, 169, 171
Advance on profit, 147
Advances on earnings, 148
Anticipated earnings, 148
Anticipated gain, 147
Applicability of market value accounting, 224
Articles of association, 170, 173
ASBJ, 14, 217
Asset and liability view, 68, 87–89, 91, 93, 96–97, 102, 211, 245, 263
Asset revaluation method, 155, 158, 160, 162, 164, 166, 174
Asset verification, 185
Audit objectives, 181
Audit principle, 179

B

Bad debt accounts, 255
Bad debts, 172
Balance sheet, 180, 183
Balance sheet audit, 191
Bilanzio, 132, 150, 249
Bolton v. Natal Land and Colonization Co., 171
Bookkeeping audit, 180–181
British Library, 112
Business Accounting Deliberation Council, 214, 216
Business investments, 235

C

Certain level of dividend assets, 175

Classical inflation accounting, 204, 206, 215
Commercial Code, 212
Commodity account, 113
Comprehensive income, 11, 28, 69, 154, 246, 261
Concept of fairness, 253
Conceptual framework for financial reporting, 211
Contagion, 228
Contract role, 64, 78
Corporate risk, 100, 101
Corporate value, 246
Cost allocation, 118–119
Cost method, 238
Cost-realization principles, 15
Cost-realization principles model, 27
Current exit value in orderly liquidation, 92, 96
Current net income, 15
Current valuation, 150
Current valuation of inventory assets, 144
Current value, 250, 254, 257
Current value accounting, 43

D

Datini company, 136, 144
De Paula, 183, 186, 188
Debt covenants, 78
Deemed sale, 147
Deficit of divident assets, 168
Depreciation and renewal of stock fund, 165–166, 168
Depreciation of fixed assets, 157, 174
Depreciation of rolling stock assets, 155
Dicksee, 180, 184, 186
Discounted present value, 247, 254
Distributable earnings, 164
Distributable income, 11, 18, 30

Dividend, 125
Dividend assets, 174
Doctrine of the capital immutability, 21
Double account system, 161
Double-entry bookkeeping, 133, 247–248
Doubtfull detters, 136
Dowling, 146

E

Early recognition of purchase cost, 148
East India, 113
East India Company, 111
Economic concept of income, 210
Economics mind, 102
Emergency market value, 226
Enron, 47
Entity specific assumptions, 212, 218
Entity-specific measurement, 93–96
Equity valuation model, 15
Excess earnings, 156, 158–162, 164–166, 168, 174
Existence of assets, 185
Exit value, 252
Expanded revenue and expense view, 100, 103
Expected exit value in due course of business, 99
Exposure Draft of Accounting Standard, 205
External report accounting, 246

F

Fair value, 93–96, 216–217, 219, 250, 254, 257
Fair value measurement, 76, 208, 219
Faithful representation, 247, 261–262
Family partnership, 249
FASB, 263–264
Fiar value view, 211
Financial crisis, 225
Financial instruments, 76, 210, 216
Financial investments, 235
£5,000 Fixed Amount Method, 155–156, 158–159, 162, 164, 166–167, 174
Florentine banker in 1211, 134
Fraud detection, 181
Future cash in-flow, 246
Future value, 252

G

GAO, 43
General balance sheet, 161
General registered companies, 155
Going concern, 260
Grand Junction Railway Co., 154–155

H

Hamilton, 143, 148
Hardness, 65
Hayes, 147
Historical cost, 90, 97, 150, 250
Historical value, 255
Holding company, 236
Hybrid type of accounting, 15
Hypothesis testing type survey, 63

I

IAS No.32, 209
IAS No.39, 55
IFRS, 72, 79, 262
IFRS No.13, 209
Imported goods, 116
Imported goods accounts, 114
Improved Method, 139
Incremental information content study, 70
Information provision, 244, 246
Information role, 64, 68
Interest adjustment, 246
Inventory, 118
Inventory quantities, 197
Irrecoverable portions of receivables, 135
Iustum pretium (fair price), 239

J

Joint stock company, 110, 127

L

Lack of liquidity, 226, 229
Land of Natal Land and Colonization Co., 154
Land revaluation gain, 172
Land revaluation to offset bad debts, 174
Ledger closing, 117
Lee v. Neuchatel Asphalte Co., 169, 171
Lehman Brothers, 53
Lender of Last Resort, 229
Level 1, 69, 76
Level 2, 69, 76
Level 3, 69, 76
Life insurance companies, 230
Life Insurance Securities Company, 232
Liquidity, 227
London Birmingham Railway, 162
London East India Company, 137
Lower of cost or market basis, 18

M

Maintenance of capital, 21
Mair, 141
Malcolm, 140
Market liquidity, 224
Market participant assumptions, 212, 218
Market price, 163
Market revaluation gain, 174
Market valuation of land, 173
Market value, 137, 150, 169, 171, 254
Materiality, 248
Measurement attribute, 89, 92, 94
Memorandum on receivables and debts, 132, 247
Mining rights' depletion, 169
Mixed attribute accounting, 252, 257
Mixed attribute model, 15, 28
Mixed cost-fair value approaches, 209
Mixed model, 264
Money dynamics, 90
Monteage, 138
Montgomery, 191, 194–195, 198–199

N

Natal Land and Colonization Co., 171
National standards, 72
Net income, 69
Neuchatel Asphalte Co., 154, 169
New financial instruments project, 208
Normal market value, 226

O

Other comprehensive income, 15
Overall fair value accounting, 18, 24–25, 29

P

Pacioli's *Summa*, 135
Paradox of the liability, 87, 102
Past accounting, 246
Past value, 251, 257
Peele's second book, 136
Perfect markets, 254
Physical tests, 199
Pie in the sky, 258
Pixley, 179, 186
Practical bookkeeping, 139
Pre-disposal earnings, 156, 160, 163
Predominance of historical value, 254
Present market price, 147
Present value, 251, 257
Present value of expected cash flows, 92, 96
Professional audit, 179, 182
Project on accounting for financial instruments, 44

R

RAP, 42
Realised gains, 258
Realization and earnings process, 18
Realization principle, 97, 99–100, 102–103
Really worth, 141

Relative information content study, 70
Reliability, 150, 245, 248, 259, 261–262
Reliability's demise, 247
Reliable profit calculation system, 245
Replacement assets, 158
Reserve fund for contingencies, 161
Restricted asset and liability view, 100, 103
Revenue and expense view, 68, 87, 89, 91, 97, 99, 102, 212, 245, 265

S

S&Ls, 39
Sale price, 120–121, 123
Securement of dividend resource, 168
Securities and Exchange Law (SEL), 212
SFAC No.1, 38
SFAC No.2, 38, 259
SFAS No.15, 252
SFAS No.33, 207
SFAS No.89, 208
SFAS No.105, 44, 208, 264
SFAS No.107, 45, 208, 264
SFAS No.115, 208
SFAS No.119, 45
SFAS No.130, 244
SFAS No.133, 50
SFAS No.157, 55, 209, 217, 264
Showa Panic, 230
SOX, 51
Speculators, 260
SPEs, 49
Spicer and Pegler, 185, 187
Staet proef, 250
Status and issues clarification type survey, 63
Statute against usury, 133
Statute company, 154
Stevin, 249
Stewardship view, 211
Stock account, 159, 163

Stock valuation, 125, 126
Subprime loan, 52, 225
Substitute amount of distributable income, 32

T

Term partnership, 248
Transaction, 180, 182
Transaction price, 137, 150, 256
Transactions, 191
Triangle relationship, 13

U

Unrealised earnings, 258
Unsalable merchandise, 118
Usefulness, 245, 262

V

Value-in-use, 25
Value relevant, 67
Verifiability, 248, 259, 261
Verification of assets, 185, 190, 193
Verification of values, 187–188, 193, 196, 198–199
Verificatory procedure, 184, 192
Vouching, 180, 182–183

W

Wealth dynamics, 90, 91
Window-dressing, 247
World of occurrences, 133
World of things, 133

Y

Ympyn, 145

Z

Zaibatsu, 236

Fair Value Accounting In Historical Perspective

2014 年 2 月 16 日　初版第 1 刷発行

編著者　©　渡　邉　　　泉
発行者　　　菅　田　直　文

発行所　有限会社　森山書店　東京都千代田区神田錦町
　　　　　　　　　　　　　　1-10林ビル（〒101-0054）
　　　　TEL 03-3293-7061 FAX 03-3293-7063　振替口座 00180-9-32919

落丁・乱丁本はお取りかえ致します　　　印刷／製本・シナノ書籍印刷
　　　　本書の内容の一部あるいは全部を無断で複写複製する
　　　　ことは，著作権および出版社の権利の侵害となります
　　　　ので，その場合は予め小社あて許諾を求めてください。

ISBN 978-4-8394-2139-7